Anorexia and Bulimia Nervosa

Anorexia and Bulimia Nervosa

PRACTICAL APPROACHES

Edited by
Derek Scott

London Sydney
CROOM HELM

First published in 1988 by
Croom Helm Ltd,
11 New Fetter Lane, London, EC4P 4EE

Typeset by LaserScript Limited
Mitcham, Surrey.

Printed in Great Britain by
St. Edmundsbury Press Ltd,
Bury St. Edmunds, Suffolk

ISBN 0 7099 5430 1

British Library Cataloguing in Publication Data

Anorexia and bulimia nervosa: practical
approaches.
1. Anorexia nervosa – Treatment
2. Bulimarexia – Treatment
I. Scott, Derek
616.85'2 RC552.A5

ISBN 0 7099 5430 1

Contents

Contributors

Mary Elizabeth Allen, MSc, OTR, is presently Assistant Director of the Occupational Therapy Programme at the University Hospital of Wisconsin, Madison, USA. Her publications in the area of eating disorders includes two chapters elsewhere.

Francis Biley, BNurs. (Wales), RMN, SRN, FET Cert., now works as an Individualised Care Facilitator for South Manchester Health Authority, UK. He has extensive clinical experience in the nursing care and treatment of patients with eating disorders, and has previously published on the subject in the nursing press.

Carol Bowyer, RD, from the Atkinson Morley Hospital, London, is a qualified dietician who has gained considerable experience in the specialist area of eating disorders.

Rachel Bryant-Waugh, BA, PhD, is a clinical psychologist employed in the Department of Psychological Medicine, St Bartholemew's Hospital, London. Her doctoral thesis was on the subject of early-onset anorexia nervosa and publications include a number of chapters and papers on this topic. She is now engaged in setting up a number of long-term projects investigating different aspects of childhood-onset anorexia.

Nina Butler, BA, MA, is currently working on her PhD thesis on anorexia nervosa with Dr Peter Slade (Reader in Clinical Psychology and specialist in eating disorders) at Liverpool University, UK, a position made possible by a grant from the Leverhulme trust.

Ivan Eisler, PhD, is a lecturer in clinical psychology at the Institute of Psychiatry, London, and an Honorary Senior Clinical Psychologist at the Bethlem Royal and Maudsley Hospitals. His speciality is family therapy.

Gordon Giles, BA, Dip COT, OTR, is a qualified occupational therapist who has published extensively in occupational therapy and psychology journals. He now works at the Bay Area Head Injury Recovery Center, Berkeley, California, USA, and is currently working on his second book.

Pat Hartley, PhD, BA Psych., BA Gen Arts, Cert Ed, is project leader of the Eating Disorders Project at Salford College of Technology, England, and the Founder/President of Anorexic Aid, having set this up in 1974. Her previous publications include a chapter on self-help groups in *Current issues in clinical psychology* (E.Karas (ed), Plenum, 1983).

Clive Hollin, PhD, is a clinical psychologist and lectures at the University of Leicester, England.

Peter Lambley, PhD, BA, BSc, is a clinical psychologist who held various academic and clinical positions in South Africa before taking up residence in Greece in 1978. He has a part-time private practice in psychotherapy. He has published extensively and his books include *The psychology of apartheid* (Secker and Warburg, 1980), *The headache book* (WH Allen, 1982), *Insomnia and other sleep problems* (Sphere, 1983), *How to survive anorexia* (Muller, 1983) and *The psychology of cancer* (Futura/MacDonald, 1987).

Vivien Lewis is a clinical psychologist based in Wolverhampton, England and has extensive practical experience within eating disorders.

Phillip Proctor, BA, is a psychologist whose areas of counselling experience spans fifteen years.

Sally Savage, BA, is a trainee clinical psychologist and also has extensive clinical experience in the nursing care and treatment of patients with eating disorders.

Janet Sayers, PhD, lectures in psychology at the University of Kent, England, and also does occasional work as a clinical psychologist. Her books include *Biological politics* (Tavistock, 1984) and *Sexual contradictions* (Tavistock, 1986).

Derek Scott, BSc, is a research psychologist at the Team for the Assessment of Psychiatric Services, Friern and Claybury Hospitals, London. He has previously published articles in the areas of food and alcohol abuse, psychosexual factors within eating disorders, genetic factors within anorexia, anorexia nervosa within the male, catastrophy theory and autism.

Mark Strasser is a professor of philosophy at Washington University, St Louis, USA.

Janet Treasure, PhD, MB, BS, MRCP, MRC Psych., is a lecturer in psychiatry at the Institute of Psychiatry, London, and also an Honorary Senior Registrar at the Maudsley Hospital, London.

Preface

This book was compiled in response to the many people on both sides of the Atlantic who felt that a gap existed for a concise account of the *practical* approaches to eating disorders. Available books fell within two camps. One was the multi-authored heavyweight tome, full of specialist research information and seeming more at home on the university library shelf. The others were single-authored idiosyncratic views full of personal anecdotes and not really having a place in the pocket of the person who needs information and advice on dealing with these individuals on a day-to-day basis. It is hoped that this book provides both the background information necessary for a full understanding of anorexia nervosa (AN) and bulimia nervosa (BN), but also provides something of a 'how to go about it' guide. It is particularly aimed at a wide range of professional carers and also towards those who find themselves having to provide structure and support to the anorexic or bulimic.

Part One contains overviews of aspects of eating disorders. As overviews, referencing is plentiful for follow-up reading. Nina Butler opens the book for us and provides a novel slant whilst covering our present knowledge of AN. The general overview of BN is supplied by Peter Lambley and Derek Scott. In order to be sure of what we are dealing with, and to provide a baseline for treatment, assessment is necessary. Examples of assessment tools for use by the practical therapist are therefore included. To round off this section of the book, discussions on sex differences and psychosexual factors are provided.

This carries us into Part Two and Janet Sayers' chapter, which integrates psychodynamic and feminist approaches to eating disorders. The theme of the various approaches is followed by Ivan Eisler outlining the subject of family therapy and then by Clive Hollin and Vivien Lewis explaining cognitive-behavioural methods. Janet Treasure, a psychiatrist, concludes with a section of up-to-date evaluation of psychopharmacological approaches.

The final part is naturally the least theoretical and contains an account of what various practical therapists may respectively do. Contributions from nurses, occupational therapists, counsellors and a dietician are presented. Pat Hartley then discusses the role of self-help groups and Rachel Bryant-Waugh warns us of some special considerations when dealing with children. Finally, Mark Strasser and Gordon Giles leave some thought-provoking remarks for those of us, of whatever profession, who may find themselves having to counsel and deal with these, at-times, desperate people.

Part One
An Overview

1

An Overview of Anorexia Nervosa

Nina Butler

INTRODUCTION

Anorexia nervosa (AN) is a state that few in the helping professions will not, at some time or other, encounter. It may be that you have been already involved professionally, perhaps nursing someone with AN, and have experienced intense frustration towards the person you are trying to help. Alternatively, it may be that you have had direct personal experience of the problem, having been yourself afflicted. If this is the case then you will understand its complexities in a unique way. Or possibly, you know someone who has been, as they say, 'anorexic', and see that person as so normal that you wonder that this could ever have been the case. Mostly I will refer to AN not as an illness (although it may be that at certain times in its course it is not inappropriate to call it that) but as a state. This is because I believe it is not as inaccessible to others as its Latin name would imply. Indeed, I would imagine that there are few women today who have not been touched by the anorexic state in some way or other. Thus, AN is a very private manifestation of a very public statement. I should make it clear at this point that throughout the chapter, when referring to the anorexic *state*, I will be talking about that collective experience shared by the majority of women in present-day Western society and when referring to AN, I will be talking about those individuals unfortunate enough to be afflicted by a debilitating form of the anorexic state. Only for this last group is the word 'diagnosis' applicable in its conventional sense, and only for them are the words 'sufferer' and 'illness' used. For this reason, discussion of assessment and diagnosis along with that of bulimia nervosa (BN) is deferred until Chapter 3.

To the lay person reading a newspaper in, say, 1970, AN would probably have stood out as a new and shattering illness. In fact, the reality could hardly be more different. Its clinical history dates back at least to the seventeenth century, and the literature pertaining to AN today is enormous. A ten-year computer search of medical and scientific journals, for example, shows that publications relating to AN increased from 59 per year in 1973 to 165 in 1982. A current estimate would at least double this figure and there are few reputable magazines or newspapers that have not given extensive coverage to AN over a similar period. This chapter, then, attempts to draw to your attention salient aspects of this literature. In no way is it comprehensive, and in some respects, it is almost too brief to be very meaningful. Where this is the case, I hope that it will have whetted your appetite and that you will give further thought and consideration to the issues raised. Indeed, some will be covered more extensively by other chapters in this book. You will find the most important references at the end of the chapter.

HISTORICAL ASPECTS

In 1689, Richard Morton, a Fellow of the College of Physicians, published a seminal volume, translated into English five years later, and subtitled *A treatise on consumptions* (Morton, 1694). A richly descriptive and highly detailed work, this text outlines from observation the many disease processes that cause wasting of the body tissues. Morton is best known today as the author of the first clinical account of AN and so little altered does the presenting problem appear, it is worth quoting an extract from his description:

> Mr Duke's daughter in St Mary Axe, in the year of 1684, and the Eighteenth Year of her Age, in the month of July fell into a total suppression of her Monthly Courses from a multitude of Cares and Passions of her mind... she was wont by her studying at Night, and continual poring upon Books, to expose her self both Day and Night to the injuries of the Air... from that time, loathing all sorts of Medicaments, she wholly neglected the care of her self for two full years...
> I do not remember that I did ever in all my practice see one, that was conversant with the Living so much wasted with the greatest degree of a Consumption, (like a Skeleton only clad with skin) yet there was no Fever, but on the contrary a coldness of the whole body... being quickly tired with Medicines, she beg'd that the whole Affair might be committed again to Nature, whereupon consuming every day more and more, she was after three Months taken with a Fainting Fit and dyed.

Just over fifty years later, the novelist Samuel Richardson published *Clarissa: or the history of a young lady* (1747–48). One of the longest novels in English literature (over a million words), it follows the heroine's struggle for independence in the context of her intractable family, and relates in epistolary form, her long decline and accompanying self-knowledge as she prepares for death. Though ostensibly 'fiction', we have here depicted a clear example of an anorexia-like experience. The novel was fantastically popular and its reputation in the later eighteenth century was superlative — both at home and on the Continent. And as Sherbourne (1962) pointed out, that Rousseau's *Nouvelle Heloise* was simply the most famous of numerous imitations, symbolises that, above all, Richardson was a moral novelist. This has important implications for what I shall say about AN's moral perspective later on. Sufficient here to appreciate that the public of the eighteenth century, as now, were receptive to the idea of a young lady's choice, when her back is against the wall, for abstinence to death.

In 1789, the French physician Naudeau (1789) published a description of some length, noting a fatal case of what we now know as AN. The patient's death he attributed to the influence of her mother — an unusually profound insight given what we understand today about family background in the pathogenesis of AN. The following year, Robert Willan, MD, published an account of the sickness and death of a young man who had starved himself for 78 days. The report, entitled 'A remarkable case of Abstinence', notes this to be the longest fast 'recorded in the annals of physic' (see Silverman, 1987).

There was much interest during the Victorian era in an 'illness' of the body resulting from food refusal in the absence of either fever, or (more crucially), the other signs associated with consumption. A lithograph in Ipswich, for example, depicts one Elizabeth Squirrel of Shottisham 'taken from life the 21st of September 1852, after 153 days total abstinence from food and drink'. Other famous cases would include, in 1871, Sarah Jacob of Wales and in July 1831, a young woman admitted to the Warneford asylum, Oxford, in an extremely emaciated state. On admission she appeared 'to be delirious from disability rather than insane', with a history of refusing food and drink, constipation and menstrual irregularity. She was tube-fed and given stimulants, but died twelve days later. A 26-year-old draper's assistant, however, admitted to the Littlemore asylum, Oxford, was discharged and recovered. The case entry made in November 1862 reads as follows:

> Has refused food and medicine, unless given by force has taken nothing. On admission has the appearance of a person who has suffered greatly from want of food, being extremely emaciated, scarcely able to turn in bed, circulation extremely feeble, extremities cold... is sensible of all that is said to her.

As we come to the first specifically defined case of AN, we begin first to encounter some of the problems of diagnosis (see Chapter 3). These will always have been present, but it is here that they become immediately apparent. It was in April 1873 that the French physician Charles Laseque clinically described an illness related, he thought, to appetite, and which he placed firmly in the realms of hysteria: 'l'Anorexie Hysterique' (an hysterical anorexia). Almost simultaneously, in October 1874, Sir William Gull, in a paper submitted to the London Clinical Society, described a morbid mental state characterised by a want of appetite — anorexia nervosa. Translated from Greek etymology this means roughly 'loss of appetite from nervous origins'. As it will later become clear, this, strictly speaking, is a misnomer; people with AN in fact very rarely lose their appetites. But, as also will become clear, it is no fault of Gull that he believed they did.

After Gull and Laseque's first descriptions, the medical literature began, over the next decade, to contain many accounts of such cases. Dally (1969) notes that physicians of this time showed remarkable understanding of both their patients and their treatment. Indeed, Hovel (Decourt, 1954) points out both how helpless sufferers were to make themselves eat, and how harmful it was to criticise them unjustly. Although de la Tourette had in 1895 attempted to distinguish between primary and secondary AN (*anorexia mentale* and *anorexia gastrique*), Janet in 1907, was the first seriously to postulate two types of AN — obsessional and hysterical — a distinction that has now been more-or-less abandoned. In 1914, Simmonds described an emaciated woman who died and subsequently was found to have destruction of her pituitary gland. The consequence of this was that until the mid 1930s, cases of AN commonly were mistaken for, and treated as, Simmond's disease — frequently with fatal results! The final and clear distinction between AN and Simmond's disease emerged with the work of Ryle, Richardson, Sheldon and others in the late 1930s, and it was this that re-established AN as a 'disease of psychological origin'.

During the 1940s, AN became a stamping ground for the psychoanalysts, whose posture regarded the illness as a defence against sexuality (see Chapter 6). Although Theander (1970) noted a five-fold increase in incidence in Malmo, Sweden between the 1930s and 1950s, it was not until the 1960s, with the advent of Twiggy and the miniskirt that the condition caught the public imagination. Why this should be is not, as yet, clear. For although Crisp (e.g. 1980) has convincingly argued for a view of AN as a phobic avoidance in relation to normal body weight and its biological and social consequences, recent findings at least partially challenge this view. For example, in 1986, Silverstein, Peterson and Perdue correlated the mean bust-to-weight ratios of women appearing in *Vogue* and *Ladies Home Journal* at four-year intervals since 1901, and have shown that the mean was *less* in 1925 than in 1965. That is to say, the public's perception of the feminine ideal showed her to be more slender in the 'flapper-girl' era than in the miniskirt era.

THE CHANGING NATURE OF ANOREXIA NERVOSA

It has been often said that neither the Greeks nor the Old Masters would have understood our modern emphasis upon slimness as a key to beauty. And although, as I have already pointed out, we have no reason to suppose that AN did not then exist, the emphasis that sufferers now place upon *thinness* was possibly subsumed at least partially by other concerns or even neuroses. It is the case, for instance, that neither Gull nor Laseque, emphasised those features now recognised as central to its pathology, namely the morbid preoccupation with body weight and dread of fatness. And Parry-Jones (1986) is not alone in suggesting that since amenorrhea and adolescent onset was specific also to chlorosis, this last may, in the nineteenth century, have been an analogous condition to AN in the twentieth. It was, after all, one of the most prominent symptoms of teenage girls in the general hospital material of that time. Russell (e.g. 1970) has taken this idea a stage further. He rejects the notion that chlorosis and AN represent a kind of continuum, since chlorosis was characterised by a greenish-yellow tinge, hypochromic anaemia and was common amongst girls living in poor social conditions. Instead, he defines AN in 'pathoplastic' terms. This term was introduced by Burnbaum, who applied it to the causal factors that contributed to the structure of an illness. It is an approach that encourages a study of personality traits and/or social factors capable of moulding an illness into its specific form.

I have already spoken about some of the changing attitudes towards and interpretations of AN under the heading 'historical aspects'. As well as determining management, these can be understood also as illustrative of 'pathoplasticity' — of society's recording of illness in different ways. It is noted that in recent years, there is an impression that sexual inhibition in anorexic women is a less regular feature (see Chapter 5), although it may still occur. Instead, the emphasis has shifted to stress the sufferer's morbid preoccupation with weight and dread of fatness. This of course begs the question as to whether it is the clinicians themselves who are more receptive to certain theories, or 'mini-paradigms', at some times rather than at others. The work of Freud, for example, is now far less influential than it was in the 1940s when Waller, Kaufman and Deutsch (1940) construed AN as a defence against unconscious fantasies or oral insemination. Such a theory today seems almost absurd, and it is easy to imagine that these clinicians were less than receptive to their patients' protestations against, and fear of weight gain. After all, it was only one year after Meyer (1961) had pointed out that most sufferers consciously reject sexuality (thus continuing Waller's theme) that Hilde Bruch first noted the 'disturbance of body image' and 'pursuit of thinness' that we recognise today as fundamental to AN. I cannot help wondering whether this important recognition occurred because a woman was in a position to listen to what her patients were telling her. There is little doubt, however, that our present fashion for slimness has accentuated this basic fear, and as such, Russell's hypothesis is not without important implications.

DIAGNOSIS

This issue is discussed in detail in Chapter 3. Here, we mention the proposed American DSM-IV criteria as depicted in Table 1.1. What is stressed within these flexible criteria is the 'intense fear of becoming overweight' and a loss of only 15 per cent of body weight for height is necessary. Insofar as it is not unlikely that at some point many girls or women will lose substantial amounts of weight and will naturally be hesitant of becoming overweight, this seems rather inclusive. Moreover, many women report that menstrual irregularity of two to three cycles need not be uncommon — especially if stress is present. The criteria predict that AN will increase, perhaps dramatically, and if adopted, a distorted statistical profile with respect to incidence is bound to result. Such an outcome may be double-edged. On the one hand, if it has the effect of alerting us to the problems women face in achieving independence in a world that undervalues the true measure of femininity, then this is well and good. Conversely, if the result is a society of 'sick' women, then we need to be our guard; the symptom will be undermining itself, and can only confirm those patriarchal impulses from which so frequently it originates. More will be said of this later.

Table 1.1: Proposed DSM-IV criteria for anorexia nervosa

A. Refusal to maintain body weight for age and height and which results in maintenance of body weight 15% below expected; failure to make expected weight gain growth period which also results in maintenance of body weight 15% below expected for height and age.
B. Intense fear of becoming overweight, even when underweight.
C. Body-image disturbance — claiming to 'feel fat' even when emaciated (this usually takes the form of the patient believing parts of the body, the hips for example, are fat when they are in fact obviously underweight).
D. In females, the absence of at least three consecutive menstrual cycles when otherwise expected to occur — primary or secondary amenorrhea.

Source: American Psychiatric Association (1987).

To distinguish between AN and the anorexic state, and to perceive the inherent dangers of an overly inclusive diagnosis, seem to me to be the cardinal features of diagnosis. Just one of these dangers is being currently demonstrated by many of the schools of nursing. Despite the recognition that sufferers of AN rarely neglect their work, and tend to be profoundly dedicated people, these schools now specifically ask on their application forms whether or not the applicant has a personal history of AN. If the answer is yes, the chances of being accepted are vastly diminished. This is clearly an instance of discrimination, and an example of women undermining their own symptoms. That it is the nursing profession that now asks this question is in itself significant. A hierarchical profession to begin with, it has tended always to collude with the medical profession's patriarchal values. The present would seem to be no exception.

An anecdote should further illustrate, albeit a little cryptically, this hesitancy of mine with respect to diagnostic criteria. I was recently lecturing on AN to a group of about 30 trainee community nurses. It was a joint lecture, in which a consultant psychiatrist spoke about the clinical mangement of AN, while I talked about its wider issues. At the end, I replied to one question by saying that unless a person's weight is critical and that the person was clearly fulfilling the Feighner criteria for AN, I did not see why we should interfere with the 'thin person's' life. While it may be the case that such a person would *benefit* from some form of co-counselling or insight-directed therapy, it was nevertheless that individual's choice to be thin (unless, of course, some pathology was involved). The psychiatrist pondered on this aloud and considering the audience, demonstrated what I think is a tremendous capacity for humility: 'I hadn't thought of it like that before. Yes — there does seem to be something rather odd about middle-aged men insisting that thin, young women should gain weight'. I will leave you to ponder this further!

INCIDENCE

Simply because AN as such was rarely heard of at the turn of the century, or in the 1950s, does not mean that it did not then exist. Equally, the increased incidence that the experts are so eager to report may be the result of those deep cultural changes that have given rise to the anorexic state, and not at all an accurate reflection of AN. Also, as the anorexic state comes to the fore in public consciousness, so an identification of the anorexic state with AN will occcur. This in turn will result in an apparent increase in AN. Public exposure will result in more referrals, and more referrals will have a tendency, not only to bias the statistical profile, but also to confuse the classification procedures.

The work of Theander (1970), Duddle (1973) and others who have comprehensively searched hospital records, insists that a significant increase has, in fact, occurred. However, other investigators are less convinced. Parry-Jones (1986), for example, exploring hospital archives has found that many of the ill-defined conditions of patients admitted to asylums in the South of England in the nineteenth century and included features such as vomiting, amenorrhea and debility, were tantalising in their possible clues to AN.

As an illness, AN has frequently been said to be of middle- and upper-class origins, but investigation has not always borne this out. A now classic study from 1973 analysed data from three case registers over roughly the same period of time: North-East Scotland, Camberwell in London and Monroe County, New York. The findings, with respect to a social bias for the problem, were equivocal, with substantially more of the Camberwell referrals coming from upper-class families than was the case for Scotland and New York. Also, estimates of new cases varied from 0.37 per 100,000 per year in Monroe County to 1.6 per 100,000 in Scotland. Another study (Szmukler, Eisler, Gillies and Hayward, 1986) reported the results of an examination of the 238 cases of AN on the North-East Scotland case register over the period 1965 to 1982. One of the aims of this study was to note changes in numbers and patient characteristics over time. A highly significant increase in the number of cases was found (for the period 1978 to 1982, 4.06 per 100,000 of the population), and a social-class bias in favour of the upper and upper-middle class was confirmed in this study.

Further support for such a bias comes from a study by Crisp, Palmer and Kalucy (1976), which directly investigated a number of schoolgirl populations. In its severe form, AN was found to be relatively common in the UK 'independent' sector, possibly implying a higher social-class tendency. In all such schools, the prevalence amounted to about one severe case in every 200 girls. In those aged 16 and over it was about one severe case in every 100 girls. Overall, one 'new' severe case in every 250 pupils over 16 years of age was encountered in the independent schools, in contrast to only one case in the group aged over 16 in the two comprehensive schools studied. Further, Crisp reports that only 15 per cent of his patients attend comprehensive schools. Palmer (1980), too has said that AN seems more probable in the upper and middle classes. Although he acknowledges the biasing effects of classification reflected in referral patterns, he offers no evidence for his conclusions. Dally and Gomez (1979) link the pressures for educational achievement with the upper social groups (in their sample 77 per cent of anorexics are from the higher social classes), and Selvini-Palazolli (1974) indicates that in Italy, anorexics tend to come from families in cultural transition. This latter point would suggest that a greater emphasis upon educational achievement would be placed upon the offspring of such families and that this, in turn, would create not only a sense of disjuncture, but also conflicting loyalties for the young women of these families.

In a very important recent chapter, Lawrence (1987) continues this theme and, I think rightly, draws our attention to the possible confusion of social status and educational achievement. Moreover, she points out that in none of these studies is there analysis of the effect of education itself upon young women, regardless of social class. Her own clinical findings indicate not a true social bias, but an educational bias, and she proposes that AN and education are coincidentally linked. Crucially, this is not to mean that education is denied to girls, as could be interpreted, but rather that education itself must begin to address the difficult situation faced by so many young women within its compass. On no account is this difficulty to be underestimated, and this is a contribution to the AN literature that no interested persons should overlook.

There exists a syndrome, again reflecting some of the problems pertaining to classification, which has come to be regarded as 'subclinical anorexia nervosa'. In effect, this refers to individuals who, while not fulfilling any of the strict criteria for AN, present serious problems of eating and weight control. These would seem to be rather worse than those commonly experiencing the anorexic state, but not so severe as to warrant the classification of AN. As a syndrome, this has been noted by several investigators (e.g. Nylander, 1971). However, it has been suggested that the identification of subclinical cases may be facilitated by the use of standardised screening procedures such as the 'eating attitudes test' (EAT; see Chapter 3). For example, Button and Whitehouse (1981) administered this test to 578 students (446 female and 132 male) at a college of technology and to a sample of anorexics. Although no male student scored highly, a total of 28 female students (6.3 per cent of the female student sample) scored within what is known as the 'anorectic range'. These 'high scorers' were interviewed subsequently. This procedure revealed that the symptoms of AN were common in the high-scoring group but almost absent in the student control group. The investigators conclude that a substantial proportion of adolescent females go on to develop subclinical AN. This is a statistic that will, I believe, further distort the prevalence and incidence of AN proper.

Mitigating against this finding, however, is a study by Garner and Garfinkel (1979) that recorded a finding that AN, diagnosed according to rigorous criteria, occured in 6.5 per cent of a sample of dancers from three national-calibre professional ballet schools. Szmukler and his colleagues (1986) conducted a similar study. Their findings differed from Garner and Garfinkel's but have critical implications for the management of subclinical syndromes. The investigators found that of 100 students at a British ballet school of the first rank, the diagnosis of AN was common. What was almost impossible, however, was defining a 'case' of AN, since the environment of these girls lent itself so readily to 'caseness'. For example, 37 per cent of the girls thought they were 'fat', and 35 per cent who weighed less than approximately 80 per cent mean matched population weight for height (MMPW) believed themselves to be of a 'normal' weight.

Nearly all the girls interviewed, moreover, were reported to be preoccupied with their body shapes and those who were already thin wanted to be still thinner. Further, to obscure the relevance of diagnosis (although its occurrence correlated significantly with EAT scores), amenorrhea was common. Szmukler *et al.* therefore point out that pathology must always take account of background; when 'symptoms' are common in a population that nevertheless seems to be functioning well socially (and in this instance physically also), then caution must be exercised in the significance attributed to them.

Their one-year follow-up proved most valuable in ascertaining the implications of 'caseness'. Most importantly and most significantly was the tendency to improvement in terms of weight gain without medical intervention. This was consistent with the observation made by staff that only once every few years was a girl in need of referral to a specialist for AN. What impressed these investigators was the pressures towards maintaining a slim figure and those pressures simultaneously brought into play to reverse the processes of *abnormal* weight loss (that is, less than 80 per cent MMPW). The matron insisted that a marked weight loss be regained immediately, and friends were similarly concerned. Enough here to say that this is an excellent illustration of the care to be assumed both when considering diagnosis, and when citing incidence.

THE FEMINIST APPROACH

Szasz (1971) has said that addiction, obesity and starvation (AN) are political problems, not psychiatric, since 'each condenses and expresses a contest between the individual and some other person in his environment over the control of the individual's body'. And as Gill Edwards (1987) points out, it is because women are not only identified by society and by gender with their bodies, and stereotypically linked with food and the kitchen, that 'this struggle for control is all too naturally expressed via eating disorders'. In this most lucid essay, Edwards examines the way in which a young woman with AN experiences herself as powerless and out of control, despite appearances to the contrary. The anorexic part of her tends to 'split off' so that she is caught between the terror of being, on the one hand, overwhelmed by her needs (most often manifest in a desperate desire for food), and on the other, the relentless drive for self-denial and chastisement. This dualism, which becomes a recurrent theme in AN, is brilliantly described by MacLeod (1981) in her autobiographical account of AN (see Chapter 6).

Edwards joins with Eichenbaum and Orbach (1984) and to a certain extent

MacLeod, in believing that a feminist approach is absolutely essential for the understanding of AN. She describes the way in which women have profound difficulties in coming to terms with their needs, dependencies and longings. They are taught early on that their role will be to minister to other's needs at the expense of their own. And it is precisely this denial of one's needs that occurs in AN, so that the problems a sufferer faces (and thus paradoxically avoids) are similar too, although more intense than the difficulties faced by most young women in our present society.

The existential philosopher, Tillich, illuminates this paradox when he says that 'neurosis is the way of avoiding non-being by being', and in *The divided self* (Laing, 1969) Laing is able to explain this for us further:

> The trouble is that the individual may find that the pretence has been in the pretending and that, in a more real way than he had bargained for, he has actually lapsed into that very state of non-being he has so much dreaded,... 'self-consciousness' is implicated in this paradox.

Self-consciousness implies two things. It implies an awareness of oneself *by* oneself, and an awareness of oneself as the object of another person's observation. Laing points out that this heightening of awareness of one's own being, both as an object of one's own awareness and the awareness of others, is practically universal in adolescents. It is almost always accompanied by shyness, embarrassment of some kind or another and perhaps blushing. A corollary of this is that a sense of 'guilt' is readily invoked to explain such awkwardness. However, guilt *per se* cannot explain why only some people become extraordinarily self-conscious and why some of these go on to develop AN. The feminist approach is able to provide the necessary link. On the one hand, the anorexic, like the self-conscious person, must be *seen*, for only by being seen can identity be confirmed; made certain. But on the other hand, to be a seeable object in what, for an insecure person, is a perilous world is to make oneself extremely vulnerable. The only way to avoid such vulnerability, therefore, is to make oneself in some way or another, invisible. And here we have the crux of AN; the necessity to become assertive and special, as is demanded by the one afflicted by the educational collective, and at the same time small and passive, as is a prerequisite of societal pressures. The sufferer of AN is almost literally competing with the sylph; that image so fundamental, in fact, to the world of dance. A world, moreover, that insists upon steely strength for performance and yet whose *raison d'etre* is lyrical ease. A world that communicates rather like the anorexic tends to communicate, not through language, but by an unspoken medium. Maybe we should cease to wonder why manifestations of AN, as related earlier under the heading 'incidence', are so common in this world. Herein lies a transient epitome of society's conflicting claims. This background has important implications for our present appreciation of what AN is about, and I offer it primarily to provoke thought.

Anorexia nervosa is thus a way of reconciling the conflicting pressures to be passive, dependent and all-giving (or feminine), and yet to be independent, successful and a high achiever. By becoming anorexic, a young woman can, for a very little while, become both. She will stand out as being special and simultaneously become small and invisible. This is what Szasz refers to as the necessity to 'define or be defined'. Or, as Sheila MacLeod has related in her own account of AN, 'One can reject all foreign substances, for which food is a metaphore, and subject them to one's will. This is power indeed'. Of course the power is little more than a transient illusion, but I think that the ascetic impulse, which is in a way the antithesis of the political, has a more enduring quality seldom spoken about, which is particularly implicated in the experience of AN.

ASCETIC VALUES

Dualism, of course, is one of the bases of asceticism. Long before Descarte's famous maxim 'Cognito ergo sum' ('I think therefore I exist'), dualism, the mind/body debate, and self-consciousness were familiar themes in philosophy. They were something that Plato, around the fourth century BC wrestled with, and partially reconciled in his famous idea of the Forms. Eight centuries later, St Augustine was not only able to make use of Plato's ideas in his great spiritual autobiography, the *Confessions*, but was to locate self-consciousness as being fundamental to identity; to what it is to 'be' in the world. I mention these two great thinkers primarily for the profound and lasting claims that both continue to have upon Western thought and Western culture. The point is also to enable one to recognise that not only does AN have a traceable history from the Middle Ages onwards, but that it is a condition conceptually rooted both in classical and Christian antiquity. Without this appreciation, any understanding of AN seems to me to be incomplete or partial.

In the context of AN, Rampling (1986) has drawn attention to the fact that fasting is a principal expression of the asceticism practised by extremes of the faithful. He cites Mogul's work (1980) in drawing on Anna Freud's concept of asceticism as a characteristically defensive attitude of young people, to postulate a link with the development of AN. I think that this may be to undermine what it is to be faithful, but you will have recognised, nevertheless, how central to what he is saying is the recurrent theme of self-consciousness. We should always be most cautious before interpreting man's spiritual dimension — let alone the anorexic's — in terms of convenient and conventional models. It is therefore with some hesitancy that I refer to Crisp and Bhat's (1982) influential statement that the stance in AN is one of phobic avoidance. Or, that Arieti (1980), as Rampling further points out, has described one of the most important characteristics in phobias as being a dis-humanisation of the source of fear; the anxiety-provoking 'I-Thou' relation is in this context transformed into 'I-It'. The essential points to remember here are not those concerning what the equation is, but rather that an equation has been made at all.

In her book, *The anorexic experience*, Lawrence (1983) asks us to consider the idea that AN is, in a sense, food for the spirit. I think this is a very unaddressed aspect of the problem, and would agree with her in suggesting that becoming 'anorexic' involves a taking of the dualism between body and spirit literally. In this literal confusion, the body surrenders to 'It' (an ascetic ideal), and is no longer thought by the sufferer to have 'human' requirements. The purpose of asceticism has been described frequently as the process of 'freeing the soul from the body'. Thus in the pursuit of moral worthiness, the body, and especially the woman's body, may be dissociated from the self, and such separation is perceived as an act of moral dedication. An excellent illustration of this impulse comes from Simone Weil (1951), a distinguished and not insignificant devotional writer who herself died of AN at the age of 34. In her *Spiritual autobiography*, she describes just such a solution to her existential problems, which may help us to appreciate AN more clearly:

> At fourteen I fell into one of those fits of bottomless despair that come with adolescence... After months of inward darkness, I suddenly had the everlasting conviction that any human being can penetrate the kingdom of truth reserved for genius, if he longs for truth and perpetually concentrates all his attention upon its attainment... for me it was a conception of the relationship between grace and desire.

This affirmation has in its essence something of MacLeod's assertion related above.

In 1985, Bell distinguished what he refers to as 'holy' anorexia. Central to his interesting hypothesis is the notion that Italian holy women of the thirteenth and fourteenth centuries who refused food, were disobedient in the face of their confessors' orders, and sought their own ecstatic relationship with Christ through starvation and death. This he sees as their only alternative to succumbing to the controlling influence of the patriarchal church.

Bell presents detailed case studies of Catherine of Sienna, Veronica Guiliani and Margaret of Cortona from spiritual autobiography and letters, but particularly from the *vitae* of these saintly women. These hagliographical accounts were sometimes composed during the 'holy' anorexic's lifetime, sometimes after her death. But what I find most fascinating in Bell's account, and which should have most relevance for us today, is his illumination of the attractions that this holy dedication held for a wide range of medieval Italian women, as well as the different possibilities for changing such an impulse offered alternatively by the Franciscan and Dominican orders. The latter, as recorded by Steedman (1986), influenced by the humanism of Northern Italy's urban centres, allowed its holy women much more individuality than did the Franciscans. Poor Clares (Fransicans), when ordered to eat by their confessors, usually did, and were 'cured', whereas Dominican women tended to pursue their extreme course to death. This 'outcome' may remind you of the strategies for management adopted by the ballet school in Szmukler *et al.*'s (1986) account I spoke of previously, and is a cryptic comment upon society's reaction to AN today. In a sense, what both these outcomes are suggesting is that *too* much individuality is a dangerous thing; there are other ways than the flesh to express one's uniqueness and devotion.

Interestingly, Bell draws our attention to the difference between those *vitae* written by men about holy women and those written by women. The former most frequently describe the starving saint as doing God's will, but Franciscan sisters, writing about Eustochia of Messina in the 1480s, are perfectly clear that Eustochia had starved herself. And it is this tone which is utterly essential for an appropriate appraisal of 'holy' anorexia. We must be very cautious both about diagnosing the dead (there are enough problems involved in diagnosing the living) and saintliness, by definition, is beyond common grasp. Besides, as a corrective to Bell's thesis, it should be noted that not all ascetics practise such extreme behaviour. Indeed, the English spiritual directors of the fourteenth century prescribed a moderate and wholesome diet. As a temple of the spirit, the body was to be respected, not abused.

FAMILY BACKGROUND

Minuchin, Rosman and Baker (1978) have described four factors seen as characterising the 'anorexic family': (a) enmeshment — the family members are not clearly differentiated. They become lost in the family's system, and there is great intensity in their interactions; (b) overprotectiveness; (c) rigidity — the family is unwilling to change; and (d) avoidance of conflict. These four factors equate well with the psychosocial approach to AN. Edwards (1987) considers enmeshment in some detail:

> A child who grows up in a highly enmeshed family learns to subordinate herself and her autonomy to the needs of her family; her goals will be approval and love rather than knowledge or competence... She will develop an obsessional concern for perfection (resulting in low self-esteem) and extreme self-consciousness.

She points out that not only is this a typical patriarchal way of treating girls, but that with such a model, the *potential* anorexic's body will seem not to be her own. Instead, it will be regarded in some way as family 'property'.

Lawrence (1983) writes of the 'fearful state of not being separated from one's parent', as does Bruch, and both describe the way in which the refusal to accept nourishment becomes an act of assertion. Lawrence adds, however, that families are not always crucially involved in this paradoxical struggle and, quite rightly, insists that we work from situations rather than ready-made theories. In particular, she examines in some detail the relationship between mothers and daughters, and outlines the characteristic ambivalence that so often tends to characterise this relationship in families with an anorexic member. The focus on mothers is not new. In 1884, the famous French physician Charcot saw the mother's influence as being always 'primarily pernicious' to her daughter's mental health and this is a view that has persisted, often with crippling results for mother, daughter and potential mother.

Lawrence offers a refreshing break from this pattern, and is careful to explain that she is not suggesting that difficulties between mothers and daughters *cause* AN. Rather, the relationship with the mother she has found to be central to many of her anorexic clients (and which most writers on the subject, I think, would tend to confirm), she sees as an extension of the difficulties that many women face. I feel personally, that there is a lot of sense in this argument. If, as a woman, you have ever felt the need to be nurtured and cared for, yet also experienced the conflicting desire to be autonomous and separate, you will have touched upon something of the anorexic's torment. But whereas the conflict for you may have been resolved in a surrender to the pretence of independence, the anorexic will simply have ceased to pretend. In so doing, it may be that the sufferer is being in some weird way, more honest than the rest of us. Thus, although the feelings that normally accompany the anorexic's behaviour are common, what becomes unusual for the sufferer of AN is the accompanying behaviour. It is not too extreme to say that even as her soul is crying out for care, the anorexic refuses resolutely to nurture it in any way.

Paradoxically, it is here that we find the most startling aspects of AN. In spite of its notorious resistance to treatment, it is precisely this need to be looked after and nurtured, yet simultaneously separate, that makes it treat*able*. Anyone who understands this aspect, as Lawrence manifestly does, and takes it into account when working with someone with AN, will not go far wrong.

Ironically, it is also the dichotomy between separateness and nurture that makes AN so hard for a mother to handle. Whereas sons are able to rediscover in another something of the intimate and nurturing relationship they had with their mothers, daughters are destined themselves to become nurturers. The daughter who grows up to become a mother, if she is extraordinarily fortunate, will herself have had a mother with a clearly defined identity, and with a tremendous capacity to be emotionally available to her offspring. Such a mother in our present society is rare. Most mothers are forced, both by history and by temperament, to compromise these extremes. The result is that daughters are in *general* less clear about their role, and this compromise tends to be represented in the pretence I spoke about above; in the act of compromising most of us are pretending to an ideal. After all, when all is said and done, families are an essentially *social* phenomeon. As I have pointed out previously under the heading 'feminist approaches', there are tremendous conflicts in our society as to what an adult woman should be like. Small wonder these conflicts are unconsciously mediated to daughters. As Lawrence (1983) says, 'Any theory of anorexia which starts and ends with an analysis of the family is mistaken'. At worst, the family's pointing to the anorexic and saying 'It's all your fault' is but a mirroring of the general medical profession's pointing to the family and saying that it is their fault. In turn, as must be clear, this scapegoating is simply a reflection of the sufferer's reflection of society's unresolved conflicts. Such an approach is not new, but until quite recently, it has not been taken into account when describing

AN. As mother to an anorexic daughter, Erichson (1985) places the approach in context. When she described her daughter's despair as a reflection of her own, she had also to contemplate this daunting prospect.

Perhaps you are able now to see that Minuchin *et al.*'s (1978) fourth anorexic family characteristic, 'avoidance of conflict', is quite understandable. A family that finds itself particularly racked by the kind of difficulties that I have previously discussed, will obviously feel itself very threatened by an attempt by one member to resolve them. Conflict and self-assertion will be seen, quite unwittingly, as an attempt to undermine the family's stability, and until the symptoms of AN become manifest, such a family will tend to trivialise or leave unresolved any conflict that does occur. If undesirable from the sufferer's point of view, it is surely understandable from the family's. It is, after all, also what happens in society at large. If you doubt this then just ask yourself as honestly as you can, if you have not ever wished that the sufferer you are trying to help would just 'get better' or 'go away'. If you have, you will not be alone. Indeed, the antipathy that AN creates within the helping professions has been documented.

I have said a lot about mothers, but what about fathers? Erichson (1985) has suggested that although from an outsider's point of view, the anorexic often seems more valued by her father, she in fact *feels* undervalued. I think that the father relationship in AN has been underestimated in the past. As women become slowly more equal, so the challenge of identity will be recognised by both sexes on equal grounds. Just as AN mirrors frequently the mother's unresolved need for independence, so it is possible to see it as a reflection of the father's need. Erichson outlines the way in which she sees the anorexic's relationship with her father changing as the AN intensifies, and suggests that some fathers may unconsciously cling to the problem. For the first time ever, Erichson suggests, these men feel really needed. Once more, we have an important comment upon a society that overvalues the traditional masculine qualities at the expense of the feminine. In a properly mature environment, these fathers would be no longer so cautious about expressing their needs and, as a result, would not need recourse to another's symptoms for this purpose.

Other fathers, Lawrence notes, appear to be mysterious, distant figures; people who instil a sense of deep interest and possibly awe. These are individuals whose insecurity will probably have led them to seek out public recognition and personal achievement. Although not in themselves bad, when coupled with unresolved security they will have tended to remove the 'father' from his family's emotional life. Since many fathers will have fought hard to establish this sense of superiority, any abrogation of it from within will naturally impose feelings of almost insupportable guilt. The person from whom the anorexic most needs to see a demonstration of need, thus becomes the one least capable of showing such insight. Of course, mothers and fathers are frequently husbands and wives too; less often, they are partners. Curiously, were they always partners, insofar as partners are, by definition, sympathetic to one another's freedom to function as individuals, yet mutually involved in caring, AN would be less likely to develop in their offspring.

From a practical point of view, what needs to be recognised is that while familial factors may play a role in the origin, development or perpetuation of AN, it cannot automatically be assumed that these are either of necessary or of sufficient importance. The results from another investigation by Garfinkel (1974), for example, did not confirm the prolific anecdotal reports that talk of excessive parental dieting, weight concerns and dissatisfaction with their bodies when compared with other middle-aged people of similar social class. These are commensurate with the findings of Dally in 1969, and with Morgan and Russell in 1975, who observed the condition to develop without the presence of any demonstrable familial pathology.

However, some problems within the family were identified. These were particularly to do with perceived expectations, family roles, demands for performance and problems with communication and affective expression. These areas correspond closely with the background that I have discussed in this section, and reflect also the areas of concern identified by other investigators addressing particularly high-risk groups. Although it is not possible to say whether these disturbances are a cause or a coincidence of AN, they must be acknowledged in formulating any therapeutic programme.

PERSONALITY PROFILE

Many clinicians have described the characteristics of people with AN before they become 'anorexic'. This is suprising, since it would be usually assumed that sufferers, until developing AN, would be unknown to these professionals. Most personality studies reflect, therefore, the methodological perils of retrospective analysis. However, the typical picture of someone who may later develop AN is of an introverted, conscientious and well-behaved child who has seldom presented problems either at home or at school. Many surveys note high intelligence, and superior scholastic performance, but the two almost overwhelmingly consistent personality traits are those of perfectionism and obsessionality. It is when these last are placed in the context of an overwhelming dissatisfaction with life, or life presents an individual with events for which their existing skills are inadequate, that AN becomes a viable alternative. This has been coherently demonstrated in a variety of ways by Bruch (1985), Crisp (1986), Slade and Dewey (1986) and Theander (1986).

CLINICAL PICTURE

The most obvious sign of AN is, of course, loss of body weight due to extreme fasting (caloric restriction). The second symptom most commonly reported and experienced in females, is amenorrhea. The wide range of other physical signs and symptoms include low basal metabolic rate and an abolition or reversal of the normal circadian rhythm of serum cortisol. Sleep is frequently disturbed, and clinical reports of hyperactivity have been objectively confirmed. Slade and Russell (1973) were some of the first to demonstrate that a distorted body image seems to be an almost universal finding, with sufferers insisting that they are overweight when, in fact, they are emaciated. Others have shown since, however, that irrespective of the feminist approach, this is at least in part an understandable mechanism of defence. I say understandable because it is, in a curious way, an attempt by the sufferer to protect her way of coping with life. If she were to admit that she were thin, she would be admitting that life is impossible. When she is able to recognise her true body size, she is in fact beginning to face life more effectively. The tendency to deny hunger, which gave rise to the name 'anorexia nervosa', is similarly a protective mechanism that needs to be respected by the helper instead of denied.

What is fascinating about this clinical profile is that what has so often been thought to be specific to AN, is, in fact, shared by many people who exist in a state of nutritional deprivation. A very recent article reports a clinical profile in jockeys, almost identical to that presented by AN, and Owens and Slade (1987) have positively correlated characteristics shared both by marathon runners and anorexics. I have already related the problems faced by Szmuckler and his colleagues (1986) in determining 'caseness' in a ballet school. These were shared by Vincent (1979) in his fascinating study of the pursuit of the ideal body form in dancers, and you will probably be familiar with the well-publicised disturbance in hormonal patterns of gymnasts and other women athletes. Furthermore, an extremely important study in 1955, which focused upon the effects of starvation on behaviour, demonstrated that starvation seems, in many ways, to reproduce 'anorexic' symptomatology. For example, the monotonous and eccentric diets characteristic of anorexics, their obsessional preoccupation with food and food-related items and occasional bouts of overeating, were all shared by the 36 men who took part in this experiment. Moreover, these patterns tended to persist for some time after weight had been fully restored, even though none of the men had been troubled by such unusual traits before the study. Happily though, a normal attitude accompanied by normal behaviour were eventually recorded.

I think that we must be careful not to become too carried away with these findings, however. If weight restoration were the way to cure AN, this book would not be necessary. Clearly, there are many more factors involved than nutritional status alone, many of them extremely subtle. To focus overly on the effects of starvation is further to avoid the issues that are really at stake. What a study like this is able to confirm is that most starving organisms will experience a period of chaos, a time of consuming more than seems to be required, before an equilibrium is regained. This in itself is reassuring, if also frightening, for people with AN.

What is most intriguing about this clinical profile, and what seems to distinguish it from other conditions that involve a profile of starvation, are the recent findings that immunity is *not* suppressed in AN. Quite the reverse seems to be true. This is contrary not only to popular belief, but also to intuitive physiological expectation.

It is thought that hormonal responses, in particular oestrogen, may be implicated in this phenomenon, but the precise underlying mechanisms are so far unclear.

OUTCOME

What is the long-term prognosis for people suffering from AN? A blanket answer would be 'fair', but we can be a little more specific. A classic study by Bliss and Branch (1960) showed that around two-thirds of sufferers recover or improve, with the others remaining chronically unwell or even dying. It is the mortality statistics that demonstrate the potentially serious nature of AN, ranging fom 10 per cent in 1970 (Theander, 1970) to over 20 per cent in 1975 (Halmi, Brodland and Rigas, 1975). At least half of these deaths are probably from suicide rather than starvation, which reflects the condition's underlying depression, especially following enforced refeeding. However, outcome studies are fraught with methodological pitfalls. It is often difficult to trace former sufferers; those presently ill, and who have relapsed, may be unwilling to co-operate; follow-up may be too soon; and inadequate outcome-criteria are common. In this latter respect, there is no overall agreement as to what is meant by 'normal', 'cured' or 'recovered'. Also, improvement in, say, weight status only, does not necessarily reflect improvement in other areas. Morgan and Russell (1975), for example, have shown that weight restoration after typical treatment is not directly correlated with long-term outcome.

To say that of people suffering from AN, one-third will successfully recover, one-third will revert to a chronic form of subclinical-like AN, and one-third will repeatedly relapse, would be to reflect accurately in very general terms, the outcome studies to date. When you are looking at these studies, however, you should bear in mind that those of less than a year's duration will tend not to reflect the condition's true course and as such will be biased. Also, we cannot be sure that the individuals being compared had an equally severe problem in the first place — how many people have recovered spontaneously, thus never becoming a statistic; or how many people would recover with the right kind of sympathetic and sustained help? What is important to remember is that recovery is possible and indeed likely. It is therefore appropriate to conclude this chapter with Lawrence's (1983) sage and optimistic words:

> Interestingly, recovered anorexics are rather wonderful people... For many the overcoming of it is a real point of growth. This is not to say that they will never have any difficulties in life again. But I think it is to say that they will not attempt to solve them in this particularly sterile and self-destructive way.

REFERENCES

American Psychiatric Association (1987) Diagnostic and statistical manual of mental disorders, 3rd edn (revised), American Psychiatric Association, Washington, DC

Arieti, S. (1980) 'Man's spirituality and potential for creativity as revealed in mental illness.' *Comprehensive Psychiatry, 21*, 436–43

Bell, R. (1985) *Holy anorexia.* University of Chicago Press, Chicago

Bliss, E.L. and Branch, C.H.H. (1960) *Anorexia nervosa: Its history, psychology, and biology.* Hoeber, New York

Bruch, H. (1974) 'Perils of behavior modification in the treatment of anorexia nervosa.' *Journal of the American Medical Association, 230*, 1419–22

—— (1978) *The golden cage: the enigma of anorexia nervosa.* Open Books, London

—— (1985) 'Four decades of eating disorders.' In D.M. Gardner and P.E. Garfinkel (eds), *Handbook of psychotherapy for anorexia nervosa and bulimia.* Guildford Press, New York

Button, E.J. and Whitehouse, A. (1981) 'Subclinical anorexia nervosa.' *Psychological Medicine, 11*, 509–16

Crisp, A.H. (1980) *Anorexia nervosa: let me be.* Academic Press, London

—— (1986) 'The integration of 'self-help' and 'help' in the prevention of anorexia nervosa.' *British Review of Bulimia and Anorexia Nervosa, 1*, 27–39

—— and Bhat, A.U. (1982) '"Personality" and anorexia nervosa — the phobic avoidance stance.' *Psychotherapy and Psychosomatics, 38,* 178–200

——, Palmer, R.L. and Kalucy, R.S. (1976) 'How common is anorexia nervosa? A prevalence study.' *British Journal of Psychology, 218*, 549–54

Dally, P. (1969) *Anorexia nervosa.* Grune and Stratton, New York

—— and Gomez, J. (1979) *Obesity and anorexia nervosa: a question of shape*, Faber and Faber, London

Decourt, J. (1954) L'Anorexia mentale au temps de Laségue et Gull. Press Medicine, *62*, 355

Duddle, M. (1973) 'An increase of anorexia nervosa in a university population.' *British Journal of Psychiatry, 123*, 711-12

Edwards, G. (1987) 'Anorexia and the family.' In M. Lawrence (ed), *Fed up and hungry: women, oppression and food.* Women's Press, London

Eichenbaum, L. and Orbach, S. (1984) *What do women want?* Fontana, Glasgow

Erichson, A. (1985) *Anorexia nervosa: the broken cycle.* Faber and Faber, London

Garfinkel, P.E. (1974) 'Perception of hunger and satiety in anorexia nervosa.' *Psychological Medicine, 4*, 309–15

Garner, D.M. and Garfinkel, P.E. (1979) 'The eating attitudes test: an index of the symptoms of anorexia nervosa.' *Psychological Medicine, 9*, 273-9

Gull, W.W. (1874) 'Anorexia nervosa (apepsia hysterica, anorexia hysterica).' *Transactions of the Clinical Society of London, 7*, 22–8

Halmi, K.A., Brodland, G and Rigas, C. (1975) 'A follow-up study of patients with anorexia nervosa; an evaluation of prognostic factors and diagnostic criteria.' *Life Hist. Res. Psychopath., 4*, 290

Janet, P. (1907) *Major symptoms of hysteria.* Macmillan, London

Laing, R.D. (1969) *The divided self: an existential study in sanity and madness.* Penguin, Harmondsworth

Laseque, C. (1893) 'On hysterical anorexia.' *Medical Times Gazette, 2*, 367–9

Lawrence, M. (1983) *The anorexic experience.* Women's Press, London

—— (1987) 'Education and identity: the social origins of anorexia.' In M. Lawrence (ed), *Fed up and hungry: women, oppression and food*, Women's Press, London

MacLeod, S. (1981) *The art of starvation.* Virago, London

Meyer, J.E. (1961) 'Das syndrome der anorexia nervosa: Katmnestich unter suchunger.' *Arch. Psych. Z. Nawol., 202,* 31–59

Minuchin, S., Rosman, B.L. and Baker, L. (1978) *Psychosomatic families: anorexia nervosa in context.* Harvard University Press, Cambridge, Mass.

Mogul, S.L. (1980) 'Asceticism in adolescence and anorexia nervosa.' *Psychoanalytic Study of the Child, 35,* 15–75

Morgan, H.G. and Russell, G.F.M. (1975) 'Value of family background and clinical features as predictors of long-term outcome in anorexia nervosa: four year follow-up study of 41 patients.' *Psychological Medicine, 5,* 355–72

Morton, R. (1689) *Phthisiologia, seu exercitationes de phthisi.* Smith, London

—— (1694) *Phthisiologia: or a treatise on consumptions.* Smith and Walford, London

Naudeau, M. (1789) 'Observation sur une maladie nerveuse, accompagnée d'un degôut extraordinaire pour les alimens.' *Journal de Med. Sur. et Pharm. Paris, 80,* 197

Nylander, I. (1971) 'The feeling of being fat and dieting in a school population: an epidemiological interview investigation.' *Acta Sociomedica Scandinavica, 3,* 17–26

Owens, R.G. and Slade, P.D. (1987) 'Running and anorexia nervosa: an empirical study.' *International Journal of Eating Disorders, 6,* 21–9

Palmer, R.L. (1980) *Anorexia nervosa.* Penguin, Harmondsworth

Parry-Jones, W.U. (1986) 'Archival exploration of anorexia nervosa.' In G.I. Szmuckler, P.D. Slade, P. Harris, D. Benton and G.F.M. Russell (eds), *Anorexia nervosa and bulimic disorders: current perspectives,* Proceeding in *Journal of Psychiatric Research,* Pergamon Press, London

Rampling, D. (1986) 'Ascetic ideals and anorexia nervosa.' In G.I. Szmuckler, P.D. Slade, P. Harris, D. Benton and G.F.M. Russell (eds), *Anorexia nervosa and bulimic disorders: current perspectives,* Proceeding in *Journal of Psychiatric Research,* Pergamon Press, London

Richardson, S. (1747–8) *Clarissa.* With an introduction by G. Sherbourne (1962), Houghton Mifflin Co., Boston, Mass.

—— (1747–8) *Clarissa, or the history of a young lady.* A. Ross (1985), Penguin, Harmondsworth

Russell, G.F.M. (1970) 'Anorexia nervosa: its identity as an illness and its treatment.' In J.H. Price (ed), *Modern trends in psychological medicine,* Butterworth, London

Scott, D.W. (1986) 'Anorexia nervosa: A review of possible genetic factors.' *International Journal of Eating Disorders, 5,* 1–20

Selvini-Palazolli, M. (1974) *Self-starvation.* Chaucer, London

Shehan, H.L. and Summers, V.K. (1949) 'The syndrome hypopituitarism.' *Quarterly Journal of Medicine, 18,* 319

Silverman, J.A. (1987) 'An eighteenth-century account of self-starvation in a male.' *International Journal of Eating Disorders, 6,* 431–4

Silverstein, B., Peterson, B. and Perdue, L. (1986) 'Some correlates of the thin standard of bodily attractiveness for women.' *International Journal of Eating Disorders, 5,* 895–905

Simmonds, M. (1914) 'Ueber embousche prozess in der hyperphysis.' *Archs. Path. Anat., 217,* 226

Slade, P.D. and Dewey, M.E. (1986) 'Development and preliminary validation of SCANS: a screening instrument for individuals at risk of developing anorexia and bulimia nervosa.' *International Journal of Eating Disorders, 5,* 517–38

—— and Russell, G.F.M. (1973) 'Awareness of body dimensions in anorexia nervosa; cross-sectional and longitudinal studies.' *Psychological Medicine, 3,* 188–99

Steedman, C. (1986) 'Oral history.' *London Review of Books,* 19 June, 8–9

Szasz, S.T. (1971) *The manufacture of madness.* Routledge and Kegan Paul, London

Szmukler, G.I., Eisler, I., Gillies, C. and Hayward, M.E. (1986) In G.I. Szmukler, P.D. Slade, P. Harris, D. Benton, and G.F.M. Russell. (eds), *Anorexia nervosa and bulimic disorders: Current perspectives*, Proceeding in *Journal of Psychiatric Research*, Pergamon Press, London

Theander, S. (1970) 'Anorexia nervosa: an investigation of 44 female patients.' *Acta Psychiatrica Scandinavica, (Suppl.) 214*, 1–194

—— (1986) 'Outcome and prognosis in anorexia nervosa and bulimia: some results of previous investigations compared with those of a Swedish long-term study.' In G.I. Szmukler, P.D. Slade, P. Harris, D. Benton and G.F.M. Russell (eds), *Anorexia nervosa and bulimic disorders: current perspectives*, Proceeding in *Journal of Psychiatric Research*, Pergamon Press, London

Vincent, L.M. (1979) *Competing with the Sylph.* Andrews and McMeel, New York

Waller, J.U., Kaufman, M.R. and Deutsch, F. (1940) 'Anorexia nervosa, a psychosomatic entity.' *Psychosomatic Medicine, 2*, 3–16

Weil, S. (1951) *Waiting on God.* Routledge and Kegan Paul, London

2

An Overview of Bulimia Nervosa

Peter Lambley and Derek Scott

INTRODUCTION

Bulimia nervosa (BN) is an eating disorder characterised by episodes of binge eating followed by self-induced vomiting or other means of purging the body of food eaten. The sufferer is usually aware of the pathological nature of this behaviour and it is often accompanied by depression, guilt and self-deprecation. There is also massive anxiety about food and eating and undue concern with, and misconception about, weight and body image. Although this syndrome has only recently been formally recognised as a separate and distinct disorder in its own right, it is, as is AN, by no means a new phenomenon. Nineteenth-century psychiatric textbooks describe bulimic behaviour in patients (e.g. Laseque, 1873), while in this century, the famous case of Ellen West originally published in the mid-1940s (Bingswanger, 1944) contains a number of bulimic features. Moreover, binge eating was identified as a feature of a number of eating disorders more than a quarter of a century ago by Stunkard (1959) — one of the early researchers in this area.

What has made BN of particular concern in recent times is the widespread increase in cases referred for treatment in the United States, Great Britain and other countries (Johnson, Lewis and Hagman, 1984; Szmukler, McCance, McCrone and Hunter, 1986). Particularly worrying are reports that suggest that many women suffer from BN in silence without realising the seriousness of their condition. In one study, for example, over ten per cent of a sample of 300 women shoppers reported binge eating, with three per cent also admitting to vomiting and purging. Clinical evidence is growing too, that numbers of women now in their middle or old age have regularly used purging or vomiting as a means of weight control throughout their lives. In this chapter, we will attempt to provide an overview of the current state of research — theoretical, clinical and empirical — into BN, and try to develop a coherent paradigm to help in understanding the world of the BN sufferer.

DIFFERENTIAL DIAGNOSIS

It is important to realise that most of the features described previously (see also Chapter 3 for fuller details on diagnosis and assessment) pertaining to BN are to be found to varying degrees in both normal individuals and amongst people suffering from non-bulimic eating disorders. Binge eating, obsession with body image and weight, depression, guilt and anxiety about self-control are each, on their own, relatively common experiences. For example, it has been found that 40 per cent of a sample of women working in a banking institution and 70 per cent of women in a university setting engaged in binge eating. Only one per cent and five per cent respectively of these women were bulimic. A number of other studies have also established that many women quite routinely feel despondent, anxious or disturbed by their weight or body image (Rodin, Silberstein and Striegel-Moore, 1985).

The key component of BN, which most reliably separates it from other food disorders, is the binging–vomiting/purging cycle and the role that it serves in the maintenance of body weight for the sufferer. Vomiting on its own is not an unusual occurrence. It does occur normally in people and amongst those suffering from non-bulimic eating disorders. We are all familiar with nausea and/or vomiting induced by excessive overeating and a number of people may involuntarily induce nausea or vomiting if they experience intense anxiety at mealtimes. However, these are inevitably rare occurrences. Similarly, the use of purgatives or laxatives to facilitate bowel movement is a relatively common occurrence but, once again, not as a means of losing weight, but to combat constipation.

Care must be taken also to distinguish between the vomiting associated with the bulimic ritual and other psychosomatic or organic conditions. Organic-based vomiting, for example, is usually clearly related to the presence of other physical symptoms, as in the case of gastrointestinal disorders, pregnancy, alcoholism and uraemia. However, vomiting after meals can be exhibited by people suffering from long-term disorders of the digestive tract (e.g. stomach ulcer or intestinal obstruction) and should be excluded early from consideration. Psychogenic vomiting generally occurs in young to middle-aged females and is characterised by vomiting shortly after eating even small amounts of food. The absence of binging, loss of appetite and excessive concern with weight loss are the key distinguishing components of this condition.

BULIMIA AND ANOREXIA NERVOSA

A number of terms have been used to describe the syndrome of BN within recent years: bulimia nervosa (Russell, 1979), bulimarexia (Boskind-Lodahl and White, 1978), and dietary chaos syndrome (Palmer, 1979). In fact, interest in BN developed from both research into AN and the clinical experience of therapists working with anorexic patients (see, for example, Beumont, George and Smart,

1976; Ben-Tovim, Marilov and Crisp, 1979; Russell, 1979). Briefly, it became apparent that a number of 'classical' AN patients either had features of BN alongside their severe weight loss or developed bulimic rituals following the onset of AN. In one important study, it was noted that the vomiting–purging ritual in hospitalised anorexics tended to appear in response to behavioural treatment programmes aimed solely at getting the patient to eat (Agras *et al.*, 1974). Quite simply, as the authors noted, patients 'discovered' vomiting or purging as a means of apparently reaching ward goals (eating) and thus securing their discharge from hospital while effectively fulfilling their need to be thin.

Throughout the literature on AN, reference has been made to binge eating, usually associated with vomiting and purging, as characteristic of some patients at some times. The proportion of cases believed to demonstrate such behaviour has varied from series to series. Crisp (1965) and Russell (1970) mention binging as an occasional feature, both Theander (1970) and Halmi (1974) noted it in about ten per cent of cases, and Bruch (1974) reported it as a characteristic of 22 per cent of her patients.

Nogami and Yabana (1977) presented an informative discussion on 16 cases of binge eating. A clear association with AN is seen in this sample as 50 per cent were described as having a history of dieting or anorexia, with the first symptom being food restriction rather than food binges. Seven subjects had amenorrhea and five frequently vomited. Russell's (1979) article on a series of 30 patients who revealed a history of episodic overeating, vomiting and purging, provides a source of detailed information on such patients. The usual clinical features of BN are described, and again most had a previous history of weight loss and amenorrhea. In both of these studies, an attendant depressive picture was typically found (Wardle and Beinhart, 1981).

According to Russell's (1979) findings, AN patients exhibited self-induced severe weight loss, persistent amenorrhea, and intense fear of losing control over eating and becoming obese. In contrast to the AN group, bulimics were only slightly underweight, or even normal or overweight. This characteristic has been reliably confirmed by other researchers (e.g. Fairburn, 1982; Halmi, Falk and Schwartz, 1981). Additionally, amenorrhea was found as a feature in these individuals. However, the singular feature exhibited by both groups was a pathological concern with body size and the absence of a realistic perspective of normal body size.

In summary, although both bulimics and anorexics are abnormally concerned with body weight and have a morbid fear of becoming fat, AN sufferers are characterised by a life-threatening weight loss, whilst bulimics may fluctuate between weight loss and weight gain. Overall, it is probably true to say that bulimics tend to look more normal in terms of current ideas of what constitutes an acceptable body shape. Classical anorexics are always obviously thin.

How prevalent is bulimia?

Although it has been suggested that bulimia is a common problem, its exact prevalence is unknown (Pyle, Mitchell and Eckert, 1981). Bulimia is difficult to detect for several reasons. For one thing, BN sufferers often take great pains to hide their rituals, even from their family and close friends. Secondly, family, friends and even trained professionals are unable to detect the disorder because the victim's weight and body shape stay within normal limits. Thirdly, unlike anorexics, who frequently have trouble eating in public, bulimics exhibit normal and appropriate eating habits in social circumstances (Fairburn and Cooper, 1982). The existence of BN usually becomes manifest when the individual feels that she can no longer cope with the pressure inside and so seeks help.

Using the American Psychiatric Association's DSM III diagnostic criteria (APA, 1980; see Chapter 3), Strangler and Printz (1980) reviewed psychiatric diagnoses in a sample of 500 students who had been through a university outpatient medical service. Twenty-two cases (four per cent) were diagnosed as having eating disorders, with BN diagnosed in 19 of these 22 cases. Because this study covered only those patients who actually sought treatment, it must be concluded that these findings represent a conservative estimate. More recent surveys using non-psychiatric subjects have shown a high incidence of both binge eating and BN in normal populations. Cooper and Fairburn (1983), for example, found that 2.5 per cent of women attending a family-planning clinic used vomiting and/or laxatives on a weekly basis to control their weight. Nearly seven per cent of the sample reported routine binge eating. Roughly similar or greater proportions were found by others. Working-class women in one sample had substantially lower proportions: 41 per cent binging; only one per cent bulimic. These figures suggest that, at the very least, between one and five women in every 100 suffer from BN. However, the true figure is probably much higher. Many bulimics are deeply ashamed of their rituals and few readily share their problems with other people, even close friends.

Whatever the true incidence of BN, we can be sure of one thing — the number of cases seeking help is increasing (see, for example, Szmukler *et al.*, 1986).

Who gets bulimia?

Gender

Initially, it was believed that BN was, almost by definition, a female problem. Fairburn (1982), for example, reported that all their bulimics were female, a finding repeated in other studies (Pyle *et al.*, 1981; Fairburn and Cooper, 1982). However, a recent review by Striegel-Moore, Silberstein and Rodin (1986) suggests that up to ten per cent of bulimics may be male (see also Chapter 4). It is possible with the publicity given to anorexia and BN by the media, that sufferers are more likely to recognise their disorder and seek treatment. Evidence is emerging that some men in occupations or in psychosexual contexts that demand strict weight control and a thin appearance are also likely to develp BN. Rodin *et al.* (1985), for example, have shown that there is a higher incidence of BN amongst athletes where weight is of major concern (e.g. wrestlers and jockeys) than amongst athletes in other sports. Similarly, there is some clinical evidence to suggest that homosexual men, concerned with maintaining their appearance, may be more inclined to practise BN than heterosexuals (e.g. Herzog, 1984; see also Chapters 4 and 5 for further discussion).

Race

Most early studies of BN reported that the great majority of subjects were white (Kendell, Hall, Hailey and Babigian, 1973). This applied to the USA as well as the UK. However, in more recent studies, non-Caucasian subjects have been seen increasingly, although the numbers remain small. Nwaefuna (1981), for example, reported a case of a Nigerian woman with BN, while Buchan and Gregory (1984) have since reported on other cases of Afro-Caribbean patients.

Social class

Few research reports have directly investigated the link between social class and BN. Some suggest that BN is more often found in the middle and upper classes of society (Szmukler *et al.*, 1986), although others disagree. In one of the few research reports in the area comparing prevalence rates in working-class and university (middle-class) communities in Virginia, USA, binge eating occurred much more often amongst middle-class subjects than amongst working-class subjects (five per cent versus one per cent, respectively). Similarly, a Scottish team of researchers found social-class differences in a study of psychiatric case registers in Aberdeen. They noted that most cases of BN came from social classes I and II (the upper- and middle-income range) and not from social class III.

Clinical presentation

Age of onset

Most bulimics commence binging between 15 and 18 years of age (Boskind-Lodahl and White, 1978; Russell, 1979; Pyle *et al.*, 1981; Fairburn and Cooper, 1982). It is interesting that the onset of overeating and the onset of vomiting do not usually begin at the same time, with Russell noting a three-year difference and Fairburn and Cooper (1982) reporting a one year difference. Garfinkel, Moldovsky and Garner (1980) noted that BN inevitably develops after, not before, the onset of dieting. Incidentally, it should also be noted that some cases of BN may begin later in adulthood, usually in the early- to mid-twenties.

Weight history

Bulimia may occur within all weight groups, from anorexic to the obese. Russell (1979) found that before developing BN, 17 of his sample (57 per cent) had suffered from AN, 33 per cent had shown moderate or slight weight loss, whilst ten per cent had been consistently overweight. Similarly, 74 per cent of Pyle *et al.*'s (1981) patients were below median weight for height and age, although only 15 per cent gave a history of AN. In addition, the majority of Herzog's (1984) patients had a history of being average or slightly overweight. In two further studies, it was concluded that the symptoms of BN are more likely to appear in individuals having a history of being somewhat overweight (Halmi *et al.*, 1981; Fairburn and Cooper, 1982).

Sexual history

Opinion is divided about the nature and degree of sexual experiences of BN compared to AN sufferers and to normals. Bruch (1982) suggested that anorexics in general may be prone to early maturation. This, she argued, creates conflict over weight gain and female body shape before the adolescent girl is emotionally ready to deal with her body changes. Striegel-Moore *et al.* (1986) suggest that the same may apply for bulimics. Whether there is early biological maturation in these girls, or whether the pattern of upbringing she (or he) received in the family render them ill-equipped to face adulthood is a matter of some debate. Psychoanalytic theorists have long held that anorexia is a rejection of female identity and other symbols of adulthood. The issue of psychosexual factors is discussed in depth within Chapter 5.

Frequency of binge eating and purging

The reported frequency of binge eating episodes varies in the literature. For instance, from a total sample of 499 bulimics, 27 per cent reported binge eating at least once daily and 33 per cent reported binge eating at least once weekly (Fairburn and Cooper, 1982). Of Pyle *et al.*'s (1981) 34 cases, the majority engaged in binge eating daily. Russell's (1979) conclusions are consistent with other writers in that frequency of binging varies from individual to individual. Certain patients are able to impose strict controls of their food intake over a period of time, with binging episodes only every week or two. On the other hand, exceptionally frequent binging episodes of three to 30 times per day have been reported (Fairburn, 1982).

The most commonly used method of purging is vomiting and then laxative and diuretic abuse (Halmi *et al.*, 1981; Pyle *et al.*, 1981). The frequency of vomiting has also been found to be higher than that of binge eating (Fairburn and Cooper, 1982). Fifty-six per cent of their sample reported vomiting at least once daily, and a further 17 per cent more than once weekly (Schlesier-Stropp, 1984).

Duration of BN

In Fairburn and Cooper's (1982) study of almost 500 women, the mean duration was 5.2 years, with the mean duration of vomiting being 4.5 years. Herzog (1984) found the average duration of symptoms to be longer than six years. Individual cases have been recorded where binging and vomiting persisted for 15 to 20 years (Lambley, 1983).

Preoccupation with food and the urge to eat

The bulimic's life is generally heavily centred on food and eating to the extent that concentration and concern for everyday issues and attitudes is impaired (Russell, 1979; Fairburn, 1982; Pyle *et al.*, 1981; Fairburn and Cooper, 1982; Herzog, 1984; Rosen and Leitenberg, 1982). For the majority, the most alarming symptom is fear of losing control over eating (Russell, 1979; Fairburn, 1982; Pyle *et al.*, 1981; Fairburn and Cooper, 1982). As an example, they frequently report that if they allowed themselves only a small quantity of some favourite food, a binge would ensue (e.g. Russell, 1979). A binge of one to two hours is typical, but may continue for an entire day with sugary or starchy foods being favoured. Single binges consuming 15,000 to 20,000 calories are known (Russell, 1979).

Preoccupation with body and weight image

In addition to preoccupation with food, bulimics report a preoccupation with their weight and body size (Wermuth, Davis, Hollister and Stunkard, 1977; Palmer, 1979; Russell, 1979; Fairburn, 1982). These patients often report an exaggerated fear of becoming overweight and a feeling of being fat when they are simply not (Pyle *et al.*, 1981; Fairburn and Cooper, 1982; Garfinkel and Garner, 1982). Having lost the sense of a realistic body image, most bulimics desire to be thinner than is normal or healthy for their height. A distorted body image is evident in the bulimic's discrepancy between what society generally regards as a 'healthy' weight and their desired weight (Russell, 1979; Pyle *et al.*, 1981).

Mood and other personality states

Alongside preoccupations with eating, dieting and weight, depressive symptoms and high levels of anxiety are prominent symptoms (Pyle *et al.*, 1981; Fairburn and Cooper, 1982). Herzog (1984), for example, found that more than 75 per cent of bulimics reported significant depressive symptoms and Fairburn (1982) found that depressive symptoms in bulimics increased as weight increased or if there were no opportunities for vomiting after eating. Depressive symptoms may therefore be due, in part, to weight gain (or perceived weight gain), or they may result from failure to control compulsive binge eating and vomiting. Similarly, differences of opinion exist regarding the source of anxiety. It has been postulated by Rosen and Leitenberg (1982) that binge eating and vomiting are linked in a vicious cycle by anxiety, as the anxiety created by eating (increased fear of gaining weight) is reduced by vomiting (Schlesier-Stropp, 1984). Other researchers have linked anxiety to the bulimic's anticipated lack of control (Rau and Green, 1975; Palmer, 1979). In addition to anxiety, bulimics experience overriding feelings of guilt, shame and self-contempt following a binge (Rau and Green, 1975; Wermuth *et al.*, 1977; Fairburn, 1982; Pyle *et al.*, 1981; Herzog, 1984). Although researchers generally agree that bulimics do experience high levels of depression and anxiety, they disagree on the cause. Williamson *et al.* (1985) studied several personality characteristics of bulimics, obese and normal subjects and noted that bulimics manifested more psychopathology than either of the other two sets of subjects. In particular, bulimics were more anxious, more depressed, more impulsive and generally more neurotic. Strober, Salkin, Burroughs and Morrell's (1982) study found bulimics to be more labile, impulsive and susceptible to mood disturbances than non-bulimic anorexics.

Family history

Data gleaned from bulimics indicates the presence of alcoholism and weight problems in first-degree relatives (Pyle *et al.*, 1981; Herzog, 1984). In Herzog's study of 30 bulimic patients, 43 per cent had a first-degree relative with either alcoholism or affective illness, and 37 per cent reported having a family history of obesity. Pyle *et al.* similarly noted that about 50 per cent of bulimics reported alcoholism in at least one first-degree family member, 68 per cent cited obesity, and 47 per cent reported that a first degree relative suffered from depression. An unexpected finding of Herzog, but one not corroborated by other studies (e.g. Pyle *et al.*), was a high incidence of serious physical illness in the parents of bulimics. About 50 per cent of Herzog's patients reported at least one parent who had died or had a history of serious physical illness.

A major study conducted by Strober *et al.* (1982) in California found that the parents of BN sufferers tended to show greater psychopathology than did parents of non-bulimic anorexics. In particular, the bulimic's fathers showed more impulsivity and excitability, less frustration tolerance and more dissatisfaction with family relationships than did fathers of anorexics. Mothers of bulimic sufferers scored higher than non-bulimic sufferers' mothers on depression, hostility and dissatisfaction with family relationships. Another American study reported that parents of bulimics tended to place much more contradictory demands on their children than did normal parents. While parents of bulimics stressed high intellectual achievement, self-discipline and independence, as did normal middle-class parents, they also tended to undermine their child's attempts to be assertive and independent and so achieve these goals. The authors of this study suggested that this created sets of double-binds for the bulimic children, who were: — taught to value high achievement but not how to achieve; taught to value emotionality, openness and independency but not encouraged to be so. The families were further characterised as enmeshing and disorganised.

Aetiological considerations: or 'what causes bulimia?'

Genetic factors

Can one inherit a predisposition to bulimia? Although it is most unlikely that a 'bulimia' gene in a parent is passed on to a child, body type is an important inherited factor and this may predispose a person to being of big build, to have more than the average fat distribution in the body and to have a slow food metabolising rate.

In this sense, genetic factors may be of importance. Research does suggest that women who are heavier than their peers are more likely to develop bulimia. However, care must be taken in interpreting this fact. Family and societal influences are considered more important in the long run in determining whether a heavy woman becomes bulimic as opposed to being overweight or to simply engage in binge eating (Strober *et al.*, 1982). This complex issue is discussed at length by Scott (1986).

Physiological factors

A considerable amount of time has been spent researching the question of whether or not there are physiological factors involved in the aetiology of BN. Again, there is no simple answer. It is unlikely that physiological factors are the sole cause of BN, but they do, nevertheless, have a role to play. This is principally in the physiological effects of dieting. When an individual diets, essentially two things happen in the body. The drop in food intake causes a reduction in weight and this results in a corresponding drop in body metabolic rate. This means that the body lowers its ability to digest food. When a diet is over and the individual returns to a normal level of calorie intake, weight gain may follow because it takes some time for the body's metabolic rate to return to normal. The body simply cannot absorb the food. This is made worse if the dieter, driven by hunger, overeats. Thus, for the anxious, weight-conscious person worried about self-control, it is an easy matter to confuse the body's normal physiological response to dieting with a lack of self-control. A second, more determined diet usually follows, with more intense results. It is often this second and subsequent bout of dieting that does the most damage, by pushing the individual into a bulimic pattern. Again, however, care must be taken to use a multiple-factor framework when interpreting these findings. Psychological variables need to be employed to account for the reason why individuals who experience these physiological effects (most dieters in fact) do not go on to develop bulimia.

Finally, physiological factors play a major role in the timing of the development of BN. Endocrinological changes in adolescence result in changes of body shape. For females in particular, rounding of the hips and increased body weight all serve to make the individual more aware than previously of body image.

Social factors

Much has been written about the importance of sociocultural pressures in the development of bulimia. Clearly, in the past 20 or 30 years, with the increased levels of both education and material standards of living, people have had much more time to focus on how they look and how they feel about their bodies than was previously so. This is particularly true in the case of women where society and the media have repeatedly put forward the view that thinness and success and well-being go hand in hand. As many have argued, this stereotyping plays a central role in the development of female sex-role identity (e.g. Scott, 1987). Does it help cause bulimia?

In one sense, yes. Women are generally more body- and weight-conscious than men and this is especially so amongst adolescents. Some studies of the attitudes held by bulimic women do show that they are more inclined than normal women to stereotypical ways of thinking; valuing thinness, beauty, dependence, unassertiveness and so on. There have, however, been a number of studies that have not found this to be the case (for a useful review see Striegel-Moore *et al.*, 1986). The issue is therefore still open to question. The best that can be said at this stage is to suggest that sociocultural factors do seem to account for why women by and large suffer from bulimia and not men. However, it is probably mistaken to say that this operates in a simple, cause–effect, 'fashion-conscious' way. Sociocultural factors also shape family upbringing patterns and these, more than magazine articles, are thought likely to be involved in explaining why the majority of women exposed to the same media images as bulimics do not develop the disorder. The fact that so many middle-class women do, however, develop binge eating suggests that these sociocultural variables are of considerable importance in that particular area. Clearly, bulimics are especially vulnerable to these pressures and further factors are required to account for why this is so.

Family considerations

For some time now, research and clinical reports have revealed considerable disturbance in the families of both anorexics and bulimics. As was noted earlier, there is evidence of affective disorder in parents and grandparents, particularly a proneness to depression under stress. There is, more fundamentally, some indication that the family milieu serves to constrict the developing child psychologically. This takes the form of cutting her off from valuable psychosocial contacts with the outside world and undervaluing her attempts to learn how to be independent, achievement-orientated, disciplined and so on, characteristics supposedly valued by the family (Lambley, 1983). Schwartz, Thompson and Johnson (1981), for example, noted that bulimic patients' families exhibited tendencies towards isolation and self-preoccupation as well as a heightened consciousness of personal appearance. Food and eating has also long been known to have special significance for parents in their families with mealtimes frequently being used as the arena for resolving (or rather acting out) family conflicts (Minuchin, Rosman and Baker, 1978; Schwartz *et al.*, 1981).

The consequences of bulimia

Medical consequences

Bulimics may develop a number of medical complications. Most often, complications result from repeated vomiting rather than actual use of purgatives or from binging (Pyle *et al.*, 1981; Mitchell and Pyle, 1982). Both vomiting and purging lead to losses of body fluids and electrolytes, which often results in hypokalemia (Herzog, 1984). Other symptoms may also be present such as sore throats, swollen salivary glands and dental problems. The principal dental complaint is the destruction of dental enamel caused by acid in vomit repeatedly eroding the teeth (Russell, 1979; Fairburn 1982; Herzog, 1984). There have also been reports in the literature of epileptic fits and renal damage occurring, following prolonged use of a vomiting–purging ritual.

Psychological consequences

By far the most disturbing of the psychological sequelaa to bulimia is the fact that for as long as an individual engages in bulimic rituals, there is neither the time nor the inclination to tackle the normal demands of growth and development. Adolescence is one of the most crucial periods in a person's life for the development of personality, and if this time of growth, challenge and integration is not made proper use of, the individual will be unable to cope effectively with normal adult life. In particular, the development of a healthy mind and body identity, the establishment of adequate psychological and sexual intimacy and the development of normal stress-management skills suffer. When the bulimia sufferer later forms relationships, develops a career, marries or has children, normal stresses and anxieties become hard to bear and can place a great strain on relationships and personal stability. Guilt, anxiety, depression and the feeling of 'never being happy, never being satisfied' are common complaints of most bulimic women. In the long term, suicide must also be considered a possibility (Russell, 1979).

It is as well to bear in mind that bulimia represents two separate, although related, psychotherapeutic tasks; removing the person's dependency on bulimic rituals and ensuring that the underlying personality development previously blocked or impaired by the ritual is followed through.

CONCLUSIONS

We have looked in this chapter at the current state of our knowledge of BN. Clearly, much remains to be done but it is becoming apparent that understanding at this stage is best served by adopting a multifactorial model for BN. As we have seen, genetic, physiological, social and psychological factors all have a bearing on explaining why one person and not another develops BN. Hopefully, as time goes on, we will reach the position where we will be able to more accurately pinpoint the precise relation and balance between the factors. Until then, BN will remain a fascinating and complex subject.

REFERENCES

Agras, S., Barlow, D.H., Chaplin, H.N., Abel, G. and Leitenberg, H. (1974) 'Behavior modification of anorexia nervosa.' *Archives of General Psychiatry, 30*, 279–86

American Psychiatric Association (1980) *Diagnostic and statistical manual of mental*

disorders, 3rd edn, American Psychiatric Association, Washington, DC
Ben-Tovim, D.I., Marilov, V. and Crisp, A.H. (1979) 'Personality and mental state within anorexia nervosa.' *Journal of Psychosomatic Research, 3,* 321–5
Beumont, P.J.V., George, G.C. and Smart, D.E. (1976) '"Dieters" and "vomiters and purgers" in anorexia nervosa.' *Psychological Medicine, 6,* 617–22
Binswanger (1944) 'The case of Ellen West.' In R. May *et al.* (eds), *Existence*, Basic Books, New York
Boskind-Lodahl, M. and White, W.C. (1978) The definition and treatment of bulimarexia in college women — a pilot study. *Journal of American College Health Association, 27,* 84–97
Bruch, H. (1974) *Eating disorders: obesity, anorexia nervosa, and the person within.* Basic Books, New York
—— (1982) 'Anorexia nervosa: theory and therapy.' *American Journal of Psychiatry, 139,* 1531–8
Buchan, T. and Gregory, L.D. (1984) 'Anorexia nervosa in a black Zimbabwean.' *British Journal of Psychiatry, 145*, 326–30
Cooper, P.J. and Fairburn, C.G. (1983) 'Binge-eating and self-induced vomiting in the community: a preliminary study.' *British Journal of Psychiatry, 142*, 139–44
Crisp, A.H. (1965) 'Some aspects of evolution, presentation, and follow-up of anorexia nervosa.' *Proceedings of the Royal Society of Medicine, 58,* 814–20
Fairburn, C.G. (1982) *Binge-eating and bulimia nervosa.* Smith, Kline and French, London
—— and Cooper, P.J. (1982) 'Self-induced vomiting and bulimia nervosa: An undetected problem.' *British Medical Journal, 284*, 1153–5
Garfinkel, P.E. and Garner, D.M. (1982) *Anorexia nervosa: A multidimensional perspective.* Brunner/Mazel, New York
—— Moldovsky, H. and Garner, D.M. (1980) The heterogeneity of anorexia nervosa. *Archives of General Psychiatry, 37,* 1036–40
Halmi, K.A. (1974) 'Anorexia nervosa: demographic and clinical features in 94 cases.' *Psychosomatic Medicine, 36,* 18–25
—— Falk, J.R. and Schwartz, E. (1981) 'Binge-eating and vomiting: a survey of a college population.' *Psychological Medicine, 11*, 697–706
Herzog, D. (1984) 'Are anorexics and bulimics depressed?' *American Journal of Psychiatry, 141*, 21–4
Johnson, C., Lewis, C. and Hagman, J. (1984) 'Bulimia: review and synthesis.' *Psychiatric Clinics of North America, 7,* 247–73
Kendell, R.E., Hall, D.J., Hailey, A. and Babigian, H.M. (1973) 'The epidemiology of anorexia nervosa.' *Psychosomatic Medicine, 3*, 200–3
Lambley, P. (1983) *How to survive anorexia.* Muller, London
Laseque, C. (1873) 'De l'anorexie hysterique.' In R.M. Kaufman and M. Heiman (eds), *Evolution of psychosomatic concepts. Anorexia nervosa: a paradigm.* International Universities Press, New York, 1964, pp. 141–55
Minuchin, S., Rosman, B.L. and Baker, L. (1978) *Psychosomatic families: anorexia nervosa in context.* Harvard University Press, Cambridge, Mass.
Mitchell, J.E. and Pyle, R.L. (1982) 'The bulimia syndrome in normal weight individuals: a review.' *International Journal of Eating Disorders, 1*, 61–73
Nogami, Y. and Yabana, F. (1977) 'On kibarashi-gui (binge eating).' *Folia Psychiatrica et Neurologica Japonica, 31,* 159–66
Nwaefuna, A. (1981) 'Anorexia nervosa in a developing country.' *British Journal of Psychiatry, 138*, 270–1
Palmer, R.L. (1979) 'The dietary chaos syndrome: a useful new term?' *British Journal of Medical Psychology, 52*, 187–90
Pyle, R.L., Mitchell, J.E., and Eckert, E.D. (1981) 'Bulimia: A report of 34 cases.' *Journal*

of Clinical Psychiatry, 42, 60–4

Rau, J.H. and Green, R.S. (1975) 'Compulsive eating: a neurophysiological approach to certain eating disorders.' *Comprehensive Psychiatry, 16*, 223–31

Rodin, J., Silberstein, L. and Striegel-Moore, R. (1985) 'Women and weight: a normative discontent.' In T.B. Sonderegger (ed), *Psychology and gender: 1984 Nebraska symposium on motivation*, University of Nebraska Press, Lincoln

Rosen, J.C. and Leitenberg, H. (1982) 'Bulimia nervosa: treatment with exposure and response prevention.' *Behavior Therapy, 133*, 117–124

Russell, G.F.M. (1970) 'Anorexia nervosa: its identity as an illness and its treatment.' In J.H. Price (ed), *Modern trends in psychological medicine, Vol. 2*, pp 131–64, Appleton-Century-Crofts, New York

—— (1979) 'Bulimia nervosa: an ominous variant of anorexia nervosa.' *Psychological Medicine, 9*, 429-48.

Schlesier-Stropp, B. (1984) 'Bulimia: a review of the literature.' *Psychological Bulletin, 95*, 247–57

Schwartz, D.M., Thompson, M.G. and Johnson, C.L. (1981) 'Anorexia nervosa and bulimia: the socio-cultural context.' *International Journal of Eating Disorders, 1*, 20–36

Scott, D.W. (1986) 'Anorexia Nervosa: a review of possible genetic factors.' *International Journal of Eating Disorders, 5*, 1–20

—— (1987) 'The involvement of psychosexual factors in the causation of eating disorders: time for a reappraisal.' *International Journal of Eating Disorders, 6*, 199–213

Strangler, R.S. and Printz, A.M. (1980) 'DSM-III: Psychiatric diagnosis in a university population.' *American Journal of Psychiatry, 137*, 937–40

Striegel-Moore, R., Silberstein. L. and Rodin, J. (1986) 'Towards an understanding of risk factors for bulimia.' *American Psychologist, 41*, 246–63

Strober, M., Salkin, B., Burroughs, J. and Morrell, W. (1982) 'Validity of the bulimia-restricter distinction in anorexia nervosa: parental personality characteristics and family psychiatric morbidity.' *Journal of Nervous and Mental Disease, 170*, 345–51

Stunkard, A.J. (1959) 'Eating patterns and obesity.' *Psychiatric Quarterly, 33*, 284–95

Szmukler, G., McCance, C., McCrone, L. and Hunter, D. (1986) 'Anorexia nervosa: psychiatric case register study from Aberdeen.' *Psychological Medicine, 16*, 49–58

Theander, S. (1970) 'Anorexia nervosa: a psychiatric investigation of 94 female patients.' *Acta Psychiatrica Scandinavica, Suppl. 214*

Wardle, J. and Beinhart, H. (1981) 'Binge eating: a theoretical review.' *British Journal of Clinical Psychology, 20*, 97–109

Wermuth, B.M., Davis, K.L., Hollister, L.E. and Stunkard, A.J. (1977) 'Phenytoin treatment of the binge-eating syndrome.' *American Journal of Psychiatry, 134*, 1249–53

Williamson, D.A., Kelley, M.L., Davis, C.J., Ruggiero, L. and Blouin, D.C. (1985) 'Psychopathology of eating disorders: A controlled comparison of bulimic, obese, and normal subjects.' *Journal of Consulting and Clinical Psychology, 53*, 161–6

3

Assessment of Anorexia and Bulimia Nervosa

Derek Scott

THE PROBLEMS OF DIAGNOSIS

While most clinicians can readily recognise patients with eating disorders, there is no consensus of opinion regarding the clinical features necessary for a diagnosis. Even psychiatrists and physicians disagree amongst themselves as to the various features considered essential for diagnosis. This is, at least in part, because different people have focused on different aspects of the illness. Nevertheless, the central feature has been described in various, yet essentially similar, ways. For Bruch (1973) it is the self-inflicted starvation and *relentless pursuit of thinness*; whilst Selvini-Palazzoli (1974) describes it as 'not the lack of appetite that holds the key to anorexia nervosa — the true cause is a *deliberate wish to slim*' (p. 24). According to Ziegler and Sours (1968) it is 'the *pursuit of thinness* as a pleasure in itself and a frantic concern with establishing control over the body and its functions', whilst for Crisp (1977) AN is a 'weight phobia'. Central to Crisp's view is the 'preoccupation of the anorectic with maintaining a low subpubertal body weight and of *avoiding any weight gain.* Within the potential anorectic there emerges the increasing conviction that her body shape and volume is governing her destiny' (Crisp, 1977, p. 465). The relentless pursuit of a thin body size in spite of emaciation is thus the central phenomenon required for a diagnosis of AN. Various other diagnostic criteria have been established beyond this basic drive to be thin. Many investigators have attempted to define more objective criteria for AN. One must bear in mind that AN consists of a number of factors: (a) the drive for thinness and its related manifestations (e.g. starvation, vomiting, laxative abuse, hiding foods); (b) the effects of starvation; (c) psychopathological features; and (d) complications or sequelae (Garfinkel and Garner, 1982).

A number of objective diagnostic criteria have therefore been developed. In the case of anorexia, if they are to truly differentiate anorexics or from others who have lost weight, these criteria must focus more on the core features of AN and less on the starvation effects and sequelae. These diagnostic criteria usually require evidence of a psychobiological disturbance in addition to the fear of weight. For example, Russell's (e.g. Morgan and Russell, 1975) criteria for a diagnosis of AN are: (a) that the patient resorts to a variety of devices aimed at achieving weight loss (starvation, vomiting, laxatives, etc.); (b) that there is evidence of an endocrine disorder, amenorrhea in the female and loss of sexual potency and interest in the male; and (c) that the patient manifests the characteristic psychopathology of a morbid fear of becoming fat. This is often accompanied by a distorted judgement by the patient of her own body size. A specific degree of weight loss is not required. Dally (1969) has used similar criteria and has quantified the specific features. For instance, in addition to the refusal to eat, the patient must have lost at least 10 per cent of her previous body weight; amenorrhea must be of at least three months' duration if menses were previously regular; the age of onset should be between 11 and 35 years. Dally also required that there be no evidence of pre-existing schizophrenia, severe depression, or organic disease. Rollins and Piazza (1978) have attempted to integrate both psychopathology and physical changes in their diagnostic criteria. According to these authors, the essential psychopathology consists of: (a) evidence of weight phobia and/or a distorted body image and (b) a 'pervasive sense of inadequacy'. Physical criteria consist of either a weight loss of 20 per cent or more body weight or weight loss to less than 80 per cent of average weight for height; and amenorrhea is a necessary feature in females (Garfinkel & Garner, 1982).

Basic to every diagnosis is a general agreement on the criteria on which it is founded. A criterion is the standard, law or rule by which a correct judgement can be made. The criteria must be logical and discriminating to the disorder under discussion, as well as being *practical* (Askevold, 1983). The two sets of criteria most in use for AN are those of Feighner *et al.* (1972) and the DSM-III (American Psychiatric Association, 1980).

Feighner's criteria

Feighner's criteria for AN consists of six main points, which are now described as critically discussed by Askevold (1983).

A. *Age of onset prior to 25 years.* This seems a purely arbitrary figure to choose. All practitioners within AN will be able to think of exceptions to this and the main decrease in incidence is after 20. The clinical fact is that AN has become increasingly difficult to differentiate from depressive loss of appetite with increasing age. So what about the lower limit? Difficulties have also emerged in differentiating this as the age of onset decreases. One can expect to see most cases in the 13 to 20 age bracket, although true cases outside of this age bracket will also be seen.

B. *Weight loss of 25 per cent of original body weight.* Twenty-five per cent is another arbitrarily chosen figure. In reality, it is without logical connection to the diagnosis. It has been shown more than once (e.g. Halmi, 1974) that there are no differences in a series of parameters in patient groups with weight loss on both sides of 25 per cent. The central issue is not weight loss *per se*, but weight loss as an indicator of a determined will to alter body shape.

C-1. *Denial of illness, with a failure to recognise nutritional needs.* Obviously, this is incorrect as clinical experience shows that anorexics are very selective about which type of food they refuse. Additionally, they usually do take care of nutritional needs and are often health-food devotees.

C-2. *Apparent enjoyment in losing weight,* with overt manifestations that food refusal is a pleasurable indulgence. Most experienced practitioners would disagree with this. Although anorexics do gain a feeling of triumph in being able to control their food intake, their life as victims of anorexia is largely a miserable situation.

C-3. *A desired body image of extreme thinness,* with overt evidence that it is rewarding to the patient to achieve and maintain this state. It is not thinness in itself that is the core, but the total shape of the body, especially the fear of the mature shape. The reward rests in the feeling of control.

C-4. *Unusual hoarding or handling of food.* What is unusual in their handling of food is their choice of specific types of food and their unusual habits. Hoarding is sometimes seen, but cannot be regarded as a cardinal feature.

D. *No known physical illness* that could account for anorexia and weight loss. This is self-evident.

E. *No other known psychiatric disorder,* with particular reference to primary affective disorder, schizophrenia, obsessive–compulsive and phobic neurosis. This too is self-evident.

F. *At least two of the following manifestations* are present: (1) amenorrhea; (2) lanugo hair; (3) bradycardia of 60 or below; (4) periods of overactivity; (5) episodes of bulimia; and (6) vomiting. This is perhaps the most dubious part of the criteria as there is no logical connection between the sub-items. *Amenorrhea* is an early manifestation of AN, occuring in 80 per cent of cases before there is any real weight loss. In some cases, it occurs as early as when they decide to diet, before dieting actually commences. The typical pattern is normal dieting that results in moderate weight loss, with the amenorrhea being a psychosomatic indicator that their dieting is not like that of their peers. Then, AN seems to take over and run its own course. *Lanugo hair* is a late manifestation in only approximately 20 per cent of cases; an incidence so low as to be useless as a criterion. *Bradycardia,* like hypotonia, hypometabolism and hormonal changes, are part of the somatic changes that result from the leanness seen in all extreme starvation processes, and therefore are of no value as criteria for diagnosis of AN. *Overactivity* and *vomiting* are means to a particular end: simply thinness. The inclusion of *bulimia* is confusing these days when we readily differentiate BN from AN.

In conclusion, it must be stressed that these criteria, so often heard of and referred to when describing a patient as definitely suffering from AN were designed as 'criteria for use in *psychiatric research*' (Feighner *et al.*, 1972, my italics), and have little, if any, use for *practising therapists.*

The new DSM-IV will partly take into consideration certain diagnostic problems and, for example, no longer will specify an age of onset. While a weight loss of 25 per cent is still required for a diagnosis, this may be modified for younger children.

It is important to note that none of the various eating-disorder scales can be used in themselves to diagnose a disorder. The diagnosis of anorexia or bulimia must be established by a personal interview with the patient and perhaps parents too. In addition, it must be borne in mind that 'anorexia' patients who binge and purge will in fact have two diagnoses: (a) anorexia nervosa, and (b) bulimia nervosa. Often, bulimic patients will have additional diagnoses of major depressive disorder and alcohol or substance abuse (Halmi, 1985). Before reviewing the most frequently used eating-disorder scales, the reader may like to refer again to the most commonly used criteria for AN and BN (DSM-III) to help understand what these scales are trying to tap.

Anorexia nervosa

A. Intense fear of becoming obese, which does not diminish as weight loss progresses.
B. Disturbance in the way in which one's body weight, size, or shape is experienced. For example, claiming to 'feel fat' even when emaciated; belief that one area of the body is 'too fat' even when obviously underweight.
C. Refusal to maintain body weight over a minimal normal weight for age and height, e.g. weight loss leading to maintenance of body weight 15 per cent below expected; failure to make expected weight gain during period of growth, leading to body weight 15 per cent below expected.
D. In females, absence of at least three menstrual cycles when otherwise expected to occur (primary or secondary amenorrhea).

Askevold (1983) has proposed a new set of criteria based on intentional dieting, early amenorrhea, avoidance of sexuality and disturbance in body image. He recommends the following (p. 42):

1. The determination to diet, which then develops into a determination to reach extreme thinness, which in itself is the sign of the will to change body shape.
2. Early amenorrhea. One can arbitrarily choose six months from the beginning of dieting as the latest time to which anorexia nervosa can be assigned.
3. A drive quality to the maintenance of the anorexia.
4. Active avoidance of sexuality.
5. Disturbed body image.

The criteria could also include age, as pointed out before, but this should be avoided.

Bulimia nervosa

A. Recurrent episodes of binge eating (rapid consumption of a large amount in a discreet period of time, usually less that two hours).
B. During the eating binges, there is a fear of not being able to stop eating.
C. The individual regularly engages in either self-induced vomiting, the use of laxatives, or rigorous dieting or fasting in order to counteract the effects of the binge eating.
D. A minimum average of two binge-eating episodes per week for at least three months.

Objective and projective psychological tests

Psychological tests have long played a critical role in the diagnostic process but, unfortunately, many of the studies that have used psychological tests with anorexics have not contributed to either the understanding or categorisation of eating disorders. It has been argued (Small, 1985) that the contribution of psychological test results has been overlooked for a number of reasons. The results of studies using *objective* tests (quantitative tests allowing little room for interpretation) such as the Minnesota multiphasic personality inventory (MMPI) have added little to our knowledge of eating disorders in terms of either aetiology or prognosis. Instead, they have been primarily descriptive studies of personality traits. There is a dearth of studies using projective tests (qualitative tests allowing greater leeway for intrerpretation) such as the Rorschach tests (Small, 1985). In reviewing the literature, Small argues that quite different perspectives are gained, depending on whether objective or projective tests are used. The few reports using projective tests are 'amazingly consistent', and valuable information previously overlooked is converging with current theoretical formulations. In a way, it should not be particularly surprising that projective measures would be more useful than objective ones, given the recent emphasis on 'ego' or self-impairments, fixations, object relations and developmental theory.

We shall not go further into this debate here as the technicalities of the various tests used and interpretation of items from the Rorschach is much too complex for the average non-specialist reader for whom this book is intended. If anyone is particularly keen to follow this issue, they are referred to Small's (1985) article and the references cited within.

Diagnosis and assesment of bulimia

As has been noted by Gandour (1984), except for frequent weight fluctuations, there are no known direct clinical signs of BN. Bulimics may be obese or underweight, although most are within a normal range for their age, sex and height.

Diagnosis is usually based upon *self-reported symptoms alone*, without any supportive physical findings or 'laboratory data'. But there are, obviously, *clinical signs* associated with binging, vomiting and laxative abuse that, to the schooled observer, could indicate a possible eating disorder. There are two procedures for assessing bulimia in current use; diagnostic interviews and questionnaires. The use of the diagnostic interview was first reported by Wermuth, Davis, Hollister and Stunkard (1977). Three criteria were used to identify persons with serious binging problems, which were subsequently reworked into the diagnostic system in the DSM-III in current use for interview procedures.

Several questionnaires have been developed to assess bulimia and its symptoms, but in general, these instruments have not been widely used, and reliability and validity data are lacking. These may be potentially useful for further: (a) investigating the causes and correlates of bulimic behaviour; (b) refining the definition of bulimia; (c) individualising treatment for the various forms of the disorder (i.e. vomiting versus non-vomiting, overweight versus normal weight, mid versus severe binging); and (d) monitoring changes in the course of treatment.

Slade anorexic behaviour scale

One of the first scales devised to assess the *severity* of anorexic behaviour was the Slade anorexic behaviour scale (Slade, 1973). This is a simple observer rating scale in which two observers, usually nurses on a ward, tick the presence or absence of 22 typical anorexic behaviours. Usefully, it can also be completed by the patient's parents to assess the patient's behaviour at home. All items, which involve a judgement as to whether a particular piece of behaviour has or has not been displayed by the person, are rated 'Yes', 'No', or '?'. A score of two is allocated when the behaviour has definitely been observed, a score of zero if it has definitely *not* been observed and a score of one when there is some doubt in the rater's mind. It thus has an obvious objective observational slant. Examples of items on this scale are 'Shows obvious signs of tension at mealtimes'; 'Bargains over food (e.g. "I'll eat X if I don't have to eat Y")'; 'Does physical exercises whenever possible (e.g. press-ups)'. The scale is scored simply by adding the number of 'Yes' and '?' responses. It has been found that anorexics will score, on average, around the 23 mark (after at least one month of observation), whilst the normal score is generally under three.

This scale has been found to have a high interrater reliability, which means that it can be used by different people with confidence that they will score the individual similarly. It will detect a significant difference in typical anorexic behaviours in an AN patient group compared with a control patient group. The preliminary results with this scale were encouraging and suggested that this can be used fairly reliably to distinguish anorexic from non-anorexic patients (within the small sample sizes) and that the magnitude of this behavioural abnormality is related to the degree of 'body misperception'. This latter point suggests that this scale could be used to

Table 3.1: Anorexic behaviour scale

Instructions: Rate all items of behaviour as either 'Yes' (i.e. behaviour was shown by the patient at some point), 'No' (i.e. behaviour never shown by the patient at any stage), or '?' (i.e. not sure). Only rate items as 'Yes' if you definitely observed them or if they were reported to you.

(a) **Resistance to eating**

1. Delays as much as possible before coming to the dining table.
2. Shows obvious signs of tension at meal times.
3. Shows increased hostility at meal times (towards nurses or food).
4. Begins by cutting up food into small pieces.
5. Complains that there is too much food or that it's too rich.
6. Exhibits extreme 'food faddiness'.
7. Bargains over food (e.g. 'I'll eat X if I don't have to eat Y').
8. Picks at food (e.g. eating inside but leaving outside of potatoes, piecrusts, etc.).

(b) **Disposing of food.**

9. Vomits after meals.
10. Conceals food in serviettes, pockets, handbags and clothing.
11. Disposes of food out of windows, into dustbins, down sinks and toilets.
12. Conceals food in own room (e.g. in cupboards, drawers, flower vases, etc.).
13. Crumbles cakes into their wrapping paper.
14. Rubs food into clothes or spills liquid over own clothes.
15. Drops odd bits of food onto floor, e.g. peas.
16. Makes frequent use of purgatives or attempts to use purgatives.

(c) **Activity**

17. Stands as much as possible rather than sits.
18. Walks or runs about whenever possible.
19. Is as active and as industrious as possible (e.g. clearing tables, cleaning own room, etc.).
20. Chooses the more strenuous activity when given the choice (e.g. table tennis rather than watching television).
21. Makes unnecessary journeys for extra exercise.
22. Does physical exercises whenever possible (e.g. press-ups, etc.).

Source: Slade (1973). *British Journal of Psychiatry, 122,* p. 85. Reproduced with permission.

measure changes in the severity of the disorder and to monitor the effects of different types of therapies. However, Halmi (1985) comments that it has not been satisfactorily tested for use as a diagnostic scale. One of the difficulties in using this scale is that after a patient is hospitalised, many of the behaviours described in this scale decrease immediately because of the structured hospital setting. A false impression of a 'psychologically improved' patient may therefore emerge.

Some of the other scales have been designed to assess severity of eating-disorder behaviour and are used mainly to measure *changes* in the patient over time and treatment rather than provide a *screening* diagnosis. The serious pitfall in the use of such measures in eating-disordered patients is their typical denial of illness. It has been repeatedly observed that even the most seriously ill anorexics will rate themselves as normal on self-rating eating-disorder scales (Halmi, 1985).

Eating-attitudes test

Perhaps the most extensively used self-rating scale for the eating-disordered patient is the 'eating attitudes test' ((EAT) Garner and Garfinkel, 1979). Although Slade's rating scale appears to have utility in an inpatient setting, its major limitation is that it taps only three dimensions of anorexic behaviour (resistance to eating, methods of disposing of food and overactivity) and so does not provide an index of other characteristic behaviours that may be equally representative in the disorder. Other idiosyncratic attitudes and behaviours surrounding food, disturbances in body image and various psychobiological symptoms such as amenorrhea and sleep irregularities have also been described. The EAT was developed to evaluate a broad range of target behaviours and attitudes found in AN. It was originally designed with 40 items, but later abbreviated to 26 (EAT-26). Subjects are simply instructed to place an 'X' under the column that applies best to the statements. These columns are labelled 'Always', 'Usually', 'Often', 'Sometimes', 'Rarely', 'Never'. Each extreme response in the 'anorexic' direction is scored three points, with the adjacent alternatives given two points and one point, respectively. Examples of items are 'Am terrified about being overweight', 'Feel extremely guilty after eating', and 'Feel that food controls my life'.

The initial validation of the EAT compared clinical cases of AN with a normal population, in which possible anorexic cases were screened out. This showed a very high efficiency for the test in allocating subjects to patient or control group. Garner and Garfinkel (1979) demonstrated that a cut-off point of 30 on the EAT differentiated normal-weight female controls from those with clinical AN. It has been demonstrated too that EAT scores of 30 or above tap some of the criteria of bulimia, and scores of about 20 or above on the EAT-26 are probably worthy of further investigation. Studies in which the EAT has been validated against a diagnostic interview, the positive predictive value (the proportion of those identified as anorexic cases by the test who turn out to be true anorexic cases) has been rather low. Such studies provide evidence that the only valid way of diagnosing AN is by a personal interview. The EAT test is most effectively used as a measure of the severity of anorexic symptoms and the change in the symptoms over treatment and time (Halmi, 1985). 'The EAT appears to have utility as a *screening device* for assessing the symptoms commonly found in anorexia nervosa. However, those appearing to be anorexic on the EAT should be *clinically interviewed*, to confirm the diagnosis' (Garfinkel and Garner, 1982, p. 30; my italics). A recent study (Carter and Moss, 1984) concluded that although in the Garner and Garfinkel (1979) study the EAT was able to discriminate between two distinct 'known' groups, it may not be successful as a screening device in the

Table 3.2: Eating attitudes test

Instructions: Please circle the letter in the column which applies best to each of the numbered statements. All of the results will be strictly confidential. Most of the questions directly relate to food or eating, although other types of questions have been included. Please answer each question carefully. Thank you.

A = Always
U = Usually
O = Often
S = Sometimes
R = Rarely
N = Never

A U O S R N	1. Am terrified about being overweight.
A U O S R N	2. Avoid eating when I am hungry.
A U O S R N	3. Find myself preoccupied with food.
A U O S R N	4. Have gone on eating binges where I feel that I may not be
able to	stop.
A U O S R N	5. Cut my food into small pieces.
A U O S R N	6. Aware of the calorie content of the foods that I eat.
A U O S R N	7. Particularly avoid foods with a high carbohydrate content.
A U O S R N	8. Feel that others would prefer if I ate more.
A U O S R N	9. Vomit after I have eaten.
A U O S R N	10. Feel extremely guilty after eating.
A U O S R N	11. Am preoccupied with a desire to be thinner.
A U O S R N	12. Think about burning up calories when I exercise.
A U O S R N	13. Other people think that I am too thin.
A U O S R N	14. Am preoccupied with the thought of having fat on my body.
A U O S R N	15. Take longer than others to eat my meals.
A U O S R N	16. Avoid foods with sugar in them.
A U O S R N	17. Eat diet foods.
A U O S R N	18. Feel that food controls my life.
A U O S R N	19. Display self-control around food.
A U O S R N	20. Feel that others pressure me to eat.
A U O S R N	21. Give too much time and thought to food.
A U O S R N	22. Feel uncomfortable after eating sweets.
A U O S R N	23. Engage in dieting behaviour.
A U O S R N	24. Like my stomach to be empty.
A U O S R N	25. Enjoy trying new rich foods.
A U O S R N	26. Have the impulse to vomit after meals.

Source: Public domain. Reproduced with permission of Garner, D.M. and Garfinkel, P.E. (note: item 25 is reverse scored) general population. The EAT score may nevertheless serve as an index of improvement, since recovered patients have normal scores.

Much more research is necessary to establish the validity of using EAT scores in the assessment of bulimia, particularly considering the careful tailoring to AN during the test's development. Nevertheless, the EAT may be particularly useful in exploring the relationship between AN and BN. As the designers themselves state, while the EAT measures symptoms commonly found in AN, *the diagnosis of AN remains a clinical one*, based upon criteria outlined earlier in this chapter. A high score on the EAT does not invariably reflect AN nor does a low score invariably rule it out (on a self-report questionnaire people may not respond honestly). In practice, nevertheless, the EAT has been shown to be quite accurate in predicting group membership.

Anorexic attitudes questionnaire

A number of attitude dimensions have been hypothesised on the basis of clinical experience and so Goldberg *et al.* (1980) constructed this scale that would, hopefully, reflect the hypothesised attitudes. For instance, there has always been the suspicion that the term anorexia nervosa is a misnomer, because a substantial number of individuals do not lose their appetite, but instead, starve themselves in the face of severe hunger. This 63-item scale has been used to measure changes in typical anorexic attitudes in several large treatment studies. The instructions read: 'Here is a series of statements which may or may not describe your feelings and attitudes about things. Please indicate how much each statement is true of your own feelings'. The subject can tick off along a four-point scale of 'Not at all' (1), 'A little' (2), 'Quite a bit' (3), and 'Extremely' (4). Goldberg *et al.* give no overall scores for anorexics or, for that matter, controls. However, it is possible to obtain meaningful scores by simply adding the total of 'confirming' scores (1 to 4) for each item. It must be noted that some items are reverse scored (numbers 3, 4, 7, 15, 18, 22, 30, 35).

Table 3.3: Anorectic attitudes questionnaire

Instructions: Here is a series of statements which may or may not describe your feelings and attitudes about things. Please indicate how much each statement is true of your own feelings (1 = not at all, 2 = a little, 3 = quite a bit, 4 = extremely.

1. There was nothing really wrong with me that a few days rest couldn't cure. ( )
2. If I could choose an age to be, it would be 10 or 11. ( )
3. One of the nicest things that can happen to a woman is having a baby. ( )
4. I feel hungry by the time mealtime comes around. ( )
5. Young men my age are usually silly fools. ( )
6. If I eat too much, I just can't hold it down. ( )
7. I have complete confidence in the way the medical staff is treating me. ( )

8. My figure looks much better now than when I was heavier. ( )
9. I wouldn't have this problem if my mother weren't so demanding. ( )
10. Most people eat too much. ( )
11. I have trouble keeping warm. ( )
12. I have to work harder than others to accomplish things. ( )
13. Exercise is excellent for preventing overweight. ( )
14. A child shouldn't be allowed to go out on her own before she is really ready. ( )
15. If I hadn't been hospitalised, I think my life would really have been threatened. ( )
16. Frankly, the treatment I am getting here seems confused and inconsistent. ( )
17. Even the smallest amount of food fills me up. ( )
18. When you get right down to it, a girl's best friend is her mother. ( )
19. Fate pretty much determines what happens to a person. ( )
20. Most people don't get nearly enough exercise. ( )
21. It's a good idea to regularly clean yourself out of excess water. ( )
22. My problems are more mental than physical. ( )
23. A few of the medical staff here are OK, but the rest don't seem to know what they're doing. ( )
24. It wasn't really necessary to hospitalise me for this illness. ( )
25. Most people eat too quickly. ( )
26. Sex appeal in men is vastly over-rated. ( )
27. I feel cold much of the time. ( )
28. Many of my problems can be traced to my father. ( )
29. I have the urge lately to stuff myself with sweets. ( )
30. I feel hungry right now. ( )
31. The trouble with parents is they butt into your business. ( )
32. They're treating me almost like a criminal here. ( )
33. I think my illness will make my parents sorry about how they have treated me. ( )
34. I wouldn't mind having a baby but I don't like the idea of being pregnant. ( )
35. I accomplish a lot without too much work because things come easy to me. ( )
36. Yes, I did lose some weight but not enough for everybody to get as worried as they did. ( )
37. My mother is usually helpful when giving me advice. ( )
38. Sweets and starches are really bad for you. ( )
39. The medical staff is overly suspicious of everything I do or don't do. ( )
40. My mother is an important source of my problems. ( )
41. I don't know why I lost all that weight; I didn't eat a lot, but I ate enough. ( )
42. The medical staff here have gone out of their way to help me. ( )
43. I wish I knew how to be more independent of my parents. ( )
44. A person has to be very careful in what she eats because so many things that are fattening. ( )
45. My real problem was not one of loss of weight, but fatigue and overwork. ( )
46. The medical staff here seem more intent on giving me a hard time than in treating me. ( )
47. My mother is taking my illness too hard. ( )
48. My problems have nothing to do with my mental condition. ( )
49. It's a good idea to clean out with a laxative fairly regularly. ( )
50. The medical staff make me feel that my medical condition is all my fault. ( )
51. I wish my parents would leave me alone. ( )
52. If I eat too much I get sick to my stomach. ( )
53. The medical staff often blame me for their own goof-ups. ( )
54. It is far better to be underweight than overweight. ( )
55. I just can't get enough exercise here. ( )

Table 3.3: contd

56. The medical staff try to take advantage of my weaknesses. ( )
57. I rarely feel hungry during the day. ( )
58. I wouldn't mind learning to cook as a hobby. ( )
59. The medical staff 'butter me up' to get their own way. ( )
60. I lost all that weight because some parts of my body are not working right. ( )
61. The medical staff here often make me angry. ( )
62. The medical staff here don't give me any respect. ( )
63. If I didn't really watch my diet, I'm afraid I would get fat. ( )

Source: Goldberg *et al.* (1980). 'Attitudinal dimensions in anorexia nervosa,' *Journal of Psychiatric Research, 15,* 243-44.

A useful aspect of this questionnaire is that it allows determination of particular factors within the individual case that are relatively salient. Various groups of questions with a common factor have been identified. Note that a few items do not fall into any of these clusters. These consist of:

1. *Staff exploits*. This dimension is an attitude that the hospital staff treats her like a criminal, is overly suspicious of everything that she does, is intent on giving her a hard time, tries to take advantage of her weaknesses, and does not give her any respect. This attitude may be described as being exploited, dominated, and coerced by the hospital staff. Examples would be: 'Frankly, the treatment I am getting here seems confused and inconsistent' and 'The medical staff here don't give me any respect' (items 7, 16, 23, 32, 39, 46, 50, 53, 56, 61, 62).
2. *Fear of becoming fat or thin ideal.* For example, 'If I didn't really watch my diet, I'm afraid I would get fat' (items 8, 13, 38, 44, 54, 55, 63).
3. *Parents at fault.* This negative attitude towards parents is represented by such items as 'I wish my parents would leave me alone' and 'I wouldn't have this problem if my mother weren't so demanding' (items 9, 18, 28, 31, 33, 40, 43, 51).
4. *Denial of illness*. These attitudes are an expression of denial or a minimisation of the severity of one's illness, for example, 'There was nothing really wrong with me that a few days of rest couldn't cure'. The patient simply does not believe she is as badly off as everyone else thinks she is and denies the need for hospitalisation. It is not, for instance, uncommon that an anorexic individual attending university, high school or college will attend the student health centre because of amenorrhea or a persistent cold. If the staff suggest that she remain and be hospitalised in order to regain some weight, she will often deny that weight loss is her main problem and that it is not severe enough for extended treatment (items 1, 15, 24, 36, 47).
5. *Hunger*. This factor is an expression of hunger as opposed to a loss of appetite (items 4, 17, 30, 57).
6. *Hypothermia*. This is a self-evident expression of feeling cold (items 11, 27).
7. *Bloated*. This cluster may also be interpreted as a desire for purgatives and

diuretics, including such items as 'It's a good idea to regularly clean yourself out of excess water' (items 14, 21, 34, 49).

8. *Poor self-care.* This may be summarised as 'People don't take as good care of themselves as they should'. There is an attitude that most people eat too much, don't get enough exercise and eat much too quickly. If interpreted as a projection, it would read 'I don't have good self care' (items 10, 20, 25).

9. *Effort for achievement.* In this, the person describes how much effort is required for her to get anything done (items 12, 35).

10. *Food is sickening.* These items were originally considered as part of the 'hunger' dimension, but these items are obviously different (items 6, 52).

11. *Problems are mental.* The person indicates that her problems are mental, rather than physical (items 22, 48).

12. *Helpful authority.* The patient indicates that both her mother and the ward staff have been helpful to her (items 37, 42).

13. *Unknown physical cause of illness.* The individual does not seem to recognise that she is severely underweight, but invokes some kind of mysterious physical cause for it not apparent to her, denying that it is failure to eat that has led to her being underweight (items 41, 60).

14. *Cooking.* This is simply an expression of attitude towards cooking for others as a hobby (item 58).

15. *Heterosexual disinterest* (items 5, 26).

Eating disorder inventory

The 'eating disorder inventory' (EDI; Garner, Olmstead and Polivy, 1983) is another self-rating scale designed to assess psychological characteristics relevant to AN and BN. It was devised to avoid reliance upon existing personality measures, since conventional tests did not adequately address the cognitive and behavioural characteristics often observed clinically in AN. It was also aimed at discriminating between AN and BN. Although the authors claim that this is in contrast to the more behavioural/symptoms measurements in other self-rating scales for eating disorders, there is in fact considerable overlap of psychological and behavioural characteristics of all scales. As the authors state, the EDI represents an attempt to isolate and objectively measure specific psychological features viewed as important in the AN syndrome. Also, they readily acknowledge that there are other personality features such as obsessionality, rigidity, compliance, depression, interpersonal insensitivity, and excessive control that are not assessed by this test (Halmi, 1985).

The EDI is a 64-item self-report scale consisting of eight subscales. Examples of the 64 items are: 'As a child, I tried very hard to avoid disappointing my parents and teachers', 'When I am upset, I don't know if I'm sad, frightened or angry', and 'I am preoccupied with the desire to be thinner'. Consistent with their multidimensional concept of AN, questions were generated by the Garner and

Garfinkel team for behavioural and psychological constructs that have been described as relevant to the disorder. The EDI subscales do not represent an exhaustive sampling of the cognitive–behavioural features of AN.

Garner *et al.* (1983) supply a short description of each subscale and the clinical sources from which it was derived.

1. *Drive for thinness.* This indicates excessive dieting, preoccupation with weight, and entrenchment in an extreme pursuit of thinness. This has been described as a cardinal feature of AN. Items reflect both the ardent desire to lose weight as well as a fear of weight gain.
2. *Bulimia* indicates the tendency towards episodes of uncontrollable overeating (binging) and may be followed by the impulse to engage in self-induced vomiting.
3. *Body dissatisfaction.* This reflects the belief that body parts associated with change of shape or increased 'fatness' at puberty are too large (e.g. hips, thighs, buttocks). This fact has been found to be related to other body image disturbances in AN and are considered a basic feature of AN. It has been suggested that dieting in AN is a response to dissatisfaction with pubertal 'fatness' and the symbolic meaning that it has for the individual.
4. *Ineffectiveness* assesses feelings of general inadequacy, insecurity, worthlessness, and not being in control of one's life; a feature that has been described by some as the fundamental disturbance in AN.
5. *Perfectionism* indicates excessive personal expectations for superior achievement. The struggle to live up to perfectionist achievement standards has also been suggested as a characteristic theme of AN.
6. *Interpersonal distrust* reflects a sense of alienation and a general reluctance to form close relationships and it has been identified as important in the development and maintenance of AN. It may be distinguished from paranoid thinking and relates to an inability to form attachments or feel comfortable expressing emotions towards others.
7. *Interoceptive awareness* reflects one's lack of confidence in recognising and accurately identifying emotions and sensations of hunger or satiety. Again, this has been described as a deficiency fundamental to AN.
8. *Maturity fears* measures one's wish to retreat to the security of the pre-adolescent years because of the overwhelming demands of adulthood. It has been suggested that the central psychopathology of AN is an avoidance of psychological maturity through the mechanism of carbohydrate avoidance.

The test format is similar to that of the EAT where subjects respond to six-point, forced-choice items by rating whether each item applies 'always', 'usually', 'often', 'sometimes', 'rarely', or 'never'. The scoring is identical to the EAT with the most extreme 'anorexic' response (always or never depending on the keyed direction) earning a score of 3; the immediately adjacent response 2, the next response 1 and the three choices opposite to the most 'anorexic' response receiving no score (0). Scale scores are the summation of all item scores for that particular scale.

AN patients are differentiated from a female comparison group on all subscales, and clinically recovered AN patients score similarly to female controls. In addition, there was good agreement between patient's self-report profiles and the judgements of experienced clinicians. The EDI differentiated between individuals with AN and obesity as well as formerly obese subjects recruited from a weight-loss programme.

While the EDI may have utility as a prognostic screening instrument, its designers have emphasised several cautions. Firstly, like all self-report instruments, the EDI is vulnerable to distortion due to inaccurate reporting by the subject and the defensive set of the patient may invalidate self-evaluation data. Secondly, the EDI should not be considered to represent an exhaustive sampling of the psychopathological characteristics of AN. Other personality features such as obsessionality, rigidity compliance, depression, introversion, interpersonal sensitivity, poor ego strength, excessive control and others have been identified. Thirdly, while some of the psychological dimensions assessed by the EDI may have primary significance, the presence or magnitude of others may simply be by-products of the disorder. It is not justified to infer a causal relationship between the attributes observed and the development of AN. Finally, the EDI should not be employed as the sole means of screening for or diagnosing AN. Although the EDI or EAT may be useful as preliminary screening tools for identifying groups in which a high proportion of subject's have formal eating disorders, these must be confirmed by clinical diagnosis. '*Psychological tests should be an adjunct, not a replacement, for clinical judgements*' (Garner *et al.*, 1983, p.32).

Despite these qualifications, the EDI represents an attempt to isolate and objectively measure specific psychological features viewed as important in the AN syndrome and which have been previously described. The preliminary results with the EDI indicate that it is an objective and economical instrument that may be useful in assessing meaningful cognitive–behavioural dimensions in AN and BN. Further research is required to determine its validity and its utility as a predictive or outcome measure with eating disordered groups (Garner *et al.*, 1983). The EDI is the property of Psychological Assessment Resources and is obtainable from PAR, Inc., PO Box 98, Odessa, Florida 33556, USA.

Binge scale questionnaire

This was designed to measure the severity of behavioural and attitudinal parameters of bulimia (Hawkins and Clement, 1980). In addition to quantifying binge-eating tendencies, it has also been used to obtain descriptive characteristics of these tendencies and data on the psychological correlates of binge eating. There are only nine items, which are scored by adding up the marked score (from 0 to 3) under each item. The mean total 'binge-scale' scores for a sample of college females of normal weight and overweight were found to be 5.63 and 8.42 resepectively.

Clinic-treated overweight females scored 10.70 whilst control-classroom overweight females scored a little less at 8.90. As a screening measure, one is probably looking for scores of at least 13 before further investigation. This questionnaire is *not able to establish the diagnosis of BN* but it is able measure the severity of some of the typical attitudes and behaviours associated with binge eating (Halmi, 1985).

Table 3.4: Binge scale questionnaire

1. How often do you binge eat? (a) seldom, (b) once or twice a month, (c) once a week, (d) almost every day. (Scores: a (0) b (1) c (2) d (3))
2. What is the average length of a binge-eating episode? (a) less than 15 minutes, (b) 15 minutes to one hour, (c) one hour to four hours, (d) more than four hours. (Scores: a (0) b (1) c (2) d (3))
3. Which of the following statements best applies to your binge eating? (a) I eat until I have had enough to satisfy me, (b) I eat until my stomach feels full, (c) I eat until my stomach feels painfully full, (d) I eat until I can't eat anymore. (Scores: a (0) b (1) c (2) d (3))
4. Do you ever vomit after after a binge? (a) never, (b) sometimes, (c) usually, (d) always. (Scores: a (0) b (1) c (2) d (3))
5. Which of the following best applies to your eating behaviour when binging? (a) I eat more slowly than usual, (b) I eat about the same as I usually do, (c) I eat very rapidly. (Scores: a (0) b (0) c (1))
6. How much are you concerned about your binge eating? (a) not bothered at all, (b) bothers me a little, (c) moderately concerned, (d) a major concern. (Scores: a (0) b (1) c (2) d (3))
7. Which best describes your feelings during a binge? (a) I feel that I could control the eating if I chose, (b) I feel that I have at least some control, (c) I feel completely out of control. (Scores: a (0) b (1) c (2))
8. Which of the following describes your feelings after a binge? (a) I feel fairly neutral, not too concerned, (b) I am moderately upset, (c) I hate myself. (Scores: a (0) b (1) c (2))
9. Which most accurately describes your feelings after a binge? (a) not depressed at all, (b) mildly depressed, (c) moderately depressed, (d) very depressed. (Scores: a (0) b (1) c (2) d (3))

Source: Hawkins, R.C. and Clement, P.F. (1980). 'Development and construct validation of a self-report measure of binge-eating tendencies.' *Addictive Behaviors, 5,* p. 221. Reproduced with permission.

Binge-eating questionnaire

This 'binge-eating' questionnaire (Halmi, Falk and Schwartz, 1981) which was designed to cover the DSM-III criteria for diagnosis of bulimia is typical of many binge-eating survey questionnaires. It was designed specifically for use with a college population to obtain information on developmental history, dieting history and the behavioural symptoms of bulimia. Prevalence and frequency data, as well as relationships between variables, are reported in detail by Halmi *et al.* (1981). This questionnaire seems well suited to this sort of large-scale survey research on normal populations. This one does not have a total score; the diagnosis of bulimia is made by a positive answer to the criteria questions for bulimia. However, readers may find it useful for information-recording purposes. Questions are very varied in their format (see Table 3.5).

Table 3.5: Binge-eating questionnaire

1. Name and address: . . . .
2. Year in college: . . . .
3. Sex: . . . .
4. Date of Birth: . . . .
5. Age: . . . .
6. What is your present weight? . . . .
7. What is your height? . . . .
8. What is the lowest you've weighed since reaching your present height? . . . . . .
9. What is the most you've weighed since reaching your present height? . . . .
10. In your opinion, you are now (tick one):

very underweight (...)	1
underweight (...)	2
average (...)	3
overweight (...)	4
very overweight (...)	5

11. What was the most you have weighed during the past year? . . . .
12. What was the least you have weighed during the past year? . . . .
13. Do you get uncontrollable urges to eat and eat until you feel physically ill? YES/NO
14. Are there times when you are afraid that you cannot voluntarily stop eating? YES/NO
15. Do you make yourself vomit after eating too much? YES/NO
16. Do you feel miserable and annoyed with yourself after eating too much? YES/NO
17. Have you ever had an episode of eating an enormous amount of food in a short space of time (an eating binge)? YES/NO
18. Do you consider yourself a binge-eater? YES/NO
19. In order to control your weight, do you use...

Diet pills	never (...)	0
	less than once every four weeks (...)	1
	1 to 3 times every four weeks (...)	2
	once every week (...)	3
	2 to 6 times every week (...)	4
	once every day (...)	5
	more than once every day (...)	6
Laxatives	never (...)	0
	less than once every four weeks (...)	1
	1 to 3 times every four weeks (...)	2
	once every week (...)	3
	2 to 6 times every week (...)	4
	once every day (...)	5
	more than once every day (...)	6

Diuretics or water pills

never	(...)	0
less than once every four weeks	(...)	1
1 to 3 times every four weeks	(...)	2
once every week	(...)	3
2 to 6 times every week	(...)	4
once every day	(...)	5
more than once every day	(...)	6

Other? (please specify) ..... How often? .....

20. What is the average number of days between your episodes of binge eating? (If never, leave blank) .... days
21. Have you ever vomited after eating? YES/NO
22. How frequently do you vomit after eating?

never	(...)	0
less than once every four weeks	(...)	1
1 to 3 times every four weeks	(...)	2
once every week	(...)	3
2 to 6 times every week	(...)	4
once every day	(...)	5
more than once every day	(...)	6

23. Do you have any other type of eating problem? YES/NO
If yes, please describe the nature of the problem (on back).

Source: Halmi, K.A., Falk, J.R. and Schwartz, E. (1985). *Psychopharmacology Bulletin, 21,* 1013-15. Reproduced with permission.

Halmi *et al.*'s (1981) study with this questionnaire showed that six factors or clusters of variables emerged that are consistent with previous clinical views and diagnostic criteria. The first factor represented weight variables. These are the percentage of standard weight for the subject's current weight, weight categorisation based on their present percentage of standard weight, the highest percentage of standard weight reached since the respondent's present height, the lowest percentage of standard weight reached since the respondent's present height and the respondent's personal opinion of their weight. The second cluster represents the main symptoms of bulimia. These were: (a) considering oneself a binge eater; (b) an uncontrollable urge to eat; (c) feeling miserable and annoyed; (d) having had a binge-eating episode and (e) fear of not being able to stop eating. The third factor represented vomiting, whilst the fourth, fifth and sixth represented sex differences, weight change and use of diuretics, respectively. The results indicate that vomiting may be present in bulimia, but that it is not a necessary aspect of bulimia. However, the combination of vomiting with other symptoms of bulimia in an individual may represent a severe form of bulimia, demanding treatment. No cut-off points are available, but this questionnaire as presented here may prove useful for comparative purposes. As the designer readily admits (Halmi, 1985), this questionnaire has not been validated by personal interviews. Although the diagnosis of bulimia has been redefined by some as bulimia nervosa with somewhat more specific criteria, there is still a need for further studies, especially long-term, follow-up studies, to define this syndrome more specifically.

> Since bulimic behaviors also occur in half of the anorexia nervosa patients, and since most of the tests devised for anorexia nervosa contain items assessing bulimic behavior, there has not been much emphasis on devising a special bulimia nervosa diagnostic screening scale. As mentioned earlier, most investigators have developed their own screening questionnaires. Because of the problem of denial in eating disordered patients, more emphasis should be placed upon developing observational rating scales for the eating disorders.
>
> (Halmi, 1985, p. 1003)

Other schedules

Two other forms, both much more comprehensive than those described above and too lengthy for inclusion here, although less validated but nevertheless worthy of looking at, are the 'bulimia interview form' (Walsh and Gladis, 1985) and the 'eating disorders questionnaire' (Mitchell, Hatsukami, Eckert and Pyle, 1985). The former has sections on menstrual history, past history of weight loss and medical status and history. It is useful for recording client details and as a starting point for practitioners to design their own, but not yet sufficiently researched for making substantiated comparisons with normals. The latter encompasses the areas of demographic information, weight history, dieting behaviour, binge-eating behaviour, purging behaviour, other weight control measures, exercise, other behaviour, menstrual history, marriage and pregnancy, medical-psychiatric history and life-adjustment.

Also, we have the 'binging–purging questionnaire' (Coffman, in press), which was designed to assist the therapist in obtaining specific details surrounding the client's binging/purging behaviour, including related thoughts, feelings, or experiences that impinge on that behaviour. It could be used as a structured interview in the therapy session or completed by the client at home and returned next session. It would seem to be potentially useful as an efficient means of obtaining information about a bulimic client, developing a treatment plan and helping a client develop some self-understanding of the problem.

Setting conditions for anorexia nervosa scale (SCANS)

Many of the aforementioned scales and questionnaires provide direct measures of either the symptoms or the overt manifest behaviours of individuals currently presenting with eating disorders, and as such, at best only capable of identifying people who have already developed an eating disorder. Effective prevention, or even early identification, requires the recognition of those who are likely to develop such a problem before the overt symptoms are apparent. Following from Slade's (1982) 'functional–analytical model' alluded to in Chapter 1, a 'setting conditions for anorexia nervosa scale' (SCANS) was developed (Slade and Dewey, 1986).

The focus of this particular study was the development of a screening questionnaire for individuals *at risk* of developing an eating disorder. Questionnaire items were formulated to measure one of five hypothetical constructs (setting conditions) based on Slade's (1982) 'functional–analytic' model of AN and BN. These 'setting conditions' were dissatisfaction, perfectionism, social and personal anxiety, adolescent problems, and need for control. Forty items were designed to measure these constructs. These items were then administered (in the form of a questionnaire) to various normal and eating-disordered groups. Although too long for inclusion in full here, three representative items are:

1. In general how *satisfied* do you feel with your attainments to date (i.e. school, college, work, etc.)?
Very satisfied, Somewhat satisfied, About average, Somewhat dissatisfied, Very dissatisfied.
2. Over the last couple of years how *often* have you felt confident?
Very often, Fairly often, Sometimes, Almost never, Never.
3. *Think of a person* who feels a failure in life. Is this person:
Very much like you, Much like you, Somewhat like you, Very little like you, Not at all like you?

There are both similarities and dissimilarities between this scale and the EDI. In terms of the latter, the EDI has three major scales measuring the symptoms of eating disorders: 'drive for thinness', bulimia and body dissatisfaction. The SCANS has only one such (minor) component termed 'need for weight control', which comprises only the final two items of the questionnaire. Thus SCANS may have a distinct advantage of being *non-transparent* in the sense that very few people completing the questionnaire will be able to determine its focus until the end. There are definite similarities between the EDI and the SCANS, with four scales appearing to have direct comparability: (a) 'general dissatisfaction and loss of control' (SCANS) and 'ineffectiveness' (EDI); (b) 'social and personal anxiety' (SCANS) and 'interpersonal distrust'(EDI); (c) 'perfectionism' (SCANS) and 'perfectionism' (EDI); and (d) 'adolescent problems' (SCANS) and 'maturity fears' (EDI). Thus, the scales designed to measure cognitive and emotional aspects of eating disorders (other than overt symptoms) display striking similarity between the SCANS and EDI. Given the fact that these two instruments were developed entirely independently, this demonstrates a clear convergence of thinking on the psychological antecedents and correlates of eating disorders. However, there remains an obvious need for a direct comparative study between the SCANS and EDI in practice (Slade and Dewey, 1986).

With regard to the discriminatory power of the SCANS, all five scales significantly discriminate between control samples and eating-disordered patients. Furthermore, concerning the two major scales (general dissatisfaction and perfectionism), a combination of cut-off points identified 14 per cent of controls obtaining scores in excess of those that were exceeded by 85 per cent of eating-disordered patients. This subset of primarily female control subjects scoring above the combined cut-offs, represents a high-risk group for developing an eating disorder. Given that this sample has an average age of less than 20 years, it is likely that up to 4 per cent do, in fact, have an existing eating disorder. This would leave approximately 10 per cent who are theoretically at risk for developing such a problem. As Slade and Dewey remark, there is a clear need to follow up such a high-risk group and to establish more directly such eating-disorder symptoms through *individual, structured interviews.* SCANS is the latest of all the eating-disorders inventories and questionnaires and looks particularly promising.

CONCLUSIONS

It has been stressed throughout that these questionnaires and inventories are no substitute for insight gained through experience dealing with these people and clinical impressions. Such measures, nevertheless, are useful adjuncts and screening devices for indicating further investigation.

REFERENCES

American Psychiatric Association (1980) *Diagnostic and Statistical Manual of Mental Disorders,* 3rd edn, American Psychiatric Association, Washington, DC

Askevold, F. (1983) 'The diagnosis of anorexia nervosa.' *International Journal of Eating Disorders, 2,* 39–43

Bruch, H. (1973) *Eating disorders.* Basic Books, New York

Carter, P.I. and Moss, R.A. (1984) 'Screening for anorexia and bulimia nervosa in a college population: problems and limitations.' *Addictive Behaviors, 9,* 417–19

Crisp, A.H. (1977) 'Diagnosis and outcome of anorexia nervosa: the St George's view.' *Proceedings of the Royal Society of Medicine, 70,* 464–70

Dally, P.J. (1969) *Anorexia nervosa.* Grune and Stratton, New York.

Feighner, J.P., Robins, E., Guze, S.B., Woodruff, R.A.,Jr., Winokur, G. and Munoz, R. (1972) 'Diagnostic criteria for use in psychiatric research.' *Archives of General Psychiatry, 26,* 57–63

Gandour, M.J. (1984) 'Bulimia: clinical description, assessment, etiology, and treatment. *International Journal of Eating Disorders, 3,* 3–38

Garfinkel, P.E. and Garner, D.M. (1982) *Anorexia nervosa: a multidimensional perspective.* Brunner/Mazel, New York.

Garner, D.M. and Garfinkel, P.E. (1979) 'The eating attitudes test: an index of symptoms of anorexia nervosa.' *Psychological Medicine, 9,* 273–9

—— Olmstead, M.P. and Polivy, J. (1983) 'Development and validation of a multidimensional eating disorder inventory for anorexia nervosa and bulimia.' *International Journal of Eating Disorders, 2,* 15–34

Goldberg, S.C., Halmi, K.A., Eckert, E.D., Casper, R.C., Davis, J.M. and Roper, M. (1980) 'Attitudinal dimensions in anorexia nervosa.' *Journal of Psychiatric Research, 15,* 239–51

Halmi, K.A. (1974) 'Anorexia nervosa: demographic and clinical features of 94 cases.' *Psychosomatic Medicine, 36,* 18-26.

—— (1985) 'Rating scales in the eating disorders.' *Psychopharmacology Bulletin, 21,* 1001–3

—— Falk, J.R. and Schwartz, E. (1981) Binge-eating and vomiting: a survey of a college population. *Psychological Medicine, 11,* 697–706

—— —— —— (1985) 'The binge-eating questionnaire.' *Psychopharmacology Bulletin, 21,* 1013-15

Hawkins, R.C. and Clement, P.F. (1980) 'Development and construct validation of a self-report measure of binge-eating techniques.' *Addictive Behaviors, 5,* 219–26

Mitchell, J.E., Hatsukami, D., Eckert, E. and Pyle, R. (1985) 'Eating disorders questionnaire.' *Psychopharmacology Bulletin, 21,* 1025–43

Morgan, H.G. and Russell, G.F.M. (1975) 'Value of family background and clinical features as predictors of long-term outcome in anorexia nervosa: four year follow-up study of 41 patients.' *Psychological Medicine, 5,* 355–71

Rollins, N. and Piazza, E. (1978) 'Diagnosis of anorexia nervosa: a critical reappraisal.' *Journal of the American Academy of Child Psychiatry, 17,* 126–37

Selvini-Palazzoli, M. (1974) *Self-starvation.* Chaucer, London

Slade, P.D. (1973) 'A short anorexic behaviour scale.' *British Journal of Psychiatry, 122,* 83–5

—— (1982) 'Towards a functional analysis of anorexia nervosa and bulimia nervosa.' *British Journal of Clinical Psychology, 21,* 67–79

—— and Dewey, M.E. (1986) 'Development and preliminary validation of SCANS: A screening instrument for identifying individuals at risk of developing anorexia and bulimia nervosa.' *International Journal of Eating Disorders, 5,* 517–38

Small, A.C. (1985) 'The contribution of psychodiagnostic test results towards understanding anorexia nervosa.' *International Journal of Eating Disorders, 5,* 23–31

Walsh, B.T. and Gladis, M. (1985) 'Bulimia interview form.' *Psychopharmacology Bulletin, 21,* 1017–23

Wermuth, B.M., Davis, K.L., Hollister, L.E. and Stunkard, A.J. (1977) 'Phenytoin treatment of the binge-eating syndrome.' *American Journal of Psychiatry, 134,* 1249–53

Ziegler, R. and Sours, J.A. (1968) 'A naturalistic study of patients with anorexia nervosa admitted to a university medical center.' *Comprehensive Psychiatry, 9,* 644–51

4

Sex Differences within Anorexia Nervosa

Derek Scott

INTRODUCTION

As long ago as 1689, Richard Morton, the doctor who is credited with first describing AN in females, also first described a case of AN in the male — the son of a minister who, at about the age of sixteen, 'fell gradually into a total want of appetite, occasioned by his studying too hard, and the passions of his mind, and upon that into a universal atrophy, pining away more and more for the space of two years, without cough, fever, or any other symptoms of distemper'. In his more extensive description, William Gull (1874) also acknowledged that AN occasionally occurred in males. The term 'anorexia nervosa' was, in fact, then preferred over 'anorexia hysterica' because of the existence of male sufferers, as the term 'hysteria' was not applicable within its contemporary meaning. The disorder in the male therefore seems to have been around for as long as it has in the female. Indeed, Roger Slade in his *Anorexia nervosa reference book* (1984) remarks that the number of male anorexics appearing in early medical accounts raises the interesting question of whether it is only in the last hundred years that AN has been a predominantly female illness!

Nowadays, the typical picture of an adolescent female with AN is readily recognised by families and health-care professionals, leading of course to earlier diagnosis and treatment. Despite considerable advances in identifying female anorexics, comparable development in recognising AN in special groups such as older people, coloured people, and the male population has been lacking (Andersen, 1977). Swann (1977), for instance, has presented certain case histories that illustrate the difficulty in diagnosing the condition in males.

In earlier accounts, particularly during the first part of this century, the diagnosis of AN in males was often neglected for at least four identifiable reasons: (a) Most clinicians saw far too few cases of the disorder in females, let alone males, to be sufficiently familiar with it to make an accurate diagnosis; (b) theoreticians who believed that it was necessary to identify the psychodynamic notion of 'fear of oral impregnation' before firm diagnosis could be be made, obviously excluded males (Kessler, 1966); (c) others excluded males because of diagnostic criteria requiring amenorrhea to be present; and (d) certain authors have stated that although food refusal is undoubtedly found in some male patients, they do not show the complex psychopathology of the syndrome — their eating behaviour being secondary to other psychiatric disorders. Four reasons can also be proposed as to why AN in males remains underdiagnosed: (a) Men may assume themselves not to be vulnerable because of the prevailing view in the media that AN only occurs in adolescent females. (b) Similarly, even some doctors may not be disposed to spot the condition in a male and may be more likely to launch an extensive medical investigation into progressively more obscure causes of weight loss. For instance, it is most surprising that 40 per cent of internists and 25 per cent of psychiatrists still believe that AN is only to be found in the female sex (Bhanji, 1979). In addition, a recent study amongst psychiatrists and psychologists indicate that at least 25 per cent of both professional groups consider the female sex as a basic characteristic of AN (Whyte and Kaczkowski, 1983). (c) Clinicians may find it difficult to diagnose because its presentation in males may have such features as emphasis on somatic complaints that obscure the central psychopathological symptoms. Additionally, (d) those with the disorder may be too embarrassed to report their symptoms to doctors (Andersen and Mickalide, 1983).

Proposed diagnostic criteria

One of the most commonly used (and the strictest) criteria for AN is that of Feighner *et al.* (1972). Table 4.1 outlines the signs and symptoms involved. The issue of the

Table 4.1: Feighner criteria for anorexia nervosa

A. Age of onset prior to 25.
B. Anorexia with accompanying weight loss of at least 25 per cent of original body weight.
C. A distorted, implacable attitude toward eating, food, or weight that overrides hunger, admonitions, reassurance and threats: e.g., (1) denial of illness with a failure to recognise nutritional needs; (2) apparent enjoyment in losing weight, with overt manifestation that food refusal is a pleasurable indulgence; (3) a desired body image of extreme thinness, with overt evidence that it is rewarding to the patient to achieve and maintain this state; and (4) unusual hoarding or handling of food.
D. No known medical illness that could account for the anorexia and weight loss.
E. No other known psychiatric disorder, with particular reference to primary affective disorder, schizophrenia, and obsessive-compulsive and phobic neurosis. (The assumption is made that even though it may appear phobic or obsessional, food refusal alone is not sufficient to qualify for obsessive-compulsive or phobic disease.)
Note: For a diagnosis of anorexia nervosa, *A through to E* are required and
F. At least two of the following manifestations: (1) amenorrhea, (2) lanugo, (3) bradycardia (persistent resting pulse of 60 or less), (4) periods of overactivity, (5) episodes of bulimia, or (6) vomiting (may be self-induced).

Source: Adapted from Feighner *et al.* (1972). 'Diagnostic criteria for use in psychiatric research.' *Archives of General Psychiatry, 26*, 57–63.

requirement of amenorrhea appears to have been resolved by this date in that this symptom has been relegated to secondary significance. The DSM-III criteria, although rather less complex, suffers from the problem of consensus of opinion over the necessary degree of weight loss (see Chapter 3).

Russell's (1970) three basic criteria brings us into circular problems on the item of 'the specific psychopathology' of AN. Beumont, Beardwood and Russell's (1972) three diagnostic criteria suggested for the disorder are: (a) behaviour to induce weight loss, including dieting, self-induced vomiting and purgation and strenuous exercise, all often carried out secretively; (b) marked fear of gaining weight, preoccupation with body size, and disturbance of body image; and (c) an endocrine dysfunction analogous to that found in females with the condition.

Perhaps the best solution is simply to delete symptom 'C' from Table 4.2 (that concerning the weight loss/age equation), which leaves us with a compromisingly tight list of criteria.

Table 4.2: DSM–III diagnostic criteria for anorexia nervosa

A.	Intense fear of becoming obese, which does not diminish as weight loss progresses.
B.	Disturbance of body image, e.g., claiming to 'feel fat' even when emaciated.
C.	Weight loss of at least 25 per cent of original body weight; or, if under 18 years of age, weight loss from original body weight plus projected weight gain expected from growth charts may be combined to make the 25 per cent.
D.	Refusal to maintain body weight over a minimal normal weight for age and height.
E.	No known physical illness that would account for the weight loss.

Source: Feighner *et al.* (1972). 'Diagnostic criteria for use in psychiatric research.' *Archives of General Psychiatry, 26,* 57–63.

THE CLINICAL PICTURE

The work of Beumont, Beardwood and Russell (1972)

In 1972, Beumont and his associates reviewed the literature on male AN. In all, 84 papers were traced, in which there were reports of a total of 250 male patients. These 250 were placed in four categories.

1. In many cases, the information given was inadequate and it was not possible to assess the diagnosis. Where sufficient details were given, an attempt was made to classify the case.
2. No evidence was given to support the diagnosis in more than half of the papers traced. In other cases, the patients appeared to be suffering from disturbances other than AN.
3. In Beumont's third group, the evidence was compatible with a diagnosis of

AN, but inadequate for confident assessment.

4. In only 25 (10 per cent) of these patients were phenomena sufficiently described to warrant the label 'probably anorexia nervosa'.

The clinical picture which emerged from Beumont *et al.*'s (1972) compilation of 25 male bona fide cases of AN is that: (a) the illness usually started in late childhood or adolescence. Fifteen of the patients were between the ages of nine and 15 at onset, and in eight between the ages of 16 and 20. Only one patient was older (38 years) and the age of one was not stated. (b) Eleven of these patients had previously been considered, by themselves or others, to be obese. (c) In seven, food refusal was rationalised on the grounds of constipation, abdominal discomfort or other somatic complaints. (d) In two, food refusal was clearly related to fears about sexuality. (e) A further thirteen also showed other features, including purging, vomiting, strenuous exercise and subterfuges to dispose of food. (f) There was evidence in fourteen that the patient consciously sought to be thin and was afraid of gaining weight; and (g) ten of the patients were described as being preoccupied with their weight or with eating. (h) Obsessional behaviour and ruminations were remarked upon in seven patients. (i) Finally, it is of note that several patients were considered to be sexually immature or to have lost their sexual interest during the course of the illness. *All these factors have previously been described in females.*

In their own series (Beumont *et al.*, 1972), male AN patients showed a consistent clinical picture. The onset of illness was just before or just after puberty in all. Two patients had previously been obese, and the dieting had commenced as an attempt to reduce their excessive weight. Although never obese, other patients had become sensitive about comments concerning their weight. Three patients had initially claimed that the reason for their food refusal was experiencing epigastric pain and discomfort after eating.

These patients did not merely refuse food, but appeared to have a morbid fear of becoming fat and to have a thoroughly abnormal attitude, not only towards eating, but also towards their own bodies, so that they considered themselves in danger of becoming obese even when they were emaciated. Their behaviour included the selection of a diet low in carbohydrates, various subterfuges to hide food or to dispose of it, self-induced vomiting and purgation and strenuous exercising.

Finally, as mentioned by Crisp and Toms (1972) amongst others, males are likely to be an overweight population just before onset of the disorder; a common feature found within the literature on females.

The work of Crisp and Burns (1983)

It has been previously suggested by Falstein, Feinstein and Judas (1956) and Bruch (1974) that the condition is more often prepubertal in the male. However, this is not borne out in other studies. Crisp and Burns' (1983) group displayed a mean age of onset of 17 years two months, which is close to the means in Crisp and Toms' (1972) and Hasan and Tibbett's (1977) series, and is in broad agreement with a number of large series of female patients. Duration of illness at presentation ranged widely from five months to over twelve years (mean = three years five months), and range of age at presentation also varied widely between twelve years eight months and 33 years (mean = 20 years seven months).

Similarly, the previously reported tendency for premorbid obesity (e.g. Crisp and Toms, 1972) was not shown; the mean weight at onset being 101.3 per cent of matched population mean weight (MPMW). The percentage MPMW at presentation ranged from 56 per cent to 96 per cent (mean = 73.4 per cent), marginally higher than that recorded in Morgan and Russell's (1975) and Hsu, Crisp and Harding's (1979) otherwise very similar series of female patients (63 per cent and 68 per cent, respectively).

All 36 patients from Crisp and Burns' study exhibited regular sustained carbohydrate avoidance and the classical attitude towards food and its components. Bulimia, vomiting and laxative abuse were found as frequently in this group as in any other male series that systematically recorded these aspects (e.g. Hasan and Tibbetts, 1977), and differed little from the comparable female series (Morgan and Russell, 1975; Hsu *et al.*, 1979).

Increased physical activity as a feature of AN has been documented by many authors and, although it is difficult to delineate accurately what is 'excessive', several have attempted to estimate its frequency within their groups. Nevertheless, from the case notes, 44 per cent of Crisp and Burns' series were judged overactive as a feature of their illness. Whilst this overactivity was usually a generalised 'rushing around sorting things out', 42 per cent of these males were also judged to be premorbidly active in sports.

The work of Vandereycken and Van den Broucke (1984)

In order to obtain a representative sample of case studies dealing with male anorexia, Vandereycken and Van den Broucke (1984) examined 48 publications yielding a total of 107 individual cases. In general, they found a similar clinical picture in these males and a matched female group. At assessment, male patients were significantly younger and presented a greater weight loss; though not if calculated in per cent of premorbid or ideal body weight. Also on the 'differences' side, males seemed to be more obsessional and manipulative, whilst females were more often labelled as immature and hysterical. However, one must be wary of interpreting a 'soft' variable such as personality.

Much more was found in the way of similarities: (a) The onset of the disorder in males occurs in (pre)puberty, adolescence or in early adult life (average age is 15.5 years). (b) The time of presentation, assessment, diagnosis or treatment is about two to three years after onset of illness. (c) In about a third of cases, the patient had been overweight before the onset of the anorexic symptoms. (d) A considerable weight loss occurs (an average of 20kg, or 30 to 35 per cent of the premorbid weight, or 25 to 30 per cent of the ideal body weight). (e) The patient evidences so-called 'anorexic behaviour', i.e. a complex pattern of behaviour aimed at inducing or maintaining weight loss (e.g. dieting, physical hyperactivity, vomiting or laxative abuse). (f) The patient evidences fear of losing control of his weight. Often this fear and preoccupation with his own weight is related to a distorted body image. (g) In about half of the cases, episodes of bulimia occur. (h) Physiological changes, as well as specific physical symptoms (e.g. lanugo, bradycardia, absence of secondary sexual characteristics) may be noticed. It cannot be precisely determined, however, how often these phenomena occur in the population of male AN patients.

These researchers are able to confirm Beumont *et al.*'s (1972) conclusion that from the clinical point of view *AN in the male and in the female are strikingly similar*. There may be a difference between the sexes, nevertheless, concerning the seriousness of the symptoms and the uniformity with which they occur, since some publications indicate that for males the syndrome is usually characterised by more pronounced symptoms and a poorer prognosis. If a general comparison is made of male and female AN patients, some symptoms (e.g. weight loss as a function of premorbid weight) are certainly more serious for the males. Also, on average, the diagnosis is made at an earlier age for males, whereas the age of onset barely differs at all. This may indicate that the more evident seriousness of the syndrome amongst males can, at least in part, be attributable to a more selective way in which they are diagnosed. In other words, in order to receive the diagnosis of AN, males who manifest an anorexic behaviour also have to fulfil more rigorous criteria regarding weight loss. Presumably this is not the case for females; perhaps because they display (often early in the illness history) amenorrhea, a symptom of which the males have no clear clinical equivalent.

Vandereycken and Van den Broucke also established three variations of male AN:

1. *A (pre) pubertal variant*, in which the patients are fairly young at the onset of the disorder (about 13 years old). These stem from all social classes and from relatively normal families.
2. *A lower-class variant*, in which the patients are characterised by very serious weight loss after having been mostly overweight. Their siblings often show psychiatric problems and in a considerable number of cases, one parent was deceased.
3. *A middle-class variant* in which less pronounced AN symptoms are combined with family problems — a 'broken home' situation and a high incidence of eating/weight disorders in siblings.

The work of Herzog, Norman, Gordon and Pepose (1984)

Herzog *et al.* (1984) compared 27 anorexic and bulimic males and 142 anorexic and bulimic females treated in an eating-disorders unit. There was a trend for males to weigh less compared with their female counterparts if weight was expressed as a percentage of ideal weight for height. No differences between the sexes in age of illness onset, duration of illness or previous history of overweight were significant. Both samples of anorexic patients were almost equally distributed across socioeconomic classes. However, significantly more males reported experiencing sexual isolation, sexual inactivity and conflicted homosexuality.

Some other studies

In 1969, Dally reviewed some of the literature on male AN and described six other cases. In a report on 13 male AN patients, Crisp and Toms (1972) concluded that the disorder has the same features as the female version and includes active avoidance of normal weight, elective carbohydrate starvation and emaciation. Other aspects of behaviour described by researchers such as Crisp and Toms include the typical preoccupation with diets and cooking, general hyperactivity that is sometimes incorporated into ritualistic behaviour, nocturnal restlessness, propensities for drug dependence (e.g. alcohol abuse) and the absence of sexual activity at either the behavioural or fantasy level.

In Crisp and Toms' (1972) group, patterns of vomiting and purging were predictably associated with severe electrolyte disturbance, most noticeably so in hypokalemia. In addition, symptomatic epilepsy, due to such metabolic disturbances, was a feature of at least one case and was described as reminiscent of similar findings in the female population (Crisp, Fenton and Scotton, 1968).

Hasan and Tibbetts (1977) found an interest in providing food for others to be common, and three of their ten young men had expressed a wish to become chefs or to take up catering as a career. Restlessness and overactivity were noted and affective disturbance was common. Suicidal ideas were expressed in three cases.

Overview of previous studies

Scott (1986) has compiled 59 cases spanning more than the past half-century. In this compilation, it was found that 36 per cent used exercises as an aid to weight reduction, 22 used various subterfuges to avoid food, binging and vomiting were noted in 24 and 25 per cent respectively, whilst purging was reported in only six per cent. Of those 49 cases where some indication of outcome is given, about 55 per cent had a favourable outcome and about 45 per cent an unfavourable outcome (including death in certain cases).

BINGE EATING

In Hasan and Tibbett's (1977) group, intermittent overeating occurred in five patients (50 per cent) and induced vomiting in three patients (30 per cent). No abnormal purging was admitted. The prevalence data for binge eating, as defined by an affirmative response to the question 'Do you binge eat?' indicated that 38 per cent of the male college students in Katzman, Wolchik and Braver's (1984) sample reported binge eating. This figure is similar to the findings of other researchers (45 per cent — Hawkins and Clement, 1980; 30 per cent — Halmi, Falk and Schwartz, 1981; 41 per cent — Pyle *et al.*, 1983) on binge eating amongst college males.

Incidence of reported binge eating amongst equivalent female samples has varied from 50 per cent (Halmi *et al.*, 1981) through 57 and 56 per cent (Pyle *et al.*, 1983; Katzman *et al.*, 1984) to 78 per cent (Hawkins and Clement, 1980). About 24 per cent of males in Scott's (1986) compilation of individual case studies showed binge eating.

Therefore, all studies seem at first glance to concur in that significantly more women than men binge eat. However, no significant differences have occurred in the percentages of men and women reporting frequent consumption of large quantities of food at times other than meals, yet women are more likely to label their behaviour as binge eating (Katzman *et al.*, 1984). This finding suggests that it is only the *subjective labelling* of one's behaviour as binge eating that occurs more often in women.

EPIDEMIOLOGICAL FACTORS

The epidemiological features of AN in males are similar to those of female anorexics in many ways, although there are the inevitable inconsistencies between some reports. The epidemiological finding that has been the most consistent has been the sex distribution. Studies of AN repeatedly note that 90–95 per cent are female (see Bemis, 1978; Jones, Fox, Babigian and Hutton, 1980).

Social class

It has been repeatedly noted that AN is over-represented in the upper social classes (Kendell, Hall, Hailey and Babigian, 1973; Morgan and Russell, 1975; Crisp, Palmer and Kalucy, 1976; Dally and Gomez, 1979; Jones *et al.*, 1980), although other investigators such as Garfinkel and Garner (1982) offer evidence that in recent years, the disorder is becoming more equally distributed through all social classes. In addition, Palmer (1980) states that the social class bias may be less evident, with relatively more males coming from working-class homes. Others, however, feel that male anorexics tend not to display this social-class skewing (Crisp and Toms, 1972; Marshall, 1978). Crisp and Toms (1972), for instance, reported exactly 50 per cent of their males to come from a social class I or II background and the other 50 per cent from a social class III, IV or V background (father's occupation, Registrar General's classification). This is comparable with the even greater (though not significantly different) predominance of social class I and II backgrounds (73 per cent) in their parallel series of female patients.

Familial factors

In a description rather typical of the family background of male anorexics, Sreenivasan (1978) states that these patients and their families show certain common features.

> The mothers, oversensitive and insecure, were partnered by men who project the cultural image of masculinity, including overindulgence in alcohol. The parents as a whole were overweight, but obesity was more noticeable in the fathers. The patients were relatively immature, overdependent and obsessional, two being markedly obsessional. The families were skewed, with marital difficulties and overt hostility between fathers and patients on the one hand, and prolonged overprotection and overdependence between the mothers and patients on the other. The onset of severe calorie restriction followed real or feared obesity (p.161).

Three out of Crisp and Tom's (1972) males had siblings who also developed the disorder, in one case a brother; quite a remarkable coincidence, but perhaps within an unremarkable number of cases.

In Hasan and Tibbett's (1977) group of ten, the mother appeared to play the dominant role and also to be the more approachable parent from the patient's point of view. A family history of psychiatric illness was moderately predominant, though not invariably present; as was previously found by Crisp and Toms (1972).

ENDOCRINOLOGY

If true that AN does occur in males, then it would follow that they would demonstrate not only the characteristic psychopathology of the condition, but also an endocrine dysfunction analogous to that underlying amenorrhea in females. As such, a discussion is outside of the aims and scope of this book and the interested reader is referred to Scott's (1986) review.

Onset of puberty

It has previously been suggested that an early puberty is a contributing factor in the development of AN. But, physical and emotional maturity do not necessarily coincide. Both male and female AN patients may tend to be 'late developers' emotionally, while physical development of girls in particular is often advanced.

Over the past century, because of better nutrition and living conditions, menstruation has begun at a progressively younger age. It may be that the onset of puberty a year or two later in boys provides them with some measure of 'protection'. Incidentally, it must be borne in mind that, as in females, AN can develop in prepubertal males (e.g. Roussounis, 1971).

SOCIOCULTURAL INFLUENCES

In understanding the sociocultural influences in the expression of AN, it is important to bear in mind the reports that while the disorder has increased among females, the frequency of male cases has decreased or remained the same (Bruch, 1979; Garfinkel and Garner, 1982). As there is less societal emphasis on thinness for males, the reduced sociocultural influence in the predisposition to the disorder for males may suggest more serious pathologies in other areas, such as within the individual and his family. However, familial psychopathologies in males do resemble those of females, and many of the individual's psychopathological features resemble those of female anorexics (Crisp and Roberts, 1962; Roussounis, 1971; Beumont *et al.*, 1972; Hogan, Huerta and Lucas, 1974; Hay and Leonard, 1979).

WHAT DO THESE FINDINGS SUGGEST?

Why is AN principally (and increasingly) a disorder of women and why does it most typically appear in adolescence? It may be suggested that normal development in our culture produces differential stresses upon the sexes from early childhood throughout adolescence. Bardwick (1971) reviews evidence from numerous psychological studies indicating that, from an early age, females tend to be socially rewarded for affiliation and dependence. Consequently, their self-esteem would be strongly linked with interpersonal approval. By contrast, young boys are generally rewarded for the traits of autonomy, competitiveness and aggression, all of which are consistent with later vocational and social-role expectations. Bardwick regards boys as likely to experience many pre-adolescent social-development crises. However, 'the general tendencies of girls are not likely to lead them into serious confrontations with adults ... [and] girls are not significantly stressed nor pressured until puberty' (pp. 207–8). Puberty changes this quiescent state and simultaneously introduces stresses on several fronts. As Garner, Garfinkel and Olmstead (1983) have recently written: The rapid emergence of female sexual maturity at puberty is marked by conspicuous shape changes and the developmental milestone of menarche. Menarche is for normal women a pivotal event that may initiate heightened awareness of gender identity and differentiation (Koff, Rierden and Silverstone, 1978; Rierden and Koff, 1980a, b). Such indications of adulthood and sexuality may make denial and avoidance of the expectations that they imply more difficult for the psychologically unprepared female. Adolescence may therefore be viewed as qualitatively and quantitatively more difficult for the female than for the male. However, cultural changes may have magnified the relevant stresses. For instance, the social norms for female sexuality have substantially altered over the past three decades. The differences in sex-related attitudes and behaviour described in early reports (Kinsey, Pomeroy, Martin and Gebhart, 1953) have now virtually disappeared (Curran, 1977; DeLamater and MacCorquodale, 1979). 'The consequent change in expectations has provided freedom for most, but may precipitate a developmental crisis in those who lack the necessary psychological foundation' (Garner *et al.*, 1983, pp. 77–8).

In addition, not only is the modern female expected to achieve in a highly competitive vocational world, but she is also expected to excel in traditional feminine roles. Failure or inadequacy in either area may result in guilt. The temporal connection between the changing body shape at puberty and the intensification of the role conflicts may lead to the body becoming the focal point for the struggle to cope with conflicting achievement and psychosocial demands (Bardwick, 1971; Garner *et al.*, 1983). More details of this sociocultural framework are given in Chapter 5 on psychosexual factors.

Dally and Gomez (1979) stress the role of developing breasts and enlarging hips and what these signify as opposed to the menarche.

> Starving reverses or minimises these changes and also removes sexual feelings. It is significant that the fear females have of becoming fat so often centres around their hips and thighs. Male hips remain thin. The fear of fatness expressed by male patients usually concerns their bodies as a whole; it is not focussed on any particular body area (p. 100).

The increased incidence of female anorexics (but perhaps not of males) seen in recent years supports this cultural hypothesis and invites speculation regarding particular social changes that may have raised women's vulnerability. The increased pressure on women to meet the current thinner standard for physical attractiveness has likely provided the growing impetus for dieting and consequent AN.

Because fewer male anorexics are identified, it is more difficult to make generalisations about them than of females. However, there do appear to be a number of characteristics that are typical of this group, and a number of aspects of their experience suggestive of a similar conflict to that occurring generally in AN, and which, equally, seems to lead to passivity and emphasis on food control.

The lack of aggression in male anorexics is more pronounced. Their attitude is more self-effacing than assertive. In this respect, they are therefore likely to have found themselves feeling at least uneasy, if not explicitly inadequate, within the general social pressure to be dominant. They also tend to have wanted a creative or expressive outlet for their abilities, but their career choices have often been hampered by family values (Slade, 1984).

OUTCOME IN MALES

Conflicting views have been expressed on the outcome of AN in males — both that it is poorer compared to that of females (Crisp and Toms, 1972) and that it is better (Morgan and Russell, 1975; Hasan and Tibbetts, 1977; Dally and Gomez, 1979; Vandereycken and Van den Broucke, 1984). There have been only three previous reports of follow-ups and outcome assessments of males (Hasan and Tibbetts, 1977; Dally and Gomez, 1979; Burns and Crisp, 1984).

Hasan and Tibbett's (1977) group of ten were followed up for six months to six years (mean 27 months). One patient died. The early pattern was the familiar one of very uncertain maintenance of weight gain, often with early readmission. In the longer term, one patient was awaiting readmission at time of writing, having relapsed into a chronic anorexic condition with a generally unsatisfactory life pattern. In two other patients (20 per cent) the situation remained precarious. None had developed a bulimic syndrome.

Workers such as Dally (1969) and Crisp and Toms (1972) have commented on the rather poorer prognosis in the anorexic's male counterpart. However, Hasan and Tibbetts feel that the outcome in their male series had been rather better than in their female cases. Nevertheless, the numbers are small and it is possible that this sample, although fitting the category of AN, contained a smaller proportion of extremely severe cases compared with corresponding females.

Of their eight patients with primary AN, Dally and Gomez (1979) report that after four years 75 per cent were of normal weight, 62 per cent had a normal attitude towards food and eating, but 50 per cent were still markedly dependent upon their families.

However, the Hasan and Tibbetts and Dally and Gomez studies were based on small sample sizes of ten and twelve, and provide insufficient details of clinical history or presentation to enable reliable comparisons of outcome with that of an equivalent female series. Burns and Crisp (1984) improved upon this state by presenting the outcome of 27 consecutive male AN patients who were followed up 2–20 years after presentation. Clinical data were used to demonstrate the characteristics of the population and to derive predictors of outcome. Twenty of these accepted an inpatient refeeding/psychotherapy regime. The outcome of the series compared very closely with similar groups of female anorexics (Morgan and Russell, 1975; Hsu *et al.*, 1979). Twelve (44 per cent) had a good outcome, as measured by indices such as nutritional status, mental state and psychosocial outcome; seven (26 per cent) had an intermediate outcome; and eight (30 per cent) a poor outcome. No patient had died.

As in the female, the high proportion of those physically recovered (71 per cent whose weight was rarely 85 per cent MPMW) contained many still excessively preoccupied with diet, weight and shape. The figure of 37 per cent who were at normal weight and also fully free from weight phobia parallels findings from comparable female studies (Hsu *et al.*, 1979). Poor outcome was associated with a longer duration of illness, previous treatment and greater weight loss during illness, although not with any specific dietary behaviour.

Of various other cases scattered throughout the literature over the past half-decade, Scott (1986) notes that 46 per cent of cases showed a positive outcome, 37 per cent a negative outcome, whilst in 17 per cent, no details were given. Taking only those cases where details were given, 55 per cent were reported as showing a favourable outcome as opposed to 45 per cent with an unfavourable outcome.

CONCLUSIONS

For almost three centuries, the existence of true AN in males has been queried by some. Reasons have been outlined here as to why this could be so.

It is suggested that the diagnostic criteria for AN be modified from the commonly used Feighner criteria to something along the lines described here so that inclusion of both sexes may be accommodated.

In many ways, the epidemiological features of AN in males are similar to those of female anorexics, although inconsistencies do exist within some reports of males. However, inconsistencies between reports on females abound also.

Although more women than men appear to binge eat, findings do suggest that it is the *subjective labelling* of one's behaviour as binging and not binge eating *per se* that occurs more often in females.

Findings from endocrinological studies (see Scott, 1986 for a review) are complex and difficult to interpret. Nevertheless, it is fair to say that there appears to be much that corresponds to the female condition.

Findings from studies of male anorexics contribute to explaining the condition as a whole. A gender identity/sociocultural framework appears to explain the greater propensity amongst females to develop the disorder.

Males should not be regarded as atypical cases, but as individuals representative of the AN population and as requiring similar forms of practical therapy as females.

REFERENCES

Andersen, A.E. (1977) 'Atypical anorexia nervosa.' In R.A. Vigersky (ed), *Anorexia nervosa*, Raven Press, New York

—— and Mickalide, A.D. (1983) 'Anorexia nervosa in the male: an underdiagnosed disorder.' *Psychosomatics, 24*, 1066–75.

Bardwick, J. (1971) *Psychology of women: a study of bio-social conflicts*. Harper & Row, New York.

Bemis, K.M. (1978) 'Current approaches to the etiology and treatment of anorexia nervosa.' *Psychological Bulletin, 85*, 593–617.

Beumont, P.J.V., Beardwood, C.J. and Russell, G.F.M. (1972) 'The occurence of the syndrome of anorexia nervosa in male subjects.' *Psychological Medicine, 2*, 216–31

Bhanji, S. (1979) 'Anorexia nervosa: physicians' and psychiatrists' opinions and practice.' *Journal of Psychosomatic Research, 23*, 7–11
Bruch, H. (1974) *Eating disorders*. Basic Books, New York
—— (1979) *The golden cage: the enigma of anorexia nervosa*. Vintage Books, New York
Burns, T. and Crisp, A.H. (1984) 'Outcome of anorexia nervosa in males.' *British Journal of Psychiatry, 145*, 319–25
Crisp. A.H. and Burns, T.P. (1983) 'Primary anorexia nervosa in the male and female — a comparison of clinical features and prognosis. *International Journal of Eating Disorders, 2*, 5–10
—— and Roberts, F.J. (1962) 'A case of anorexia nervosa in the male.' *Postgraduate Medical Journal, 38*, 350–3
—— and Toms, D.A. (1972) 'Primary anorexia nervosa or weight phobia in the male: report on 13 cases.' *British Medical Journal, 1*, 334-8
—— Fenton, G.W. and Scotton, L. (1968) 'A controlled study of the EEG in anorexia nervosa.' *British Journal of Psychiatry, 114*, 1149–60
—— Palmer, R.L. and Kalucy, R.S. (1976) 'How common is anorexia nervosa? A prevalence study.' *British Journal of Psychiatry, 218*, 549–54.
Curran, J.P. (1977) 'Convergence towards a single sexual standard?' In D. Byrne and L.A. Byrne (eds), *Exploring human sexuality*. Harper and Row, New York.
Dally, P. (1969) *Anorexia nervosa*. Heinemann, London
—— and Gomez, J. (1979) *Anorexia nervosa*. Heinemann, London
DeLamater, J. and MacCorquodale, P. (1979) *Premarital sexuality: attitudes, relationships and behavior*. University of Wisconsin, Madison, Wis.
Falstein, E.I., Feinstein, S.C. and Judas, I. (1956) 'Anorexia nervosa in the male child.' *American Journal of Orthopsychiatry, 26*, 751–72
Feighner, J.P., Robins, E., Guze, S.B., Woodruff, R.A., Jr., Winokur, G. and Munoz, R. (1972) 'Diagnostic criteria for use in psychiatric research.' *Archives of General Psychiatry, 26*, 57–63
Garfinkel, P.E. and Garner, D.M. (1982) *Anorexia nervosa: a multidimensional perspective*. Brunner/Mazel, New York
Garner, D.M., Garfinkel, P.E. and Olmstead, M.P. (1983) 'An overview of sociocultural factors in the development of anorexia nervosa.' In P.L. Darby, P.E. Garfinkel, D.M. Garner and D.C. Coscina (eds), *Anorexia nervosa: recent developments in research*, pp. 65–82, Alan Liss, New York
Gull, W.W. (1874) 'Anorexia nervosa (apepsia hysterica, anorexia hysterica).' *Transactions of the Clinical Society, London, 7*, 22–8
Halmi, K.A., Falk, J.R. and Schwartz, E. (1981) 'Binge-eating and vomiting: a survey of a college population.' *Psychological Medicine, 11*, 697–706
Hasan, M.K. and Tibbetts, R.W. (1977). 'Primary anorexia nervosa (weight phobia) in males.' *Postgraduate Medical Journal, 53*, 146–51.
Hawkins, R.C. and Clement, P.F. (1980) Development and construct validation of a self-report measure of binge-eating techniques. *Addictive Behaviors, 5*, 219–26
Hay, G.G. and Leonard, J.B. (1979) 'Anorexia nervosa in males.' *Lancet, i*, 574–6
Herzog, D.B., Norman, D.K., Gordon, C. and Pepose, M. (1984) 'Sexual conflict and eating disorders in 27 males.' *American Journal of Psychiatry, 141*, 989–90
Hogan, W.M., Huerta, E. and Lucas, A.R. (1974) 'Diagnosing anorexia in males.' *Psychosomatics, 15*, 122–6
Hsu, L.K.G., Crisp, A.H. and Harding, B. (1979) 'Outcome of anorexia nervosa.' *Lancet, i*, 61–65
Jones, D.J., Fox, M.M., Babigian, H.M. and Hutton, H.E. (1980) 'Epidemiology of anorexia nervosa in Monroe County, New York: 1960–1976.' *Psychosomatic Medicine, 42*, 551–8
Katzman, M.A., Wolchik, S.A. and Braver, S.L. (1984) 'The prevalence of frequent binge

eating and bulimia in a nonclinical college sample.' *International Journal of Eating Disorders*, *3*, 53–62

Kendell, R.E., Hall, D.J., Hailey, A. and Babigian, H.M. (1973) 'The epidemiology of anorexia nervosa.' *Psychological Medicine*, *3*, 200–3

Kessler, J. (1966) *Psychopathology of childhood.* Prentice Hall, Englewood Cliffs, New Jersey

Kinsey, A.C., Pomeroy, W., Martin, C. and Gebhart, P. (1953) *Sexual behavior in the human female.* Saunders, Philadelphia

Koff, E., Rierden, J. and Silverstone, E. (1978) 'Changes in representation of body image as a function of menarchial status.' *Developmental Psychology*, *78*, 635–42

Marshall, M.H. (1978) 'Anorexia nervosa: dietary treatment and re-establishment of body weight in 20 cases studied on a metabolic unit. *Journal of Human Nutrition*, *32*, 349–57

Morgan, H.G. and Russell, G.F.M. (1975) 'Value of family background and clinical features as predictors of long-term outcome in anorexia nervosa: four year follow-up study of 41 patients.' *Psychological Medicine*, *5*, 355–72

Morton, R. (1689) *Phthisiologia: or a treatise of consumptions.* Princess Arms Press, London

Palmer, R.L. (1980) *Anorexia nervosa.* Penguin, Harmondsworth

Pyle, R.L., Mitchell, J.E., Halvorsen, P.A., Neuman, P.A. and Goff, G.M. (1983) 'The incidence of bulimia in freshman students.' *International Journal of Eating Disorders*, *2*, 75–85

Rierden, J. and Koff, E. (1980a) 'The psychological impact of menarche: Integrative versus disruptive changes.' *Journal of Youth and Adolescence*, *9*, 49–58

—— and—— (1980b) 'Representation of the female body by early and late adolescent girls.' *Journal of Youth and Adolescence*, *9*, 339–46

Roussounis, S.H. (1971) 'Anorexia nervosa in a prepubertal male.' *Proceedings of the Royal Society of Medicine*, *64*, 666–7

Russell, G.F.M. (1970) 'Anorexia nervosa: Its identity as an illness and its treatment.' In J.H. Price (ed), *Modern trends in psychological medicine, vol. II*, Appleton Century Crofts, New York

Scott, D.W. (1986) 'Anorexia nervosa in the male: a review of clinical, epidemiological and biological findings.' *International Journal of Eating Disorders*, *5*, 799–819

Slade, R. (1984) *The anorexia nervosa reference book.* Harper & Row, London

Sreenivasan, U. (1978) 'Anorexia nervosa in boys.' *Canadian Psychiatric Association Journal*, *23*, 159–62

Swann, I. (1977) 'Anorexia nervosa: a difficult diagnosis in boys.' *Practitioner*, *218*, 424-7

Vandereycken, W. and Van den Broucke, S. (1984) 'Anorexia nervosa in males.' *Acta Psychiatrica Scandinavica*, *70*, 447–54

Whyte, B.L. and Kaczkowski, H. (1983) 'Anorexia nervosa: a study of psychiatrists' and psychologists' opinions and practices.' *International Journal of Eating Disorders*, *2*, 87–92

5

An Overview of Psychosexual Factors in Eating Disorders

Derek Scott

INTRODUCTION

It has long been suggested that psychosexual factors play a contributory part in the development of eating disorders. The earliest description of the syndrome noted heterosexual-relationship difficulties as precipitating AN, and Janet (1929) regarded anorexia as a hysterical variant due to sexual frustration. It has often been alleged that those with the illness are psychosexually immature, and that the condition results from a failure to cope with problems of adolescence; that they cannot accept their own physical and sexual maturity, and are incapable of assuming an adult female role (e.g. Beumont, Abraham and Simson, 1981). Thus, it is commonly regarded that AN develops as a way of dealing with conflict between instilled attitudes and the biological and social demands of puberty.

This chapter examines gender identity from a psychological perspective. Areas covered include: (a) psychoanalytical perspectives; (b) empirical findings and associated theoretical frameworks; and (c) psychosexual factors within male anorexics.

One such anecdotal account is that of Selvini-Palazzoli (1974) who believes that some patients cannot imagine that sexual relations are a form of self-fulfilment based on personal choice and some simply ignore the whole problem by shutting themselves off whenever others broach the subject. Others (usually those in their late teens) indulge in romantic Platonic fantasies with imaginary or distant people. Selvini-Palazzoli describes one girl who confined her 'love life' to sentimental correspondences with various men who had emigrated and whose addresses she had gained from a matrimonial agency. However, she quickly broke off corresponding when one of these 'pen-lovers' announced his impending arrival in the country.

Such anecdotal accounts continue within the literature, yet obviously cannot be said to give support for the idea of psychosexual factors as playing a causal role in the eating disorders.

THE PSYCHOANALYTICAL MODEL

This model is more substantially detailed in Chapter 6, but for present purposes, the following (necessarily simplistic) details may function. The aim of the psychoanalysts has largely been to explain the underlying concealed conflicts by *one* psychodynamic formulation. Freud (1902) likened AN to 'a melancholia occurring when sexuality is underdeveloped... Loss of appetite [is] in sexual terms, loss of libido'. This link was extended by Waller, Kaufman and Deutsch (1940). AN was viewed as a form of conversion hysteria and as the symbolic expression of the repudiation of sexuality, specifically of 'oral impregnation' fantasies. During the 1940s and 1950s, this view dominated the field, and is still held by some. Such sweeping generalisations as Waller *et al.*'s have long been questioned. However, careful examination is still warranted. Thoma (1967), for instance, whilst defending psychodynamic factors in the aetiology of AN, cautiously avoids automatically giving them causal significance. He prefers to emphasise the abnormal psychic development of the patient and stresses that only seldom can a psychological trauma be elicited before the onset of illness, as opposed to characterising the family environment as pathogenic. The following psychodynamic processes are described: (a) A defence mechanism not directed against external anger but against the developmental process of puberty itself; (b) A regression so that the patient abandons the genital–sexual stage of development and sexual impulses vanish from consciousness; (c) 'Fixation at an oral level' so that thought is dominated by food and hunger; (d) Striving towards an ascetic ideal and an asexual life; (e) There would appear to result a perpetual struggle to escape from guilt and anxiety; abstinence from food may serve as self-punishment; they may also seek to protect and feed other members of their families or other patients.

As an example of a contemporary psychodynamic view on the sexual aspects of AN, one might quote Sours (1980, p.149):

> Mary's discomfort with adolescent sexuality and the persistence of tomboyism from the latency years were apparent. In early adolescence, the biosexual tendency of the girl is strong, manifest in her body-image as well as ego interests and physical activities. The adolescent ego cannot rely as much on the superego, since its authority structure is now weakened as decathexis of the object relations occurs. Withdrawal of object cathexis leads to isolation and depression in the young adolescent, who then, if adaptive and progressive in development, turns to idealizing isosexual friendships in multiple attempts at separation from the primary love object. In this phase, the young adolescent is plagued with hunger and fantasies of food and eating.

As ever, little in the way of hypotheses for experimental validation is forthcoming.

GENERAL CHARACTERISTICS

Abstainers versus vomiters/purgers

Beumont *et al.* (1976) found considerable differences in sexual history between their 'dieters' and their 'vomiters and purgers'. Fifty-three per cent of dieters as opposed to 100 per cent of vomiters/purgers had ever had a boyfriend, 33 per cent of dieters as opposed to 88 per cent of vomiters/purgers had experienced sexual intercourse and six per cent as opposed to 50 per cent of dieters/purgers had used oral contraceptives. These results are consistent with the general finding that the latter group were more normal in their social interactions. Similar findings were obtained by Garfinkel (1981) in that the 'bulimic' group were more outgoing and sexually active. However, sex was rarely enjoyed and the patients often reported feeling 'used' in sexual relationships.

Adolescence

Puberty and adolescence, with concomitant evolving alterations in physical appearance, sexual characteristics, social relationships and family interactions, are viewed by some as critical transitional experiences for the future anorexic patient (e.g. Crisp, 1980). The anorexic's reaction to the biological changes of adolescence is to retreat from the demands of adulthood and an attempt to establish a sense of self-control. Casper and Davis (1977), for instance, suggest that what may have commenced as normal dieting with the aim of increasing a girl's sexual attractiveness progresses and becomes out of control. Orbach (1978) suggests that the anorexic woman both rejects and exaggerates the feminine role. Whilst the anorexic lacks prominent female secondary sexual characteristics, she has become excessively petite and fragile (Sitnick and Katz, 1984). Despite anecdotal assertions, few studies have addressed these issues in any formal way. Those that have done so are illustrated here.

One of the first such studies was that of Dally, Gomez and Isaacs (1979). They held that libido was likely normal in the majority of AN patients prior to development of the illness, but that once the illness is established, sexual interest diminishes in a majority and sexuality may be actively repudiated in a minority. Others seem to form idealised desires for an understanding and undemanding partner with whom they would eventually have children, yet could avoid direct discussion of sexual matters. Fifty per cent of these patients had experienced sexual intercourse, 40 per cent of these being married. However, only one per cent of all their patients experienced intercourse after the onset of illness. Additionally, they reported that many younger patients were sexually timid.

A recent French study (Buvat-Herbaut, Hebbinckuys, Lemaire and Buvat, 1983) demonstrated that AN does not signify the rejection of a sexually attractive and menstruating female body in every case. The proportion of these girls who wished to menstruate was the same across the three groups examined (controls, emaciated anorexics and 'recovering' (gaining weight) anorexics). Their motives for this were consistent across the groups: viz. 'to feel normal', 'to feel like a woman', 'to have children'. The proportion of women in the groups wishing to have children were very similar (91–95 per cent). More anorexic girls than controls reported fearing an idea of an enlarged stomach during pregnancy and being disgusted by this idea. However, these feelings concerned less than 20 per cent of the anorexics. Similarly, only a few more anorexic girls than controls said they feared sexuality (33 per cent versus 21 per cent). The proportion of the anorexic girls gaining weight and reporting being disgusted by sexuality was higher than that of the controls and of the emaciated girls. Nevertheless, percentages of these were much lower than many others might have imagined (controls = 14 per cent; emaciated = 18 per cent; weight-gainers = 37 per cent). It may be significant that the fear of sexuality only appears to emerge (or re-emerge) with weight normalisation and it may follow that in certain cases, weight loss could be used as a protection against sexuality. Incidently, these figures, obtained outside of hospital and after informing the subjects that they would not be treated by constraining methods, are likely to be nearer to the true picture than data gained during a hospital stay and where girls may wish to seem less ill and leave hospital as soon as possible.

Anorexia nervosa is often regarded as resulting from an inability to assume the adult female body, menstruation and sexual attractiveness. It has again been shown that this hypothesis is not supported in every case. A large percentage of anorexics assume a sexuality before (45 per cent) or during (37 per cent) their illness (Buvat and Buvat-Herbaut, 1977). In this earlier study by the French team, it was suggested that specific problems related to sexuality did not have a causally important role in more than 22 per cent of the anorexics. It must be concluded from these two studies collectively that in the majority of cases, AN does not indicate an absolute rejection of the adult female body, although a fear or a refusal of sexuality can have a causal role in 20 per cent to 40 per cent of cases.

Beumont *et al.* (1981) elicited comprehensive psychosexual histories from 31 females (mean age 21.8 years ±4.3) with AN. Although only the most salient points shall be precised here, this is quite a comprehensive account and deserves a close examination. Their subjects exhibited a wide spectrum of sexual knowledge, attitudes and behaviour, which may be summarised as follows:

1. More than half of the patients had a poor *knowledge* of sexual matters and knowledge of contraception. Whilst some deliberately avoided reading sexual materials, others actually sought sexual literature.
2. Twenty-six per cent expressed a positive *attitude* towards menstruation, 29 per cent expressed a negative attitude, whilst the others were 'unsure'. Twenty-three per cent expressed a negative attitude towards marriage, 35 per cent expressed a negative attitudc towards pregnancy and childbirth, 23 per cent had negative attitudes towards masturbation, 35 per cent showed negative attitudes towards premarital intercourse and 26 per cent towards homosexuality.

Although varying numbers are recorded as having ambivalent attitudes or being unsure on the relative dimension, in the light of previous anecdotal statements, these figures are consistently low.

3. As far as sexual *experience* was concerned, 58 per cent admitted to masturbation and six per cent admitted to having had early adolescent homosexual experiences, and 87 per cent had had at least one boyfriend whom they considered special.

In sum, there appears to be nothing in particular to substantiate a suggestion of oddities within sexual outlook or behaviour amongst anorexics.

Beumont *et al.* (1981) also reported that the sexual experience of anorexics was near that of normal girls of the same age, although a loss of sexual desire and episodes of no sexual activity often occurred during emaciation. In further contrast to commonly held views, sexual promiscuity has been noted occasionally. Cantwell *et al.* (1977) for instance, noted that 17 per cent of their 26 anorexics had reported premorbid sexual promiscuity.

It is a physiological fact that a patient who may at one time have been heterosexually active, on becoming severely emaciated will lose this interest. Two separate analyses revealed factors termed 'heterosexual disinterest' and 'psychosexual immaturity'. The expression of disinterest in the opposite sex showed a small decline under a placebo condition but a much sharper decline in the expression of that attitude under a drug condition (cyproheptadine).

In Morgan and Russell's (1975) prognostic study of 41 patients, four aspects of sexual adjustment were rated: (a) attitude towards sexual matters; (b) aims — for example, intention to marry — in sexual relationships; (c) level of active sexual behaviour; and (d) attitude towards menstruation. Heterosexual contacts ranged from a regular relationship with a boyfriend to an engagement, and were found before the onset of the illness in 49 per cent of the patients. At four-year follow-up, 60 per cent of patients were judged to be normal or near-normal in terms of sexual adjustments. Twenty-three per cent were clearly abnormal, showing, for example, aversion to heterosexual contact, denial of libido or satisfaction at continuing amenorrhea. Poor sexual adjustment was commonest in patients of low body weight, though it was also found in one obese patient. They note that the assessment of sexual adjustment presented difficulties, but it did seem that abnormal attitudes to sexual matters, or precipitating factors of a sexual nature, had occurred in only a minority of patients.

PSYCHOSEXUAL FACTORS IN MALE ANOREXICS

Recently, Scott (1986) has collated previous reports of AN in males; the general impression being that this was indeed the counterpart to female anorexia. As such, comparable psychosexual disturbances should be apparent. As stated in the previous chapter, the lack of aggression in male anorexics is often very pronounced.

Their attitude is more self-effacing than assertive. In this respect they are therefore likely to have found themselves feeling at least uneasy, if not explicitly inadequate, within the general social pressure to be dominant.

That food refusal in the male is related to fears about sexuality in certain cases has been noted by Beumont *et al.* (1972). It is of note that several of their patients were considered to be sexually immature or to have lost their sexual interest during the course of their illness (as of many female anorexics). In all of Beumont's series, the onset of illness was either just before or just after puberty. Absence of sexual activity at either the behavioural or fantasy level was also observed in Crisp and Toms' (1972) male group. Of the 59 cases spanning more than the past half century reviewed by Scott (1986), 32 per cent exhibited some form of sexual disturbance.

Homosexual conflict?

Some authors have remarked on the presence of homosexual conflict preceding the onset of AN in up to 50 per cent of the male patients (e.g. Crisp and Toms, 1972). Crisp (1970) suggested that homosexual conflict in the male might play a comparable role to that of the heterosexual threat in the female. Crisp (1983) maintains that there is usually profound gender uncertainty present at the outset, which may be either a recent pubertal phenomenon or chronically entrenched within an older adolescent. Males develop shape consciousness either within this context or else within that of 'massive' adolescent obesity. Limited sexual activity has been found with groups such as Hasan and Tibbetts' (1977). Although there was no evidence of homosexual activity, there was a noticeable lack of assertive masculinity or identification with the normal interests and activities of the respective male age-group. It is possible that the cultural pressure on the homosexual male to be thin and attractive places him at greater risk for eating disorders. Perhaps intrapsychic factors, as yet unknown, are more central to the association between conflicted homosexuality and eating disorders in men (Herzog, Norman, Gordon and Pepose, 1984).

Until further work is done within this area, the case for psychosexual conflicts within the development of male anorexia must remain unproven.

CONCLUSIONS

The questions of why AN is principally a disorder of the female sex and why it typically appears in adolescence have been discussed in Chapter 4.

Psychodynamic formulations usually offer little other than to prompt areas for empirical evaluation (although see Chapter 6). Some psychoanalytically minded writers acknowledge that within eating disorders, causal significance is not attributable to psychosexual factors (e.g. Thoma, 1967). Even outside of the psychoanalytical perspective, many writers have described distorted psychosexual attributes within the eating-disordered patient (e.g. Boskind-Lodahl, 1976; Crisp, 1977). However, many empirical studies have demonstrated normal or near-normal psychosexuality. For instance, Buvat-Herbaut *et al.* (1983) have shown that AN generally does not signify a rejection of the female body. In addition, Beumont *et al.* (1981), in examining knowledge, attitudes and sexual experience of eating-disordered patients, generally found nothing to substantiate commonly held views of oddities within sexual outlook and behaviour.

Sexual adjustment was found to be reasonably good in a surprisingly high proportion of patients, although there remained an excessive emotional dependence of the patient on her family in over half the cases (Morgan and Russell, 1975). Furthermore, reports such as those of Beumont, George and Smart (1976) and Garfinkel (1981) suggest that *bulimics* are more 'normal' in their sexual outlook.

It is often difficult to assess sexual attitudes because of the youth of many subjects. Additionally, it is difficult, although important, to try to distinguish between morbid attitutes to sexual matters that might follow weight loss from those antedating onset of illness. The reliability of data referring to sexuality is always suspect, and must be particularly so from anorexics due to their likelihood of 'faking good'.

Because fewer male than female anorexics are identified, it is more difficult to make generalisations about them. However, there do appear to be a number of characteristics that are typical of this group, and a number of aspects of their experience suggestive of a similar conflict to that occurring generally in AN, and which equally seems to lead to passivity and emphasis on food control.

Several authors have commented on homosexual conflicts preceding the onset of anorexia in up to 50 per cent of males, and Crisp (1970) has suggested that this may play a comparable role to the alleged heterosexual threat in the female. However, the possible homosexual factor is probably not some *specific* sexual inclination, but rather a *general* lack of sexuality (Scott, 1987). It has not yet been established if there is a greater proportion of homosexuals within male anorexics than within the general population. Until this is done, such notions remain purely speculative and based only upon anecdotal statements.

REFERENCES

Beumont, P.J.V., Abraham, S.F. and Simson, K.G. (1981) 'The psychosexual histories of adolescent girls and young women with anorexia nervosa.' *Psychological Medicine, 11,* 131–140

——, George, G.C.W. and Russell, G.F.M. (1972) 'The occurrence of the syndrome of anorexia nervosa in male subjects.' *Psychological Medicine*, 2, 216–31

——, George, G.C.W. and Smart, D.E. (1976) '"Dieters" and "vomiters and purgers" in anorexia nervosa.' *Psychological Medicine, 6,* 617–22

Boskind-Lodahl, M. (1976) 'Cinderella's step-sisters: feminist perspective on anorexia nervosa and bulimia.' *Signs: Journal of Women, Culture, and Society, 2,* 35–41

Buvat, J. and Buvat-Herbaut, M. (1977) 'La sexualite de l'anorectique mental(e).' *Nouvelle Presse Medicale, 6,* 859–61

Buvat-Herbaut, M., Hebbinckuys, P., Lemaire, A. and Buvat, J. (1983) 'Attitudes towards weight, body image, eating, menstruation, pregnancy, and sexuality in 81 cases of anorexia compared with 288 normal control school girls.' *International Journal of Eating Disorders, 2,* 45–59

Cantwell, D.P., Sturzenburger, S., Burroughs, J., Salkin, B. and Green, J.K. (1977) 'Anorexia nervosa: an affective disorder?' *Archives of General Psychiatry, 34,* 1087–93

Casper, R.C. and Davis, J.M. (1977) 'On the course of anorexia nervosa.' *American Journal of Psychiatry, 134,* 974–8

Crisp, A.H. (1970) 'Anorexia nervosa, "feeding disorder", "nervous malnutrition", or "weight phobia"'? *World Review of Nutrition and Dietetics, 12,* 452–504

—— (1977) 'Anorexia nervosa.' *Proceedings of the Royal Society of Medicine, 70,* 464–9

—— (1980) *Anorexia nervosa: let me be.* Grune and Stratton, New York

—— (1983) 'Some aspects of the psychopathology of anorexia nervosa.' In P.L. Darby. P.E. Garfinkel, D.M. Garner and D.Y. Coscina (eds.), *Anorexia nervosa: Recent developments in research,* pp. 15–28, Alan Liss, New York

—— and Toms, D.A. (1972) 'Primary anorexia nervosa or weight phobia in the male: Report on 13 cases.' *British Medical Journal, 1,* 334–8

Dally, P., Gomez, J. and Isaacs, A. (1979) *Anorexia nervosa.* Heinemann, London.

Freud, S. (1902) *The origins of psychoanalysis. Letters to Wilhelm Fliess, drafts and notes.* Hogarth Press, New York.

Garfinkel, P.E. (1981) 'Some recent observations on the pathogenesis of anorexia nervosa.' *Canadian Journal of Psychiatry, 26,* 218–233

Hasan, M.K. and Tibbetts, R.W. (1977) 'Primary anorexia nervosa (weight phobia) in males.' *Postgraduate Medical Journal, 53,* 146–51

Herzog, D.B., Norman, D.K., Gordon, C. and Pepose, M. (1984) 'Sexual conflict and eating disorders in 27 males.' *American Journal of Psychiatry, 141,* 989–90

Janet, P. (1929) *The major symptoms of hysteria.* MacMillan, New York.

Morgan, H.G. and Russell, G.F.M. (1975) 'Value of family background and clinical features as predictors of long-term outcome in anorexia nervosa: four-year follow-up study of 41 patients.' *Psychological Medicine, 5,* 355–71.

Orbach, S.C. (1978) *Fat is a feminist issue.* Paddington Press, New York.

Scott, D.W. (1986) 'Anorexia nervosa in the male: A review of clinical, epidemiological and biological findings.' *International Journal of Eating Disorders, 5,* 799–820

—— (1987) 'Psychosexual factors in anorexia nervosa: time for a reappraisal?' *International Journal of Eating Disorders, 2,* 199–213

Selvini-Palazzoli, M. (1974) *Self starvation.* Chaucer, London.

Sitnick, T. and Katz, J.L. (1984) 'Sex role identity and anorexia nervosa: brief report.' *International Journal of Eating Disorders, 3,* 81–7

Sours, J.A. (1980) *Starving to death in a sea of objects.* Vason Aronson, New York

Thoma, H. (1967) *Anorexia nervosa* (trans. G. Brydone). International Universities Press, New York

Waller, J.V., Kaufman, M.R. and Deutsch, F. (1940). 'Anorexia nervosa: a psychosomatic entity.' *Psychosomatic Medicine, 2,* 3

Part Two
Some Frameworks

6

Psychodynamic and Feminist Approaches to Anorexia and Bulimia Nervosa

Janet Sayers

INTRODUCTION

Freud wrote little of anorexia. What little he did write is mostly confined to his pre-psychoanalytic writings, in which he attributed AN to the prior occurrence in the sufferer's life of traumatic events associated with food and eating, specifically to the trauma of childhood seduction involving oral sex. Neurotic symptoms, he said, involve the reliving of this trauma in hallucinated somatic form, the trauma's mental content having been repressed from consciousness because of its conflict with social propriety as mediated by the ego. These symptoms could therefore only be relieved, in his view, through enabling the patient to recall to consciousness the repressed memory of their traumatic origin, either through hypnosis or through free association, so that its repressed mental and emotional content might thereby be discharged through verbalisation and catharsis.

At first, Freud accorded greater centrality to the father, later to the mother in the genesis of women's psychological disorders. This shift of focus has been adapted in current psychoanalytic and feminist approaches to the understanding and treatment of AN. These approaches are divided, as was Freud himself, as to whether this condition is determined by fantasy elaborated on the basis of the drives, or by actually occurring traumas such as that of parental seduction or deprivation understood by feminists as reflecting the more widespread deprivation and abuse suffered by women as an effect of sexual inequality.

FANTASY AND DRIVE APPROACHES

Perhaps the most notorious drive approach to the understanding and treatment of anorexia is that of Waller, Kaufman and Deutsch (1940). They argued that anorexia stems from disapproval by parents of their adolescent daughter's sexuality resulting in her defending against it by regression to the orality of infantile sexuality. As evidence, Waller *et al.* cite the cases of two nineteen-year-old girls whose anorexia was preceded by compulsive eating, which they associated with becoming pregnant. They then foreswore food; the first girl because her father disapproved of her boyfriend, the second because of the similarity of her boyfriend to her father. Both girls accordingly turned against their adolescent sexuality in the name of their father's authority. They refused food, according to Waller *et al.*, because of the symbolic equation they unconsciously made between sex and eating on account of their defensive regression from adolescent genitality to infantile orality.

This approach was reiterated by Helene Deutsch in the late 1940s (Deutsch, 1981). She described the case of a twenty-two-year-old girl whose anorexia she traced to the girl's feeling of rejection by her stepmother. This, says Deutsch, had caused the girl to turn to her father, symbolically expressing through compulsive eating her desire for impregnation by him. Her subsequent anorexic self-starvation, argues Deutsch, stemmed from fear lest she were actually to become pregnant by her father like her hated stepmother. Her anorexia, says Deutsch, expressed repudiation of this possibility and of the incestuous desire for her father seemingly realised, albeit unconsciously, through eating.

Deutsch's paper is symptomatic of a movement from implication of the father to implication of the mother in the genesis of anorexia. This change of emphasis is still more marked in Thomae's (1963) classic drive theory account of over 60 hospitalised anorexics. He makes no mention of the role played by the father in the aetiology of anorexia. Instead, his focus is entirely on the mother. Like other analysts before him, he argues that anorexia is a defence against the sexual drives of adolescence involving regression to the oral stage of infancy. But, his attention is on the ambivalent relation to the mother involved in this phase of development, on the desire both for union with, and for separation from, the mother. By starving herself, he says, the anorexic becomes as physically dependent as the infant on being cared for and unified in this sense with the mother. Therapy should therefore seek to make conscious those unconscious determinants of anorexia. But, he acknowledges, this is no mean task given the counter-transference reaction that anorexics evoke in the therapist. This reaction, writes Thomae, includes both anxiety at the anorexic's physical dependence, and hostile control in response to her negativism. Only by hospitalising the anorexic during treatment, he argues, can these untoward counter-transference reactions be allayed.

Others link AN with achievement, and with greed and envy stirred up by experience of separation and difference. An example is a patient of mine who has spent much of her life seeking to live up to her own and her mother's social aspirations by becoming both an accomplished writer and actor. She dreads getting better lest she thereby becomes ordinary and boring. She also records:

> I would like to be the thinnest of the thin. Then I would be relaxed because then I would only want a little to eat... I feel so sorry for fat children. I envy mothers whose children are thin. They want their children to be the same as mine. I want mine to be the same as theirs.

If the anorexic seeks to do away with difference and the longing and envy that it evokes by instead evoking these feelings in others, then it is no help for the therapist to collude in this process by envying the patient and longing for her to eat. For, as Boris (1984) points out, the therapist then becomes flawed in the anorexic's eyes. This has the effect of enabling her still further to evade the task of experiencing and working through the envy and longing for help that would be evoked in her were she to experience the therapist not as flawed, but as capable of providing such help. This task can only be achieved through enabling the anorexic to experience the therapist, not as enmeshed and fused with her own longing and envy, but as separate and different from herself. Some support for this view comes from feminist Sheila MacLeod's account of her recovery from a recurrence of her teenage anorexia following her mother's death:

> For weeks afterwards I was inconsolable, my defences completely eroded. Then one day, I found myself so weak that my legs had become paralysed and I couldn't walk upstairs... A few days later I remembered my mother having said, the last time I saw her, 'I sleep down here these days because my legs won't carry me upstairs'. It was shockingly clear to me that I had been identifying with my mother... It was only when I could tell myself, 'You are not your mother', and believe myself, that I could see the meaning of my anorexic stance.
>
> (MacLeod, 1981, p. 158)

Recognition of separation and difference, however, poses particular problems for women because of their social subordination. At least this is the view put forward by Marie Maguire (1987) from the London Women's Therapy Centre. She echoes Melanie Klein's (1957) claim that the first recognition in infancy of difference from the mother evokes a sense of emptiness and deprivation relative to her. It provokes envy of what she seemingly possesses and the infant lacks and wants, leading to attempts enviously to spoil and destroy her and her mothering capacity. Boys and men, writes Maguire, can deal more constructively with envy of the mother's capacities through realising their own capacities in work outside the home. This option is not so available to girls and women. Instead, they often find themselves competing on the same terrain as the mother, the feelings of envy and emptiness involved in this competition being so destructive and painful that they are often suppressed along with the recognition of difference that triggered these feelings in the first place.

Applying this perspective to the treatment of eating disorders in women, US feminist Kim Chernin (1986) argues that they stem from the guilt that women feel about competing with, and surpassing their mothers in a society that still accords this right less to women than to men. Women's guilt in this respect, she argues, like fellow Berkely-based therapist Michael Friedman (1985), is fuelled by the depletion their mothers express about providing the mothering that enables their daughters to surpass them, having felt neither able whole-heartedly to embrace nor to refuse this as their sole role as perhaps their mothers could before them when society faced women with a more straightforward choice between mothering and self-liberation. So drained do today's mothers often feel by mothering, says

Chernin, that their daughters can unconsciously experience the destructive fantasy of enviously devouring the mother, described by Klein (1957) as universal in infancy, actually to have taken effect. Eating disorders both express this fantasy of the 'primal feast' and defences against it; the bingeing, purging and self-starvation of bulimia and anorexia expressing the contradictory forces towards attacking and making reparation to the mother, towards regression and development and towards affirmation and denial of identification with the mother as female.

Treatment, in her view, accordingly depends at the individual level on undoing the resistances involved in AN to recalling positive as well as negative experiences of the mother and of food. It also calls, she insists, for widespread social change towards a generally more positive image of womanhood into which adolescent girls might be initiated without succumbing to the eating disorders that currently plague them now that they are offered no other ideal but quasi-male slenderness to which to aspire.

SOCIAL REALITY APPROACHES

Some therapists and feminists have sought to integrate Kleinian understanding of AN (in terms of the drives and fantasies of deprivation to which these drives give rise) with recognition of the social realities of family life and sex inequality that also contribute to the genesis of anorexia. Others virtually abandon all consideration of the drives and of unconscious fantasy. Instead, in so far as they adopt a psychoanalytic perspective of anorexia, they adopt the more socially oriented perspective of object relations theory and self-psychology.

Klein (1946) argued that the infant's psychic incorporation of the mother as an 'internal object' within the self is an effect of the infant's inborn drives; specifically of its supposed destructive instinct and of the elemental fear of self-annihilation to which this instinct supposedly gives rise. Object relations theory takes issue with Klein on this point. It argues that it is actual deprivation, not any inborn instinct, that gives rise to internalisation or introjection of the mother. The Scottish psychoanalyst, Fairbairn (1944), generally regarded as the founder of object relations theory, argues that introjection of the mother is first triggered by her failure to meet the baby's needs. Faced with this real deprivation, the baby seeks to deal with it by taking its mother in fantasy into itself; by internalising both her frustrating and exciting aspects. These then become split-off parts of the self that the infant's 'central ego' seeks to master and control.

Perhaps the best-known application of this theory to AN is that of the Italian psychoanalyst, Selvini-Palazzoli (1974). Anorexia, she says, stems from the mother's failure to meet and validate her child's need for autonomy and independence. Instead, the mother substitutes her own needs for those of the child. The child's first experience of feeding, therefore, is one of frustration rather than of gratification; the child coming to identify its body in the process with the mother now felt to be both bad and invasive. The bodily changes of adolescence compound and exacerbate this process. The anorexic responds as though the conflict with the mother first triggered by actual deprivation were intra- rather than inter-psychic; the anorexic using her central ego to fight off the frustrating and exciting aspects of the mother now experienced as one with her body ego.

Selvini-Palazzoli does not specify exactly how this theory might be applied in the treatment of AN. This has been left to her followers, notably John Sours in the USA. Like Selvini-Palazzoli, he argues that the anorexic lacks self-integration and differentiation from the mother. Anorexics, he writes, 'fear merger of self with an infantile inner object', using 'magical devices to save the self from passivity and merger' (Sours, 1980, p. 343). He combines this perspective with hospitalisation, behaviour modification and family therapy, aimed not least at getting the anorexic to eat; the psychological symptoms of starvation thereby being removed. As regards individual therapy of the anorexic's other psychological symptoms, he argues that once a therapeutic alliance is established, it often becomes necessary to interpret and make conscious to the anorexic the character of her internalised objects so as to enable her to begin to accept and integrate the good and bad aspects of herself, thus strengthening her ego and its integration with her body. And, in common with the Freudian and Kleinian drive approaches, Sours' object-relations perspective leads him to emphasise the necessity of working through the anorexic's ambivalence towards her mother as this ambivalence is transferred onto the therapist.

As well as drawing on the early work of Selvini-Palazzoli, Sours also draws on that of Bruch. Bruch (1973) too attributes anorexia to real deprivation rather than to fantasies of deprivation elaborated on the basis of the drives. She identifies three cardinal symptoms of anorexia: delusional body image, disturbed perception of bodily needs and a paralysing sense of ineffectiveness. She attributes the origin of these symptoms to the mother's failure to respond appropriately to her child's expression of need in infancy. In effect, she implies that the child is seduced into compliance with the mother's needs, seeking to know what others want of her rather than what she herself wants. This results in lack of a sense of self distinct from others; a lack of 'ego boundary', which Bruch says is rendered acute by the onset of adolescence with its pressure on the individual to develop an identity separate from the parents.

Bruch (1977) has subsequently put more stress on the fact that anorexics tend to come from highly successful families. The particular parental failure in relation to anorexia that Bruch now emphasises is that stemming from the very high achievements that the anorexic's parents seemingly expect of their children. The anorexic, states Bruch quoting one of her patients, accordingly feels hemmed in and constricted as it were in a 'golden cage' of felt parental expectations that she shine, feeling that she is not loved for herself but only for her achievements. Adolescence exacerbates this feeling because it both pressurises the individual into independent achievement and also scotches once and for all any illusions that the girl might entertain of either being a boy, or of being able to secure the same achievements as boys. The response of the anorexic is an achievement-orientated struggle; to be 'as good as a man', say, or to be 'super-special by being super-thin' (Bruch, 1977, p. 78).

Illustrative here, perhaps, is again the case of Sheila MacLeod (MacLeod, 1981). She attributes the origin of her anorexia to her parents' ambition that she obtain Oxbridge entrance, leading them to insist that she continue at boarding school after 'O' levels, even though she told them that she wanted to return home. Today, she feels enormous rage and anger against her parents, at least if the spirit of her book is anything to go by. As a teenager, however, her response was to stop eating. She recalls revelling in her achievement in this respect, driving herself to the very limits of physical endurance, seemingly also, outwitting her biology by ceasing menstruating, all the while dwelling on the superiority of her intellectual and athletic achievements compared to those of her peers.

Believing that AN stems from parents forcing their perceptions, ambitions and needs on their children, Bruch opposes the use of psychoanalytic interpretation in the treatment of anorexia lest it also be experienced as an attempt to interpose the therapist's experience in place of that of the anorexic. Instead, Bruch (1977) advocates that the therapist focus on authenticating the anorexic's own experience, meeting and validating her expression of need so as to make good the apparent failure of the parents in this respect. Only thus, she argues, can the anorexic's genuine self be enabled to emerge from its glittering but hollow facade, from its golden cage.

Bruch (1977) implies that the anorexic's parents fail to be the self-objects that their children need them to be. Instead, they interpose their own narcissistic needs, looking to the anorexic to be a self-object that will meet their needs (Bemporad and Ratey, 1985). They thereby fail to provide the mirroring and idealising affirmation of their child's grandiosity necessary to its developing a firmly based narcissistic sense of self. Hence the anorexic's precarious narcissistic grandiosity.

Applying this perspective to the treatment of anorexia, US psychiatrist Alan Goodsitt (1985) argues that the therapist should act as the self-object that the parents seemingly failed to be; that this includes the therapist sometimes acting as the patient's 'alter ego', stepping in for instance to supervise and manage her eating. This approach is likewise advocated by Lerner (1986), drawing on the work of British psychoanalyst Winnicott. Winnicott also argues that integrated self development depends in the first instance on the mother recognising, reflecting and meeting the baby's needs rather than frustrating these by interposing her own needs such that, in order to survive, the baby then has to fit in with the mother's needs. In Winnicott's (1960) terms, such maternal failure results in the baby forming a compliant 'false self' facade split off from its 'true self'. Attributing anorexia to 'failures in maternal holding behavior, particularly empathic mirroring' (Lerner, 1986, p. 41), Lerner urges the use of a treatment method that first and foremost provides anorexics with the empathic holding of which he says they have been deprived in infancy. Classic analytic interpretation of the anorexic's conflicts and defences should only be used once a therapeutic alliance has been established on this ground.

Some feminists also draw on self-psychology and object relations theory in understanding and treating AN. But, they situate the deprivation held by this theory to be causative of anorexia within the context of the deprivation suffered generally by women in our sexually unequal society. Women thereby become alienated from, and fearful of their own needs, claims Orbach (1986), unable to respond to them either in themselves or as they see themselves reflected in their daughters. The latter, accordingly, grow up equally cut off from their 'needy little girl self' and this results *in extremis* in total anorexic refusal of need.

Orbach (1986) and others such as Mira Dana (1987) therefore advocate a therapeutic approach in which the therapist provides the mirroring of which they say the anorexic was deprived in infancy. The therapist, they argue, should respond to and thus authenticate the anorexic's needs so that they are no longer cut off and refused. Orbach seeks to heal the mind–body split of the anorexic by establishing, through free association, the meaning that food and the body have for her. She thereby hopes to enable the anorexic to become conscious of the needs her food avoidance is intended to satisfy so that these needs might be met more effectively. This involves working against the anorexic's resistance which, like her symptoms, is erected in defence against the danger of rejection she believes to be inherent in her needs being expressed; a belief sustained by society's ubiquitous message to women to this effect. Hence Orbach's (1986) insistence, like Chernin (1986), on the importance of securing social as well as individual change to counter the anorexic's alienation from her needs; an alienation that, in Orbach's view, stems not only from maternal failure but also from the social repudiation of women's needs that cause this failure, and from the use of women's bodies in marketing, whereby women come to experience their bodies not from within but from the alien and external perspective of advertising.

CONCLUSIONS: FROM INTERNAL TO EXTERNAL REALITY

It is now generally recognised that AN involves psychological as well as organic factors. In this chapter, I have detailed the approaches to its psychology developed by psychoanalytically minded therapists, both feminist and non-feminist. This has involved documenting two conflicting currents and approaches in psychoanalysis; one that focuses on the fantasies underlying anorexia elaborated on the basis of biologically-given drives and needs; the other focusing on the actual deprivations suffered by the anorexic – deprivations that are attributed by feminists to those suffered generally by women as an effect of sex inequality.

The first approach involves a treatment method designed to make conscious the unconscious fantasies that seemingly sustain anorexia by interpreting these fantasies as they are expressed in the anorexic's transference relation to the therapist. The second approach, by contrast, involves the therapist in providing the empathic holding which, behind her hostile or compliant facade, the anorexic craves and of which she feels deprived.

The evidence of the consulting room cannot decide between these two approaches. The story that the anorexic tells of the deprivations she has suffered, and the transference of this sense of deprivation and of the defences against it on her relation with the therapist, are compatible both with the hypothesis that these deprivations actually occurred, and with the hypothesis that they are the fantasied effect of the comparison made by the anorexic between the felt strength of her needs and drives and the capacity and willingness of her family and the therapist to gratify them. Nor is the evidence of the consulting room sufficient on its own to determine the relative efficacy of the different treatment methods to which these two approaches have given rise. This can only be determined through short- and long-term follow-up studies, studies that are singularly lacking as regards both the non-analytic and analytic psychotherapy of anorexia (Garner, 1985).

The little evidence that is available has led Selvini-Palazzoli to abandon psychoanalysis altogether. Looking beyond the anorexic's behaviour in individual therapy to the current interactions of her family, she finds confirmation that anorexia is indeed an effect of real deprivation. She now attributes this deprivation to the drive of each member of the anorexic's family to outdo the others in terms of self-sacrifices, a strategy that mystifies the essential self-serving, competitive character of this interaction.

Having for years sought to treat anorexics psychoanalytically, Selvini-Palazzoli now finds that therapeutic change can be more quickly and effectively obtained through directive, 'strategic intervention', rather than through non-directive interpretation and empathy. Observing, for instance, that a central dynamic in the anorexic's family is the attempt by each parent to draw the anorexic into collusive alliance against the other — an alliance concealed out of concern for the second parent — she sometimes suggests that the mother go away on holiday. This can have the effect of exploding, without need of interpretation, the unspoken and shared fantasy of father and daughter that they would realise perfect harmony were it not for the mother's presence. For in her absence, it quickly becomes obvious to all that what the father most wants is her return!

Ironically, in the very process of abandoning the interpretative methods of psychoanalysis, Selvini-Palazzoli, in a sense, reiterates Freud's discovery of the triangular roots of psychopathology in the Oedipus complex (see also Dare, 1985), in the pairing of child and parent against the other parent; a pairing that Freud believed is first repressed in the name of patriarchal authority. Paradoxically, despite the concern of feminists to understand and challenge the present ordering of society in terms of this authority, the place of the father in the genesis of AN is virtually ignored by feminists now involved in its psychoanalytically-based treatment. This may reflect their sex, with anorexics being less likely to transfer on to a female therapist, feelings experienced in relation to the father. It also reflects the movement of psychoanalysis generally away from concern with the triangular father–mother–child relation of the Oedipus complex to concern with the pre-Oedipal mother–child relation; a concern that now informs the work of male and female psychoanalytically minded therapists alike. This concern is comprehensible given that the mother is so much more physically present than the father in the child's early years and therefore appears to exert a more formative influence on its psychological development. But the absence of men from the home, as a result of, say, the exigencies of work or divorce, does not entail that they are not implicated in the aetiology of AN. Indeed, their involvement becomes immediately obvious, as Selvini-Palazzoli (1974) demonstrates, once their interactions with the anorexic and her family are actually observed.

Illustrative of the father's involvement in anorexia is the case of Catherine (Dunbar, 1987). The tale her mother tells of Catherine's short life dwells mostly on her day-to-day care of Catherine, her father being away at work during the day and indeed, being abroad during many months of her illness. Nevertheless, Catherine dated its onset to the time when his business collapsed with the aftermath of the 1974 world recession, resulting in him then becoming depressed and violent towards her mother. Her anorexia first started, she told her mother: 'To protect you... The only way I could make myself ill was to stop eating and the only way I would be allowed home [from boarding school] was for me to become ill. I was so frightened about you being alone with daddy' (Dunbar, 1987, p. 88). Her illness, it seems, at least from her mother's account of it, essentially involved the attempt to regain the unity enjoyed by the infant with the mother through starving herself into child-like, physical dependence in defiance of her father's and doctor's strictures to the contrary.

Catherine never received psychotherapy during her hospital treatment, a fact much regretted by her mother. I hope that through the above review of recent psychoanalytical and feminist writings about AN I have conveyed the willingness of psychoanalytically minded therapists to provide such therapy and to combine it with hospital-based, organic, behavioural and family-based approaches to treatment. In the process, I have sought to demonstrate the variation between psychoanalytically minded therapists in the extent to which they go beyond the internal reality of the anorexic's drives and fantasies to engage with the external reality both of her family and of society and its sexual divisions and inequalities.

REFERENCES

Bemporad, J.R. and Ratey, A. (1985) 'Intensive psychotherapy of former anorexic individuals.' *American Journal of Psychotherapy, 39*, 456–66

Boris, H.N. (1984) 'On the treatment of anorexia nervosa.' *International Journal of Psychoanalysis, 65*, 435–42

Bruch, H. (1973) *Eating disorders.* Basic Books, New York

—— (1977) *The golden cage.* Open Books, London.

Chernin, K. (1986) *The hungry self.* Virago, London

Dana, M. (1987) 'Boundaries: one-way mirror to the self.' In M. Lawrence (ed), *Fed up and hungry*, Women's Press, London

Dare, C. (1985) 'The family therapy of anorexia nervosa.' *Journal of Psychiatric Research, 19,* 435–43

Deutsch, H. (1981) 'Anorexia nervosa.' *Bulletin Menninger Clinic, 45*, 499–511

Dunbar, M. (1987) *Catherine*, Penguin, Harmondsworth

Fairbairn, W.R.D. (1944) 'Endopsychic structure considered in terms of object-relationships.' *Psychoanalytic studies of the personality*. Tavistock, London, 1952

Friedman, M. (1985) 'Survivor guilt in the pathogenesis of anorexia nervosa.' *Psychiatry, 48*, 25–39

Garner, D.M. (1985) 'Individual psychotherapy for anorexia nervosa.' *Journal of Psychiatric Research, 19*,, 423–33

Goodsitt, A. (1985) 'Self psychology and the treatment of anorexia nervosa.' In D.M. Gardner and P.E. Garfinkel (eds), *Handbook of anorexia nervosa and bulimia*, Guildford Press, New York

Klein, M. (1946) 'Notes on some schizoid mechanisms.' In *Writings of Melanie Klein*, vol.3, Hogarth Press, London

—— (1957) 'Envy and gratitude.' In *Writings of Melanie Klein*, vol.3, Hogarth Press, London

Lerner, H.D. (1986) 'Current developments in the psychoanalytic psychotherapy of anorexia nervosa and bulimia nervosa.' *Clinical Psychologist, 39*, 39–43.

MacLeod, S. (1981) *The art of starvation*. Virago, London

Maguire, M. (1987) 'Casting the evil eye — women and envy.' In S. Ernst and M. Maguire (eds), *Living with the sphinx*, Women's Press, London

Orbach, S. (1986) *Hunger strike*. Faber and Faber, London

Selvini-Palazzoli, M.S. (1974) *Self-starvation*. Human Context Books, London

Sours, J.A. (1980) *Starving to death in a sea of objects*, Jason Aronson, New York.

Thomae, H. (1963) 'Some psychoanalytical observations on anorexia nervosa.' *British Journal of Medical Psychology, 36*, 239–48

Waller, J.F., Kaufman, M. and Deutsch, F. (1940) Anorexia nervosa: a psychosomatic entity. In R.M. Kaufman and M. Heilman (eds), *Evolution of psychosomatic concepts*, Hogarth Press, London (1965)

Winnicott, D.W. (1960) 'Ego distortion in terms of and false self.' In *The maturational processes and the facilitating environment*. Hogarth Press, London, 1972

7

Family-Therapy Approaches to Anorexia

Ivan Eisler

INTRODUCTION

Descriptions of AN from the earliest days have included comments on the families of the starving youngster. Generally, the parents of anorexic patients have been presented in a very negative light, variously described as being emotionally overinvolved, overprotective, controlling and excessively preoccupied with weight and food themselves. This, combined with the parents' apparent inability to feed their child, seemed to indicate a need to protect the patient from these negative parental influences. Indeed, one of the first controversies appearing in the literature on AN concerned the question of whether it was at all possible to treat anorexic patients without isolating them from their families (Myrtle, 1888; Playfair, 1888). The view that the individual suffering from anorexia is in some ways a 'victim' of a poorly functioning family was by no means restricted to those writing a hundred years ago. For example, Bliss and Branch (1960), while concluding that the pattern emerging from the studies of the families of anorexics was not specific to this condition, say: 'One can only conclude that a large number of these patients are nurtured in family environments which tend to produce emotionally impaired individuals' (p. 48).

In recent years, influenced by the developments in the field of family therapy, the interest in the study of families of individuals suffering from AN has grown considerably. It is also more and more common to involve other family members in treatment, mostly in the form of family therapy. This might be seen simply as a logical extension of the idea that the root causes of AN are to be found in the family. The term 'family therapy' will suggest to some that the family rather than the individual is the 'patient' and therefore that it is the family that is disturbed and in need of treatment. Before discussing the contributions of family therapy to the understanding of AN, it is important to dispel such a notion. It is true that family therapy was originally conceived of as a treatment of families, but most practitioners nowadays would describe what they do as treatment *with* families, remaining more neutral to the question both of the origin and current location of the disturbance. There are several reasons for this.

Firstly, increasing feelings of guilt does little to encourage a working treatment alliance and so attaching blame to the family tends to be therapeutically counterproductive. This is because however much the parents or child blame themselves for what is happening to them, they also feel that it is not within their power to change things.

Secondly, a variety of factors, including biological, psychological and social ones, are involved in the genesis of AN (Garfinkel and Garner, 1982). Treating these factors as additive and singling out one as being of prime importance ignores the complex interactions that exist between them and also the fact that the relative contribution of each factor will vary from individual to individual. The evidence that AN always appears within a particular family constellation is at best tenuous. Even if such a constellation did exist, it does not follow that AN develops as a consequence of it. The most commonly described features of the 'anorexic family' (see Minuchin, Rosman and Baker, 1978) include overclose, enmeshed family relationships, avoidance of overt conflict, overprotective attitudes between family members and rigidity of interactional patterns. Each of these characteristics, however, can be seen as much a consequence as a cause of the anorexic behaviour. Take, for instance, the observed overclose parent–child relationship. The youngster says that she feels smothered by it but is unable to find an appropriate area in which to assert herself. Asserting her independence by starvation, however, only has the effect of drawing the parents ever closer to her. One mother commented on this vicious cycle as follows: 'I know I hover over her too much and I know she hates it, but I can't stop. I can't just watch her starve herself and do nothing.'

The final point is the most important one. It is sometimes difficult to draw a clear separating line between cause and effect in the context of family interaction. This in itself challenges the question of whether families 'cause' AN. In the above example, parental overinvolvement and the anorexic behaviour influence each other in a circular manner and in that sense can be said to be in a causal relationship. To ask whether one caused the original appearance of the other is like asking the old question about the chicken and the egg. If the anorexic behaviour can both influence and be influenced by what other family members do, then to try and pinpoint the origins of this complex chain of events is about as feasible a task as that of the teacher trying to find out which of the two kids was at fault for starting a fight. As Hoffman (1986), in discussing the location of the disturbance to be tackled by family therapy puts it: 'The problem is whatever the original distress consisted of plus whatever the distress on its merry way through the world has managed to stick to itself.'

Family therapy is playing an increasingly prominent role in mental health in general and particularly so in the field of AN. Claims for its efficacy in AN have been made for some time, based principally on the work of Minuchin *et al.* (1978) and Selvini-Palazzoli (1974). A recent, controlled-treatment trial (Russell, Szmuckler, Dare and Eisler, 1988) gives support to these claims. It showed that in younger patients, whose onset of illness was before the age of 18 and lasted for less than three years, family therapy proved clearly superior to individual supportive therapy. However, in patients in whom the illness had either taken a chronic course or whose symptoms included frequent overeating and self-induced vomiting (BN), there was no difference between the two treatments. Moreover, in a fourth group, with a relatively late onset of illness of 19 years or more, there was some indication that individual treatment was more beneficial (although this last result was equivocal).

Whatever the merits of family therapy as a practical approach to treatment, the conceptual framework from which it is derived is equally important. For while demonstrations of the efficacy of a new approach to treatment gives some credence to it, it is just as essential to show that the shift in thinking, characteristic of the specific theoretical approach, is able to provide a new perspective on the problem at hand, giving insights as to the development, maintenance and, most importantly, ways of resolving particular problems.

Individual psychological accounts of AN aim to provide an understandable picture of the disorder. These are not necessarily conceived of as aetiological explanations but rather as explorations of psychological meaning of the symptomatic behaviour (Szmuckler, 1985). It is assumed that the disorder has a 'function' in the sense that it can be understood as an attempt by the individual to resolve the stresses of normal development (e.g. a conflict between the needs for dependence and independence). The aim of this chapter is to provide a similar account of AN, but from the perspective of family systems theory and to discuss how this relates to understandings from an individual psychological point of view. In the first part of the chapter I will outline the theoretical framework underlying a family-therapy approach and later discuss this with specific reference to AN and its treatment.

THE FAMILY AS A SOCIAL SYSTEM

Few people would dispute the importance of the social environment in shaping the development of individuals. No-one doubts that we are all influenced by our families, teachers, peers, colleagues and society in general. But our dominant perception of ourselves and of others is in terms of what we are as individuals, and so our understanding of these influences is as something that simply impinges on the individual and the 'self'. We can feel that we are targets of such influences ('I lack confidence because my parents do not let me do things for myself.') and sometimes the source of them ('My child is inconsiderate of others, because I've never been able to say no to him.'). However, we generally think of people as possessing personality characteristics so that they *are* powerful or ineffective, kind or cruel, domineering or submissive. This is clearly reflected in our language. We have many words for individual qualities but far fewer expressions for personal relationships. Yet all personal characteristics only manifest themselves in the context of social interaction as we recognise when we say for instance: 'This person brings out the worst in me.' The interplay between the individual and his social context, even at the level of moment-to-moment interaction is complex and cannot be expressed by simply describing a sequence of events in terms of A causing B causing C and so on. A child breaks a glass and starts crying. The child's crying happens both in response to the previous event and also in anticipation of his mother getting angry. His mother's response will depend not only on her experience of similar events in the past, but also on her perception of why the child is crying. For instance, if she thinks that the child is crying simply to avoid being punished, she might react even more strongly. Mother's expectation of how her own response will influence the further course of events will also be brought into play. She might feel very sorry for her child, yet also feel that if she did not express her displeasure, the child would not learn to be more careful in the future. There will be other factors; mother's concept of herself as a parent and the nature of the mother–child relationship, the value in this family that is attached to crying ('boys shouldn't cry, as it shows their weakness', or perhaps 'expressing one's emotions openly is good as it encourages closeness'), and so on. Going beyond this two-person, or dyadic context, it would be possible to explore what effect father's presence might have on the pattern of interaction. The child's anticipation would now have to include the possible responses to both parents, one of whom might perhaps be more lenient than the other. Mother, for instance, might feel that father was not strict enough and attempts on his part to play down the situation would have the effect of making her reaction even stronger. The child's crying, which in effect sparked off the ensuing parent's argument, could, in this context, also be seen as an anticipation of it. Similarly, the parents' response is governed, not only by the event itself, but also by their mutual relationship, by the role they normally take in parenting, their recollections of previous, similar situations and so on.

This brief example, portraying the complexity of social interaction, epitomises why family systems theory views the behaviour of each person, not just as an expression of that individual, but also as an expression of the role that he holds in the given context, and of his relationship with other people. It also illustrates the way events, feelings and beliefs in the present are intertwined with both the past and the future.

The concept of the family as a social system, then, draws on several related strands: (a) The limitations of viewing individuals and their personal characteristics outside of a specific social context (e.g. the dominant individual can only be dominant in relation to someone who is submissive); (b) the mutual, circular influence that individuals exert on each other (he withdraws because she nags because he withdraws...); (c) the mediating role of the individual's internal world resulting in their perceptions of the past and expectations of the future being inextricably linked with their present actions; and (d) the notion that the whole is more than the sum of its parts, in that the whole also takes account of the relationships with the parts. Researchers and clinicians working with families often note the apparent stability of certain aspects of family life; the repetitiveness of patterns of interaction within a given family and a tendency of families to react to changes in one part of the family by counterbalancing responses in other parts of the family. In giving an account of these observations, systems theorists have often likened the family to a complex cybernetic system with feedback mechanisms that control the behaviour of its component parts so that a balance in the system as a whole is maintained. Such an analogy has its limitations, as we will discuss later, but it highlights the importance of attempting to apprehend the pattern of interaction that characterises the family as a whole.

In observing interactions within a family, what is immediately discernible is the content of the discussion. A careful observer, however, is soon able to perceive patterns of interaction that emerge, regardless of the topic of discussion. Much of what happens appears to be governed by unspoken rules that sometimes become apparent only when there is a danger that they will be broken. The following sequence of interaction in a family session illustrates the way in which this family deals with potentially conflicting situations. During a 'family lunch', the therapist asks the patients to describe all that they have tried to do to help their daughter, Anne, to overcome her eating problem.

Mother We have tried everything. I have pleaded, cajoled, threatened. When she came out of hospital we let her serve herself. She did eat, but gradually she was eating less and less, her portions were getting smaller and smaller and she would end up with just a couple of peas on the plate. That's not a portion of peas.

As mother goes through the list of things she has tried, her tone of voice becomes increasingly critical.

Anne (in a sullen voice) It's not what I had either.

Mother (sounding quite exasperated) It is Anne.

Father (calmly) O.K. Anne, let's look at what happened to your weight. Since you left hospital it has continued to go down.

Anne But I haven't had much chance, have I. You are always watching what I eat and you never leave me on my own, do you.

Father's interruption is, at one level, an expression of his support for his wife's position. Anne has not been eating enough to maintain her weight. But the timing and manner of his interruption has another effect. It happens precisely at a point when a confrontation is beginning to develop between mother and daughter. Father's calmness and more detached attitude contrasts strongly with mother's irritation and greater emotional involvement. This, together with the shift of topic away from Anne's eating behaviour to Anne's weight

Father No, but that's because your weight has always gone down. Every day I look at the scales and they are never up.

Anne I've only lost two pounds.

Father Yes, but your weight is never up. It's always a bit down. In the end you will end up back in hospital, and none of us want that. It's not as if mum was trying to fatten you up as a turkey. The meal you had last night wasn't a particularly big meal and in the end, I had to come in and make you eat. And it wasn't even something you don't like.

stops the developing confrontation. Father continues for several minutes. Although father remains quite calm he is increasingly critical of Anne. During this time, Anne remains silent but has a very dismissive look on her face. On several occasions she exchanges glances with her older sister as if they had heard all this before. During her father's monologue, mother becomes increasingly restless, glancing alternately at Anne and father.

Anne (starts to object quite strongly) But you...

Mother (turning to therapist) The thing is, she does want to eat. There is a part of her that wants to and part of her resists. Some days that part is stronger.

Mother's interruption comes practically simultaneously with Anne's objection. The same pattern happens as before with only a slight difference. This time, mother stops the developing confrontation. Later, the same thing happens again when the parents begin to disagree about how much Anne should eat and Anne's own intervention changes the topic to what would happen at home.

This emergent pattern and its apparent regularity can help the observer form a picture of the way the family as a whole functions and to formulate an understanding in terms of rules that govern the interaction. These rules are obviously only constructs of the observer and are not thus experienced by the family members. Their own experience forms only a part of the whole, from which vantage point the overall pattern can be difficult to apprehend.

An analogy can serve to illustrate the point. When someone stumbles and throws out his arms to regain balance, he is not aware of the detailed sequence of his motor activity. Nevertheless, an observer could accurately describe this sequence just as an observer of interaction in families can apprehend an overall pattern, of which the participants are not aware. In the same way that the flailing arms can be said to have a 'function' (to maintain balance), so an observed family interactional pattern can be understood as serving a function within the family system. It has been shown that the clinical descriptions of interaction in families of anorexic patients as well as 'family rules' and hypotheses about the 'function' of the overall transactional pattern of interaction can be reliably identified by independent observers.

INDIVIDUAL AND FAMILY PERSPECTIVES OF ANOREXIA NERVOSA

Anorexia nervosa develops most commonly during adolescence. Accounts of the illness from an individual psychological perspective stress a variety of sources, most of which are common problems of adolescence. Szmukler (1985) lists the following: 'problems of autonomy, of separating from the family, of coming to terms with sexual feelings, of accepting one's peculiarities, of making satisfactory peer relationships and of achieving confidence in study and work'. The overriding sense of ineffectiveness and a feeling of lack of autonomy (Bruch, 1973) lead the individual to an attempted 'solution' to these problems which, however, has the paradoxical effect of also perpetuating the problem. The more the youngster attempts to regain control of at least a part of her life by not eating, the more she becomes dependent on her parents. She will complain bitterly about being treated like a little child yet she is unable to lead an independent adult life. The 'solution' is painful, but it allows many of the difficulties to be sidestepped. Sexual maturation is stopped or even reversed, leaving home ceases to be an issue, physical growth is halted, work or study often becomes impossible and social contact with peers is frequently reduced.

When placed in the context of the family, the complementarity of the individual psychological features and family features become clear. The developmental crisis of adolescence is as much a crisis for the whole family as it is for the individual. Adolescence signals an end to the family in its present form. Once their children leave home, the parents will have to relearn to live as a childless couple. The youngster's emergent sexuality challenges intimacy between herself and her parents. Attaching high values to closeness, which would have been a positive feature in earlier developmental phases, is suddenly an obstacle for the process of individuation–separation. There is uncertainty whether the family can survive the departure of the children, particularly if there is a perception that the closeness between child and parent is greater than that between the parents.

The previously discussed notion of reworking of past distressful experiences is also relevant here. If the parents' memories of their own disengagement from their family of origin is a painful one, then making the necessary adaptations when their own children reach that stage of development can also be difficult. This is both because of the fear of what is in store for their children and also because the uncertainty about the shape of their own future can make them feel that they are also once more about to 'leave home'.

These pressures are not specific to individuals suffering from AN and their families. They are universal components of the developmental pressures for change in all families. We do not know why AN develops in the context of some families. What is clear is that when it does, it addresses both individual developmental issues as well as family life-cycle issues, although in a way that does not resolve them but perpetuates them.

The youngster who feels that in her interaction with signficant others she is not able to achieve an age-appropriate independence, discovers an area of psychological being in which she can gain total control and, at the same time, remain as dependent as ever on her family. She defies her parents to take away the one area of independence that she has carved out for herself, but when they acquiesce saying 'We cannot force her to eat. It is the thing she fears most', it only reinforces her feeling that she and they are one. The parents in a desperate effort to regain some of the closeness they now feel that they are losing, ignore their own independent fears and wishes, and instead, act on what they think are their daughter's wishes to be. This, however, just maintains the same transactional pattern where the close, enmeshed relationships are manifested by 'mind-reading' and speaking to others.

One of the features described by Minuchin *et al.* (1978) as being characteristic of 'anorexic families' is the rigidity and narrowness of their transactional repertoire. Frequently, when observing such a family, the overwhelming impression is that of a 'frozen' family where time has virtually come to a standstill. The family seems poised in a balancing act where putting one foot wrong could bring everything crashing down. The pattern of conflict avoidance described earlier can be seen as part of that pattern and it illustrated how the whole family seemed caught up in it. The daughter's eating behaviour appears to challenge the family's apparent wish to maintain the status quo. Her refusal to eat with the family, perhaps even to sit down with them at meals, make it very difficult for the family to hold onto the image of the 'nice, stable family'. Her challenge, however, does not lead to diversity in the family's way of life. In order to maintain the balance, the rest of the family fit in with her, often going to quite extraordinary lengths; by allowing her to completely dictate what happens, transactions become even more restricted and rigid.

The relationship between the parents is also affected in a paradoxical way. Directly or indirectly, the young anorexic will frequently express a feeling of responsibility for her parents and their marriage, while at the same time voicing her fear that she will never recover unless her parents' marriage improves. Her self-starvation brings the parents together to look after her. This does so in a way, though, that increases their sense of failure as parents, invoking feelings of guilt that, even when they do not always lead to overt recrimination, puts a strain on the marriage, thus again distancing them. The daughter's relationship with her parents, which is mediated by her self-starvation, thus plays a pivotal role in the marriage, keeping them together yet distant at one and the same time.

Case example

Emma, 19 years old, was seen in our clinic, together with her parents and older sister Frances. The family sessions from the very beginning were unusually tense. Both parents were very critical of Emma, but also expressed their feelings of guilt about their failure as parents. There was a feeling that the family were sitting on a time bomb that was about to explode and there were hints about the possibility of the parents separating. During the course of the treatment, that is, in fact, what happened; with one day, mother just walking out on them. Emma's weight continued to drop, until finally she had to be admitted to hospital. During her stay in hospital, her father made it very clear that he could not cope with looking after her any more, and that on discharge she would not be able to return home. After she left hospital, Emma at first again lost weight, but after a long struggle, was able to reverse the weight loss, and eventually recovered. It was around this time that the parents were reunited again. Several months later, Emma moved back home. At a follow-up interview two years later, Emma was well and leading a very active social life. Although still living at home, it was more out of convenience than necessity. She was enjoying the company of her parents who, in spite of occasional disagreements, were getting on very well together.

In retrospect, Emma was able to talk about how desperately she wanted her parents to get back together and how let down she felt when, even upon her being admitted to hospital, this did not happen. Her long road to recovery started, however, only when she realised that she was not able to keep her parents together. Her parents, similarly, felt that the realisation of whether they stayed together or separated seemed to make no difference to how Emma was, helped them to face the problem they had as a couple and eventually come together again.

I am not suggesting that the resolution of the parents' marital problems led to Emma's recovery or, for that matter, that Emma's improvement brought the parents back together. Emma's recovery was a long, drawn-out and difficult struggle. Similarly, the parents' resolution of their marital difficulties did not happen overnight. Neither one preceded the other. It was striking the way the two seemed to take place in parallel and, in some sense, quite independently of each other.

PRACTICAL IMPLICATIONS

I have tried to portray the family as a continuously evolving social system whose transactional pattern is shaped in the process of interaction between individual members of the family in their attempts to define a mutually satisfying relationship. Each family member contributes to the development of their family through different stages and has a role to play in maintaining the cohesion of the family as a whole. It is assumed that the way a family functions is determined both by the needs of its individual members and by the needs of the family as a whole. At the same time, the way that the family functions constantly shapes the individuals and their needs. This theoretical approach also stresses the importance of the developmental aspects of family functioning.

Anorexia nervosa is here described as being intertwined with the transactional processes of the family. This is not in any way meant to deny the importance of individual psychological or biological mechanisms in the genesis and maintenance of the disorder. It is put forward as an alternative *perspective* rather than an alternative *explanation.*

This view of AN has a number of implications for treatment. Obviously it is most pertinent when family therapy is being used. As mentioned in the introduction, there is good evidence that with young patients who are still living with their families of origin, this is an efficacious form of treatment. There will be situations, however, when it is not possible to deploy family therapy, either because of difficulties in engaging the family in treatment (Szmuckler, Eisler, Russell and Dare, 1985), unavailability of family with older patients, or an urgent need for hospital admission for life-saving purposes. A systems view is relevant, even in such cases.

Firstly, the patient's family has a role to play whether or not they are involved directly in treatment. An understanding of the interpersonal processes in which the patient is caught up provides a useful insight for the clinician. For instance, anorexic patients are sometimes advised to leave home in order to help them separate from their families. The fact that this seldom works is readily explainable in family-systems terms. Interpersonal relations extend beyond the process of person-to-person interaction. Physical separation on its own, therefore, cannot resolve problems of individuation and can, in some cases, contribute to the avoidance of the underlying issues. In the case discussed earlier, the crucial change took place, not when Emma left home, but when she realised that she could not save her parents' marriage.

The second reason is that a systems point of view provides a new perspective on the process of therapy. In the traditional medical model, the physician is seen as someone who first identifies the source of the disturbance and then prescribes a remedy for it. Hence, as I have argued, the notion is mistaken that family therapy is a treatment for disturbed families that have caused the anorexia. Family systems theory views treatment in a very different way. The professional is never external to the system and always enters into a relationship with the patient and therefore also, either directly or indirectly with the patient's family. It is these relationships that are the vehicle for treatment. Whatever the formal setting of the treatment, be it a traditional doctor–patient framework, individual psychotherapy or hospitalisation, it is useful to consider which role the professionals have in relation to the patient and her social network. This can help the clinicians make their therapeutic interventions more effective. A comparison of the process of family therapy with the possible impact of hospitalisation on the family will illustrate this.

With the young anorexic, we generally start the family therapy by stressing the importance of the role the parents have in saving their daughter's life. We work hard to support the parents as the executive couple in the family. This strengthens the boundary between the parental and child subsystems in the family and emphasises the point that whatever differences there might be between the parents as a couple, they have a joint task as parents. Some parents raise the issue of marital discord themselves. We make it very clear that we consider that to be a separate question that cannot be dealt with as part of tackling their daughter's anorexia. At later stages of treatment, when the responsibility for weight and eating is handed back to the youngster, other problems can be focused upon. These are related to questions of independence, autonomy, the impact on the parent's life of the children leaving home, etc. If, at this stage, the parents are still wanting to discuss marital issues, it can be appropriate to offer them marital sessions. We would, however, make it very clear that this was for their benefit and not for the benefit of their child.

The therapist's understanding of the particular therapy derives, in part, from observations of the minutiae of family interaction. Of equal importance is the therapist's developing relationship with each family member, which in a sense, allows him (or her) to join the family system. In doing so, he begins to experience some of the prohibitions and restrictions that are operating in the family. The impact of the therapist's interventions depends not only on him conveying his understanding to the family directly (this is seldom effective) but rather in the way that he uses his insights to alter the way in which he relates to the family. He will ask questions that will show that he is interested in the interpersonal aspects of the problem ('Who shows their worry about your sister more; your mother or your father?'). He will block some of the accustomed transactional patterns (for instance by preventing a third person from interrupting a developing conflict), thus forcing them to explore new ways of interacting. He will use his personal authority to raise the parents' anxiety about their daughter's life, in order to underline the importance of them finding a way of strengthening the parental alliance. In fighting to save their daughter's life, the parents start reversing the paradox of AN. In taking control, they begin to act on their own fear that she might die rather than on what they thought were her fears. The parents' united front and their independent stand emphasises their separateness from the child and in turn, this helps her to struggle for differentiation. We have frequently observed how, having lost the battle over food, the adolescent suddenly finds her need for independence resurfacing in other, more appropriate areas.

Admission to hospital is frequently used as a means of helping anorexic patients to gain weight. Where there is a skilled nursing staff it is usually relatively easy to achieve restoration of weight to a normal level (Russell, 1983). Follow-up treatment is, however, usually necessary to prevent relapse requiring further admissions to hospital. Because weight restoration itself is unlikely to lead to recovery from AN, it is important to examine the long-term impact hospitalisation can have on the individual as well as on her family. Admission to hospital stresses the individual and, in particular, physical aspects of the disorder. It can also be understood by the parents to be an indication of their failure, confirming their feelings of helplessness. The focus of weight in the context of a hospital admission cannot, of course, have the same role as the one which it has within the setting of family therapy. While on the one hand, this can make the process of weight restoration easier, it is not possible to use it to address some of the important, linked problems. Thus, when the youngster leaves hospital and, perhaps starts losing weight again, it can be even more difficult for the parents to mobilise their resources, and help their child reverse the weight loss.

The hospital's relationship with the patient is in many ways a parent–child relationship, which incorporates in this case, a very strong expectation that the hospital staff will take control over the patient's eating. Obviously, the impact of the hospital taking such a role extends beyond the arena of eating. The sense of containment and safety that the hospital environment can provide (particularly when the patient also feels understood and supported) often helps the youngster to start exploring other issues and to look for new areas of independence. The psychological changes that accompany weight gain (Channon and de Silva, 1985) facilitate this process. However, because the youngster's concept of self is so closely tied up with her perception of her position in the family, and because she has not negotiated her new found concept of self within the family, there is a danger that when she leaves hospital, she and her family will gradually revert to their accustomed style of relating to one another where eating and food play a major role in maintaining a transactional pattern.

The difficulty of dealing with these issues in the context of a hospital admission can be compounded by the medical framework of the treatment with its strong emphasis on diagnosis. Thus discussions with or about the patient's family will often focus on uncovering areas of dysfunction or deviance as possible causal or contributing factors in the development of illness. This increases disabling feelings of guilt and also can lead to a competition between the hospital and the family as to who can provide better parenting.

CONCLUSIONS

When viewed from a family-systems perspective, the question of causes becomes secondary to the examination of ways in which the hospital admission can help the family utilise their own resources most effectively. Thus, from the moment that hospital treatment starts to be discussed, it is important to involve the parents in a way that is supportive and acknowledges the crucial role that they will continue to play. For instance, one or both parents might be reluctant to force their daughter to accept treatment against her will. It is easy to see this simply in a negative light, particularly if the parents are not in complete agreement. However, emphasising the positive aspects of this reluctance (their sensitivity towards their child's wishes and their desire to maintain a good relationship with her), can often help the parents to also express their joint determination to save their daughter's life. Any meetings with the family during the time of admission are best focused on the role that the family, and in particular, the parents, can have in helping to achieve the goals of the hospital treatment. In other words, it is more important to concentrate on what the family can do rather than on what the family is like.

The way in which the hospital relates to the family and the kind of role that the parents are given during their child's stay in hospital all influence the family's perception of the treatment and of themselves. It can confirm their feeling of helplessness or it can help them see the hospital stay as a time when they can gather strength in order that they are in a better position to get on top of the problem later on. It can increase their feelings of guilt that they are responsible for the problems in the first place, or it can help them face up to their own conflicting feelings and to rediscover some of the strengths that they have, but have found difficult to make full use of. This may not have an immediate influence on the course of the treatment in hospital, but the long-term impact can be crucial.

REFERENCES

Bliss, E.L. and Branch, C.H.H. (1960) *Anorexia nervosa.* Hoeber, New York

Bruch, H. (1973) *Eating disorders.* Basic Books, New York

Channon, S. and de Silva, W.P. (1985) 'Psychological correlates of weight gain in patients with anorexia nervosa.' *Journal of Psychiatric Research, 19*, 273–8

Garfinkel, P.E. and Garner, D.M. (1982) *Anorexia nervosa: a multidimensional perspective.* Brunner/Mazel, New York

Hoffman, L. (1986) 'Beyond power and control: toward a 'second order' family systems therapy.' *Family Systems Medicine, 3*, 381–96

Minuchin, S., Rosman, B.L. and Baker, L. (1978) *Psychosomatic families: anorexia nervosa in context.* Harvard University Press, Cambridge, Mass.

Myrtle, A.S. (1888) Letters to the Editor. *Lancet, 1*, 899

Playfair, W.S. (1888) 'Note on the so-called anorexia nervosa.' *Lancet, 1*, 817

Russell, G.F.M. (1983) 'Anorexia nervosa and bulimia nervosa. In G.F.M. Russell and L.A. Hersov (eds), *Handbook of psychiatry, vol. 4: the neuroses and personality disorders*, Cambridge University Press, Cambridge

——, Szmuckler, G.I., Dare, C. and Eisler, I. (1988) 'An evaluation of family therapy in anorexia nervosa and bulimia nervosa.' *Archives of General Psychiatry*, (in press)

Selvini-Palazzoli, M. (1974) *Self-starvation.* Chaucer, London

Szmukler, G.I. (1985) 'Anorexia nervosa: a clinical view.' In R.A. Boakes, D.A. Popplewell and M.J. Burton (eds), *Eating habits*, Wiley, New York

——, Eisler, I., Russell, G.F.M. and Dare, C. (1985) 'Anorexia nervosa: parental "expressed emotion", and dropping out of treatment.' *British Journal of Psychiatry, 147*, 265–71

8

Cognitive–Behavioural Approaches to Anorexia and Bulimia

Clive Hollin and Vivien Lewis

INTRODUCTION

Cognitive–behavioural approaches combine traditional behavioural techniques with more recent cognitive techniques for the treatment of psychological problems. Such approaches have particular relevance for BN and AN, where prominent features of the disorders include, not only many inappropriate behaviours, but also a vast array of dysfunctional beliefs and values concerning bodyshape, weight and food intake. In recent years, therapists and researchers alike have recognised the limitations of behavioural treatments in isolation. These limitations are evident in the high relapse rates and prevalence of residual symptoms following the more traditional behavioural interventions (Russell, 1981). Consequently, the emphasis has been on the development of 'multi-modal' treatments, which aim to integrate various treatment models — with some indication of success (Garner, Garfinkel and Bemis, 1984). Cognitive – behavioural strategies are predominant among the components of these multi-modal approaches.

Traditional behavioural approaches to treatment — behaviour modification or behaviour therapy — developed over the past 20 or 30 years, following the pioneering work of such figures as Joseph Wolpe. The treatment techniques associated with behavioural intervention such as contracting, skills training and systematic desensitisation are well known and so will not be discussed in great detail here (see Bellack, Hersen and Kazdin, 1982). Cognitive therapy is perhaps less widely appreciated and therefore merits some discussion.

Cognitive therapy was developed by Beck (1976) for the treatment of 'emotional disorders', and is based upon the relationship between behaviour, thinking or 'cognitions' and feelings or emotions. The central assumption in cognitive approaches is that dysfunctional behaviours and emotions derive from distorted thinking, and that these cognitions should therefore be the primary focus for therapeutic intervention. This contrasts with a traditional behavioural approach, in which the environmental consequences of a behaviour are seen as the determinants of behaviour. In practice, cognitive therapy is not dissimilar in procedure to other approaches. The initial stages involve collecting a detailed case history, including personal data, then formulating a preliminary assessment of the problem. Therapist and client may then discuss the influence of thinking on behaviour and emotions, using the client's personal examples. At this stage, specific thoughts leading to negative emotions can be examined, with special reference to any recurring thoughts. Other dysfunctional cognitive processes could include thinking errors, irrational and 'absolute' thoughts, inappropriate expectations, self-criticisms, and the assumptions associated with such cognitions (Beck, 1976). Eventually, therapist and client would work towards alternative ways of thinking and developing more adaptive coping responses. This would relate to meeting the client's goals, starting with easy efforts to change in order to maximise the chance of success. Like most treatments, cognitive therapy would also include a follow-up. Using this rationale, as well as methods adapted from other cognitive therapies (Ellis, 1962), cognitive approaches have been incorporated successfully into the treatment of both bulimia (Fairburn, 1981) and AN (Garner and Bemis, 1985).

One of the dangers of over-emphasis on cognition is that the same thing will happen as with traditional behavioural interventions: There will be too much attention paid to just one aspect of human functioning, to the exclusion of other important processes. Therefore, in advancing the notion of cognitive – behavioural treatment, the emphasis is on *both* cognition and behaviour. Further, rather than concentrating upon just these 'person' factors, they should be understood in relation to the individual's immediate environment as well as the culture in which they live. A schematic representation of this view, which directly follows social learning theory, is shown in Figure 8.1.

The work of Fairburn exemplifies the adoption of this cognitive – behavioural model to the treatment of eating disorder (Fairburn, 1985; Fairburn, Kirk, O'Connor and Cooper, 1986). This individualised treatment approach consists of three stages. In the first stage, there is an attempt to disrupt the pattern of habitual overeating and vomiting using behavioural techniques. Patients are required to carry out self-monitoring of food intake, situational factors and their thoughts and emotions. From this information, a self-controlled and regular eating pattern is established, and the behavioural and cognitive stimuli for eating are examined. This stage also includes the presentation of factual information about nutrition and various aspects of BN. The second stage is based on cognitive therapy. This involves cognitive restructuring procedures for irrational thoughts about body shape and weight, as well as a consideration of the problems that are avoided by eating. Hence, there is some emphasis on training in adaptive problem-solving, with special attention to setbacks. Within this stage, one aim is to minimise dietary restraint in the individual. The third and final stage of treatment is aimed at the maintenance and consolidation of progress, involving preparation for coping with future stress and measures for reducing the risk of relapse.

The cognitive – behavioural approach to the treatment of AN and BN to be described in this chapter has many features in common with the approach developed by Fairburn and his colleagues. The components of this approach will be presented in a 'step-by-step' fashion. However, there are two qualifications to

Figure 8.1: Schematic representation of the person in relation to their culture and environment

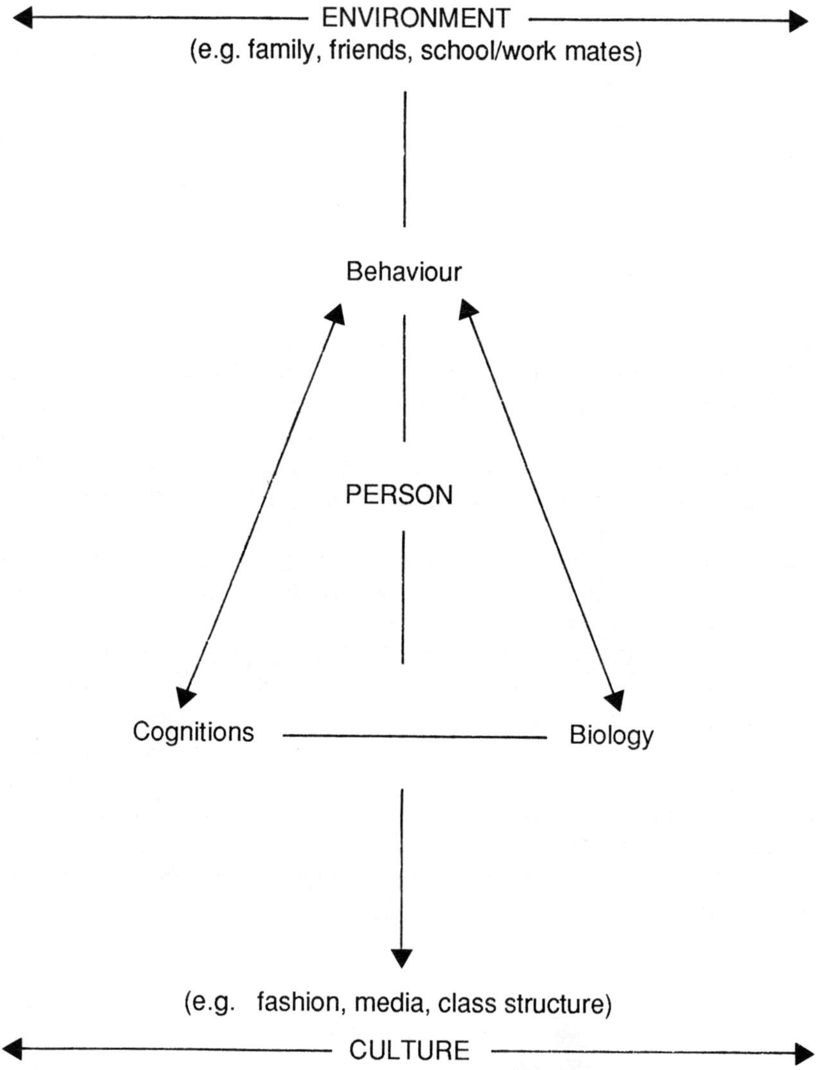

this presentation. The first is that treatment is individualised, and varies from patient to patient. Hence for a particular individual, some steps will be more important than others. Furthermore, within treatment, many of the steps will overlap. The second qualification is that AN differs from bulimia in several fundamental and important characteristics. This necessarily means that a single specific approach to both disorders is not really feasible. Therefore, some steps will have greater relevance for AN than for bulimia, and vice versa. Having made those qualifications, there are, nevertheless, sufficient common features to cognitive – behavioural functioning in AN and bulimia that a general approach allowing for variations in specific details is feasible.

THE COMPONENTS OF TREATMENT

Assessment

The style of assessment suitable for cognitive–behavioural intervention would need to examine aetiological factors, present behaviours and cognitions and the reinforcing consequences that maintain the disorder. Slade (1982) has presented a functional analysis of both anorexia and bulimia that integrates such factors as dietary restraint, the real or perceived loss of control over food intake in bulimia, cognition, background factors and behaviour. The factors are viewed in terms of the consequences they produce for the individual. This is seen in terms of positive reinforcement from feelings of control and produced from compensatory behaviours, as well as negative reinforcement from the avoidance of weight gain and distraction from negative emotions.

Using a model such as Slade's provides a useful structure for the assessment of those factors that serve to maintain the disorder. In both bulimia and AN there are many such factors that may need to be addressed in therapy. For example, any 'dieter' knows well the praise (i.e. social reinforcement) that accompanies loss of body weight and the maintenance of that lower weight. Equally well, the dieter knows the negative comments that accompany gains in body weight and changes in body shape. There is, in Western society, a cultural emphasis on thinness as the preferred body shape, particularly for women (Leon, 1980; Furnham and Alibhai, 1983; Garner, Garfinkel and Olmstead, 1983); an emphasis that extends even to the anorexic body shape (Branch and Euman, 1980). Therefore, assessment must take into account the social consequences that may be reinforcing the disordered behaviour. This will broaden the assessment to other people significant to the individual, such as family members who may, unwittingly, be acting in such a way as to maintain the disorder.

While behavioural assessment is best carried out using a combination of observation and interview (Ciminero, Calhoun and Adams, 1986), perhaps in conjunction with psychometric scales such as the 'eating disorders inventory' (Garner, Olmstead and Polivy, 1983), cognitive assessment poses a special problem. The client is the only person who knows the validity of their report on their cognitions. Additionally, it is possible that aspects of cognition are not able to be reported as they function outside awareness. These two factors necessarily limit cognitive assessment at present. While an individual client's cognitions will be unique, recent research has suggested areas to which the clinician might pay particular attention. Ruderman (1986) found that bulimia was strongly associated with 'distorted cognitions of a rigid, perfectionist and demanding nature' (p. 197).

While O'Connor and Dowrick (1987) reported that weight disorders are correlated with food- and weight- focused cognitions, the cognitions were both self-defeating, e.g. 'I have absolutely no self-control when it comes to food', and are extreme, e.g. 'I can't make it another second without eating'. Schulman *et al.* (1986) developed the 'bulimia cognitive distortions scale', which may prove to be a useful aid to assessment. Garner and Bemis (1982) discuss types of cognition common in AN.

Assessment should also involve consideration of the individual's background, personal history and dieting history. While we agree with Fairburn that emphasis should be placed on the present and future, there are at least two reasons for placing some importance on the past. The first is that if an individual can understand some causes of the disorder, then that individual is better able to come to terms with those causes, and will be better placed to prevent those causes having further effect. If AN is not to progress into bulimia and bulimia is not to be replaced by some other psychological disorder, then any event that precipitated or contributed to the problem must be considered. Many therapists experience the return of a patient with a 'new' problem, when the cause of the original problem was never addressed. The second reason for attending to past events is taken from the researcher's standpoint. The more that can be learned about the causes of any psychological problem, the greater the chances of effective treatment for future clients.

The nature of assessment in this approach is that it should be continual. As therapist and client progress together, new factors may arise or some changes may be effected that will necessitate a shift in the emphasis of treatment. This means more than simply monitoring progress, but rather being prepared to be flexible in the formulation of hypotheses and the direction of therapy. Hence, continual assessment does logically overlap with monitoring progess, and eventually merges with the clinical evaluation of the extent to which the intervention has been successful.

BEHAVIOUR THERAPY

The use of behavioural techniques in the treatment of eating disorders is most easily applied in an inpatient setting, in which there is more control over the events that influence the client. However, they can be employed elsewhere and, like all treatments, should always be used with an awareness of ethical considerations. Indeed, Bruch (1974) has pointed out some of the dangers inherent in behaviour therapy with AN, in particular, in accentuating feelings of being trapped and low self-esteem, as well as leading to a sense of depersonalisation. Murray (1986) in his review of AN suggests that behaviour-modification techniques are most effective when used as a first step in a multidimensional approach.

In AN, reinforcement has often been made contingent upon weight gain, such that privileges are linked to the gain of a certain amount of weight each day (Halmi, 1985). However, even when the individual is engaging in the appropriate behaviour, that is, eating the required amount of food, body weight may not increase consistently. Hence, in some instances, performance of the behaviour may not achieve the desired outcome. Therefore, reinforcement might better be made contingent upon food consumed rather than weight gained.

Other behavioural techniques adopted with AN may include response prevention in the case of mirror-gazing, in which, while the individual is gaining weight, mirrors are removed to inhibit gazing behaviour. Similarly, small-sized clothes may be removed from the individual's wardrobe, as these clothes may act as discriminative stimuli for the disorder.

In both AN and bulimia there may be high levels of anxiety associated with others and social interactions. In such instances, an approach involving systematic desensitisation may be appropriate. Here, the individual may be trained in anxiety management with progressive muscle relaxation, and gradually exposed to the anxiety-provoking situation. Further, as stressful life events may be associated with eating disorder (Hollin, Houston and Kent, 1985), some form of stress innoculation training may be appropriate (Meichenbaum and Jaremko, 1983).

Response prevention can be used in two ways (Rosen and Leitenberg, 1982): From self-report diaries 'danger periods' may be identified and at those times activities incompatible with, say, binging are carried out, such as seeing friends, making telephone calls and so on. Alternatively, the client may be restricted for up to two hours after eating, so that immediate vomiting may not occur. Loro and Orleans (1981) provide a useful study of binge eating, with a behavioural-treatment approach based upon a functional analysis of the antecedents and consequences of the binge-eating behaviour (see also Polivy and Herman, 1985). The component of their approach, which is strongly emphasised, is 'programmed binge-ing', involving binge eating under direction from the therapist. Loro and Orleans argue that this approach demonstrates to the client that binge eating is a 'habit under the control of antecedent and consequent events rather than the expression of personal weaknesses or a personality deficit' (p. 163). Furthermore, they argue that the individual may thus come to view the binge or relapse as a learning experience instead of a failure to control their behaviour.

The technique of stimulus control may be used to attempt to establish a regular eating pattern, so that the client eats at the same time, in the same place, for the same length of time each day (Fairburn, 1984; Yates and Sambrailo, 1984). Response delay might be attempted to insert a lapse between the decision to overeat and the actual eating. As Meyer (1973) suggests, the function of the delay would be to weaken the association between impulse and action. Social-skills training has also been used with anorexic clients (e.g. Pillay and Crisp, 1981), although at face value there seems little justification for its use (Hollin, 1986).

As with every component of this therapeutic approach to anorexia and bulimia, behavioural techniques are necessarily tailored to the individual. Reinforcers that are potent will vary between individuals; some maladaptive behaviours will be apparent in one client while others will not. In addition, the extent to which behavioural techniques can be applied will depend upon the context of therapy. That is to say, in inpatient or outpatient; if the latter, whether the individual lives alone, or with partners or family who are both willing and able to involve themselves in therapy.

COGNITIVE THERAPY

Cognitive therapy is important in this approach to eating disorders, given the assumption that unless maladaptive cognitions are addressed, the likelihood of relapse is increased. In cognitive therapy for AN, Garner and Bemis (1985) give their patients an understanding of the cognitive model, which can be readily applied to bulimia. They suggest that the five steps shown in Table 8.1, based on Beck's (1976) model, provide a structure for therapy.

Table 8.1: Steps in Cognitive Therapy

1. The client is required to monitor their thinking or heighten their awareness of their own thinking.
2. They recognise the connection between certain thoughts and maladaptive behaviours and emotions.
3. Examine the evidence for the validity of particular beliefs.
4. Substitute more realistic and appropriate interpretations.
5. Gradually modify the underlying assumptions that are fundamental determinants of more specific beliefs.

Source: Adapted from Garner and Bemis (1985).

The first stage in this cognitive approach is teaching the client to recognise their pattern of thinking, and to become aware of specific thoughts. People are generally not in the habit of examining their own thoughts, and initially, may find it difficult to identify particular thoughts. Thinking may occur in the form of images and very often is not specifically verbalised. Hence, the individual may need considerable input from the therapist to be able to attend to and articulate specific beliefs. In addition, individuals may be selective about what they are aware of and what they are avoiding. On occasions, heightened awareness of a belief may be sufficient to demonstrate its irrational nature to the individual concerned.

As clients learn to identify their thoughts, they need also to begin to examine the beliefs associated with those thoughts. Thinking patterns frequently occur as a 'chain' that can be worked through backwards to arrive at the underlying belief, and it is this belief that often becomes the focus of attention in therapy. Hence, clients can begin to perceive the connections between such beliefs and the way they are thinking, and how this in turn is associated with maladaptive behaviour. Similarly, they can learn the manner by which their thoughts and behaviours influence the way that they feel and so contribute to negative emotions.

The most difficult beliefs to address in therapy are those concerning ideal body size, and in AN this is compounded by misperceptions of body shape. As has already been noted, Western society and sometimes, even family and friends, can reinforce a body weight below that which is desirable for optimum health. Various methods can be used to demonstrate how *not* to be in contrast to healthy individuals. In AN, video feedback can occasionally correct the misperceptions. However, in general, the relationship between the therapist and the individual is used to assist the process of change. While the client may not immediately acknowledge that their thoughts are distorted, they may begin the process of change by accepting that the therapist is giving an honest appraisal of their current situation.

In many psychological disorders, thinking frequently occurs in absolute or all-or-nothing terms, and this is also the case for AN and BN. Words or phrases such as 'must', 'should' and 'can't' can often be heard, and the absolute dichotomy between 'good' and 'bad' foods is common; e.g. 'I must not eat chocolates', 'I can't eat one biscuit without eating the whole packet', and 'I can't stop myself vomiting after meals'. Rephrasing the sentences can often be helpful, and in the case of 'can't', sentences substituting 'won't' may begin to re-establish the client's control over the behaviour.

With this type of absolute thinking, the client is setting standards for perfect behaviour that cannot be achieved, especially in the case of 'must' and 'should'. Hence, since such perfection is unattainable, one instance of violating the command contributes to the client's feelings of failure and worthlessness. With 'can't' statements, the feelings of inadequacy are readily apparent; perfectionist standards are rife in the thinking of eating-disordered individuals, and there is little room for compromise. Therefore, it is not sufficient for these individuals to acknowledge that they set goals for themselves that they would never apply to others, they need to be able to accept their real successes in more modest targets and to be kind to themselves.

This extreme thinking can also be seen in the eating-disordered person's prediction of the consequences of actions or events as necessarily disastrous: 'If I gain weight, nobody will like me'; 'If I don't vomit, I grow enormously fat'. Sometimes the feared consequence actually happens as a result of the thought that predicts the disaster. Hence, the emaciated anorexic who is concerned about not being 'liked' becomes socially withdrawn and unpopular. Thus, one of the most fundamental and paradoxical effects of predicting disaster is seen in the belief that only by being thin can happiness be attained, and that gaining weight would immediately bring misery. However, the individual is not happy and lives in constant fear of the 'disaster' of gaining weight.

Another pattern of dysfunctional thinking occurs when individuals believe that they and their behaviour are the focus of other people's attention. Within this, there are certain classic thinking errors such as 'People will think I'm greedy when they notice I've gained weight'. In this instance, there are two thinking errors — the first is 'telepathy' in knowing what people will think; the second is in the assumption that a small weight gain would be noticed if, indeed, attention was focused upon the individual concerned. Thoughts of this type are often associated with the belief that the individual is more important to others than is really the case.

Once again, this is somewhat paradoxical as the person concerned typically has a very low opinion of him/herself. An examination of specific thoughts can often demonstrate that the belief is without supporting evidence. It is often worthwhile to encourage the client to try to view the situation through someone else's eyes, to see that the distorted beliefs are not supported by real evidence.

The paradox of feelings of personal inadequacy and of being the centre of attention is evident in other areas of cognitive behaviour. On direct questioning, in both AN and bulimia, being thin will often be stated as life's most important aspect, sometimes along with a desire to be perfect. However, the individual also wishes to be happy and to be a 'nice' person. This may be acknowledged as having greater priority over body shape but, as was previously stated, the two are viewed as inseparable rather than inconsistent. A useful exercise may be to elicit from clients their ideal happy future situations and to plan how to arrive at those goals. In this way, relative priorities may be shifted in a manner that is helpful to the therapeutic strategy.

Clients with AN or bulimia frequently experience significant deficits in self-esteem. Throughout therapy, this has to be taken into account and directly or indirectly addressed, again within the cognitive therapeutic framework. Low self-worth is also a result of distorted thinking and common thinking errors. These may include total self-condemnation on the basis of a single event, focusing on weaknesses and ignoring strengths, taking responsibility inappropriately, attending only to negative factors and predicting the future instead of experimenting with it. Using these examples as well as those previously mentioned, the therapist can act in such a way as to re-establish feelings of personal effectiveness and belief in one's own abilities.

Problem-solving

As progress is made with the cognitive work, experiments may be made to test traditional versus irrational beliefs. The thinking needs to be put into practice so that realistic and adaptive beliefs are maintained and consolidated. At the same time, simple tasks may be carried out in order to enhance self-esteem and increase belief in personal effectiveness. Clearly these should be achievable tasks in order to maximise the chance of success. However, while goals should remain realistic, the complexity can be gradually increased to match those that would be naturally encountered.

Consideration needs to be given, in the final stages, to preparing the individual to be able to cope with stresses and learn from setbacks once formal therapy is terminated. Within this context, and also relevant to the enhancement of self-esteem, some aspects of assertiveness training might be appropriate (Lange and Kakubowski, 1976). Behaviours associated with low self-worth are frequently either passive or aggressive, and as such, dysfunctional. With assertive behaviour, individuals will be able to communicate more openly and honestly, maintaining their own personal rights while respecting the rights of others. This is not viewed as separate from cognitive therapy, but as another variant of the cognitive–behavioural approach that can usefully be incorporated into treatment.

Given these considerations in preparation for problem-solving, a fairly structured approach can be adopted (e.g. Fairburn, 1981, 1985; Goldfried and Goldfried, 1980). In this, the specific problem is identified in detail independently, even when two or more problems occur together. The next step is to generate as many solutions as possible to the problem and then devise alternative methods for coping with the problem. It is not inappropriate to seek advice from family and friends at this stage. The greater the number of potential solutions that are available, the greater chance there is that a viable solution will be found. At this point, the client should create hypotheses about the practicality and likely success of each solution, finally selecting a single solution. The client should then plan the steps needed to carry out this solution, and reconsider the one selected, if necessary. Finally, the solution should be put into practice. Afterwards, it is important that the individual evaluates both the process and the solution in order to consider what might usefully be applied to future problems.

This problem-solving process may seem mechanical as for most people, the process is carried out without awareness. However, for an individual recovering from a psychological disorder, awareness needs to be heightened when previous irrational thinking patterns have distorted the logical processes. It is important to emphasise that the chances of success must be maximised; another failure can set back progress considerably.

INVOLVEMENT OF RELEVANT OTHERS

While the wider cultural reinforcers for thinness will not be easily changed, the more immediate reinforcement by family, partners and friends may be able to be modified. It is important to stress that those in the client's social network can help or hinder therapy, often unwittingly, and may behave in ways that maintain the disorder. For example, reinforcement for significant loss of body weight as well as the extreme apparent self-control in AN has already been referred to (Branch and Euman, 1980). School friends have been found to express a desire to 'catch' AN, which again may act as a reinforcer for the individual. During weight gain, family members may comment on the individual's improved appearance with the best of intentions, but the individual may reinterpret such comments to mean how obvious that weight gain is.

Looking at the problem from the relevant others' point of view, the behaviour of the eating-disordered individual may be seen as bizarre, frightening and incomprehensible. Parents often fear that they have been responsible for the disorder in some way. Indeed, this may have been the case, but would need to be managed in such a way as not to lose their co-operation. The point here is that family and friends often need educating about the disorder in the same way as the client, both to reduce their own distress as well as to facilitate behaviours and attitudes on their part that will be constructive rather than destructive.

Families can help in practical ways, such as by hiding mirrors in the house (response prevention for mirror-gazing) and by disposing of small-sized clothes (discriminative stimuli for the excessively thin body shape). In bulimia, there are certain times when a partner or family member can help in the prevention of binges and vomiting, although this requires careful monitoring. Clearly, the family can assist greatly in dietary planning, but again this requires considerable support as well as the proviso that the client must eventually move towards taking personal responsibility for food intake.

There are likely to have been many times during the onset and development of an eating disorder when partners or family members have felt they could not say anything right. Taking into consideration the client's distorted cognitions, this is not entirely suprising. In AN, the client may gain vicarious pleasure from catering for the family and it is not unknown for other family members to gain weight. Any rapid weight loss may be associated with irritability shown to any comment that might be interpreted negatively. In bulimia, the consequences for someone who interrupts a binge or vomiting episode can be somewhat aversive! Partners and family members 'watch' the person's eating behaviour, waiting for the secretive binges and vomiting episodes. This, in turn, may be met with hostility. In many cases, the family or partner will recognise the need for professional intervention long before the disordered individual does, in such circumstances the individual's denial of the problem can again lead to family conflict.

From another perspective, family members may, indirectly, act in such a way as to maintain the individual's eating disorder in order to avoid confronting problems of their own, and the role of the family cannot therefore be ignored. While the approach presented here would not address the role of the family to the extent that family therapy would (see Chapter 7), this form of cognitive – behavioural therapy does incorporate relevant others as an essential component of the overall strategy.

MAINTENANCE AND FOLLOW-UP

As the formal therapeutic intervention comes to an end, the frequency of therapy sessions diminishes. At this time, the emphasis shifts to the maintenance of progress and the resolution of any setbacks that may occur. Although the avoidance of dependency is necessary, it is equally important not to terminate therapy too early or too finally. Eating-disordered clients should have access to brief 'booster' sessions for times of crises. Typically the availability of such sessions will improve the maintenance of progress, and is rarely an inappropriate part of treatment.

Researchers and therapists alike differ dramatically in the length of time from the termination of formal therapy to conducting a follow-up. Indeed, some do not follow up their clients after termination of therapy. However, in the case of AN and bulimia, where the chances of relapse are comparatively high and residual symptoms common, long-term follow-up would seem to be advisable, although it need not be more than a brief telephone conversation. For the researcher, more extensive follow-ups might be desirable — but for any therapist there is a need to evaluate the effectiveness of their intervention. With eating disorders, follow-up should be considered in terms of years, rather than weeks or months.

CONCLUSIONS

As cognitive–behavioural therapy itself is a relatively recent approach to treatment, dating back only to the 1970s, there is not a great deal of empirical research on the effectiveness of the approach to the treatment of eating disorders. Indeed, it is only in the past few years that the applicability of the approach to anorexia and bulimia has been capitalised upon (e.g. Fairburn, 1981; Garner and Bemis, 1982). However, a number of evaluative studies have been reported in the literature and in this final section, we will consider the findings of a sample of these investigations.

Fairburn (1981) used cognitive-behaviour therapy with eleven women with BN. The study showed that nine of these women reduced the frequency of binging and vomiting to less than once a month, accompanied by a positive change in attitudes towards eating and physical appearance. At long-term follow-up after about eight months, eight of the women had maintained the gains made during treatment. Yates and Sambrailo (1984) carried out a study comparing the effectiveness of two types of treatment for 24 women with BN: The two treatments were cognitive–behavioural group therapy and cognitive–behavioural group therapy *plus* specific behavioural instructions on an individual basis. It was found that overall, both groups showed a reduction in binging and purging, with more of those participating in the group plus individual treatment showing this change. Other measures of cognitive change also showed positive shifts, but this did not differ between the two treatment approaches.

Kirkley, Schneider, Agras and Bachman (1985) also compared the effectiveness of two group treatments for bulimia. The two treatments were a cognitive–behavioural group and a non-directive group. In the former, specific recommendations and strategies for change were given; in the latter, the emphasis was on self-discovery and self-disclosure without instruction. The study showed that, for the 28 women who took part in the groups, the intervention was effective in changing cognitions. However, the cognitive-behavioural group had fewer dropouts and showed much more consistent decreases in binging and vomiting. At a three-month follow-up, 38 per cent of the cognitive-behavioural group and 11 per cent of the non-directive group continued to abstain from binging and vomiting. Hsu and Holder (1986) used individual cognitive-behaviour therapy with 56 bulimic women. They report that 68 per cent of this sample showed either a 'marked' or 'moderate' improvement in eating behaviour. At a one-year follow-up, 46 per cent were reported to have a 'good outcome'. Fairburn *et al.* (1986)

compared cognitive-behaviour therapy and short-term focal psychotherapy as treatments for BN. They found that the cognitive-behaviour therapy led to greater improvements over a 12-month follow-up period on measures of overall clinical state, general psychopathology, social adjustment and client assessment of outcome.

While most studies have concentrated on BN, Cooper and Fairburn (1984) report a study of cognitive-behaviour therapy for AN. They treated five female anorexic patients, measuring bulimic episodes and frequency of self-induced vomiting. They concluded that 'two patients did well, one showed some improvement, and two did not benefit at all' (p. 498). While it would be unwise to make generalisations on the basis of such a small sample, it is nonetheless interesting that the treatment appeared most effective for women who showed episodes of bulimia.

While future research will address the efficacy of the various components of cognitive-behaviour therapy, it is clear from the outcome studies that there is strong support for its use with BN, and indications that it may be beneficially applied to AN. As the benefits of future research and practice will lead to refinements of the therapy, we are confident in asserting that, in the hands of practitioners who are sensitive to theory as well as practice, cognitive-behaviour therapy will be confirmed as an effective strategy for the treatment of anorexia and bulimia nervosa.

REFERENCES

Beck, A.T. (1976) *Cognitive therapy and the emotional disorders.* International Universities Press, New York

Bellack, A.S., Hersen, M. and Kazdin, A.E. (1982) *International handbook of behavior modification and therapy.* Plenum Press, New York

Branch, C.H.H. and Euman, L.J. (1980) 'Social attitudes towards patients with anorexia nervosa.' *American Journal of Psychiatry, 139*, 1531–38

Bruch, H. (1974) 'Perils of behavior modification in treatment of anorexia nervosa.' *Journal of the American Medical Association, 230*, 1419–22

—— (1982) 'Anorexia nervosa: therapy and theory.' *American Journal of Psychiatry, 139*, 1531–8

Ciminero, A.R., Calhoun, K.S. and Adams, H.E. (1986) *Handbook of behavioural assessment*, 2nd edn, Wiley, Chichester

Cooper, P.J. and Fairburn, C.G. (1984) 'Cognitive behaviour therapy for anorexia nervosa: some preliminary findings.' *Journal of Psychosomatic Research, 28*, 493–9

Ellis, A. (1962) *Reason and emotion in psychotherapy.* Lyle Stuart, New York

Fairburn, C.G. (1981) 'A cognitive–behavioural approach to the treatment of bulimia.' *Psychological Medicine, 11*, 707–11

—— (1984) 'Bulimia: its epidemiology and management.' In A.J. Stunkard and E. Stellar (eds), *Eating and its disorders*, Raven Press, New York

—— (1985) 'Cognitive–behavioural treatment for bulimia.' In D.M. Garner and P.E. Garfinkel (eds), *Handbook of psychotherapy for anorexia nervosa and bulimia*, Guildford Press, New York

—— Kirk, J., O'Connor, M. and Cooper, P.J. (1986) 'A comparison of two psychological treatments for bulimia nervosa.' *Behaviour Research and Therapy, 24*, 629–43
Furnham, A. and Alibhai, N. (1983) 'Cross-cultural differences in the perception of female body shapes.' *Psychological Medicine, 13*, 829–37
Garner, D.M. and Bemis, K.M. (1982) 'A cognitive–behavioral approach to anorexia nervosa.' *Cognitive Therapy and Research, 6*, 123–50
—— and—— (1985) 'Cognitive therapy for anorexia nervosa.' In D.M. Garner and P.E. Garfinkel (eds), *Handbook of psychotherapy for anorexia nervosa and bulimia*, Guildford Press, New York
—— Garfinkel, P.E. and Bemis, K.M. (1984) 'A multidimensional psychotherapy for anorexia nervosa.' *International Journal of Eating Disorders, 3*, 3–46
—— ,—— and Olmstead, M.P. (1983) An overview of sociocultural factors in the development of anorexia nervosa.' In P.L. Darby, P.E. Garfinkel, D.M. Garner and D.Y. Coscina (eds), *Anorexia nervosa: recent developments in research.* Alan Liss, New York
—— , Olmstead, M.P. and Polivy, J. (1983) 'Developments and validation of a multidimensional eating disorder inventory for anorexia nervosa and bulimia.' *International Journal of Eating Disorders, 2*, 15–34
Goldfried, M.R. and Goldfried, A.P. (1980) 'Cognitive change methods.' In F.H. Kanfer and A.P. Goldstein (eds), *Handbook of psychotherapy for anorexia nervosa and bulimia.* Guildford Press, New York
Halmi, K.A. (1985) 'Behavioral management for anorexia nervosa.' In D.M. Garner and P.E. Garfinkel (eds), *Handbook of psychotherapy for anorexia nervosa and bulimia*, Guildford Press, New York
Hollin, C.R. (1986) 'Innovative clinical applications of social skills training.' In C.R. Hollin and P. Trower (eds), *Handbook of social skills training, vol.2: clinical applications and new directions.* Pergamon Press, Oxford
—— Houston, J.C. and Kent, M.F. (1985) 'Neuroticism, life stress and concern about eating, body weight and appearance in a non-clinical population.' *Personality and Individual Differences, 6*, 485–92
Hsu, L.K.G. and Holder, D. (1986) 'Bulimia nervosa: treatment and short-term outcome.' *Psychological Medicine, 16*, 65–70
Kirkley, B.G., Schneider, J.A., Agras, W.S. and Bachman, J.A. (1985) 'Comparison of two group treatments for bulimia.' *Journal of Consulting and Clinical Psychology, 53*, 43–8
Lange, A.J. and Kakubowski, P. (1976) *Responsible assertive behavior: Cognitive–behavioral procedures for trainers.* Research Press, Champaign, Illinois
Leon, A.D. (1980) 'Is it bad not to be thin?' *American Journal of Clinical Nutrition, 33*, 174–5
Loro, A.D. and Orleans, C.S. (1981) 'Binge eating in obesity: preliminary findings and guidelines for behavioral analysis and treatment.' *Addictive Behaviors, 6*, 155–66
Meichenbaum, D. and Jaremko, M. (1983) *Stress reduction and prevention.* Plenum Press, New York
Meyer, R.G. (1973) Delay therapy: two case reports. *Behavior Therapy, 4*, 709–11
Murray, J.B. (1986) 'Psychological aspects of anorexia nervosa.' *Genetic, Social, and General Psychology Monographs, 112*, 5–40
O'Connor, J. and Dowrick, P.W. (1987) 'Cognitions in normal weight, overweight, and previously overweight adults.' *Cognitive Therapy and Research, 11*, 315–26
Pillay, M. and Crisp, A.H. (1981) 'The impact of social skills training within an established in-patient treatment programme for anorexia nervosa.' *British Journal of Psychiatry, 139*, 533–9
Polivy, J. and Herman, C.P. (1985) 'Dieting and binging: a causal analysis.' *American Psychologist, 40*, 193–201
Rosen, J.C. and Leitenberg, H. (1982) 'Bulimia nervosa — treatment with exposure and

response prevention.' *Behavior Therapy*, *13*, 117–24

Ruderman, A.J. (1986) 'Bulimia and irrational beliefs.' *Behaviour Research and Therapy*, *24*, 193–197

Russell, G.F.M. (1981) 'The current treatment of anorexia nervosa.' *British Journal of Psychiatry*, *138*, 164–6

Schulman, R.G., Kinder, B.N., Powers, P.S., Prange, M. and Gleghorn, A. (1986) 'The development of a scale to measure cognitive distortions in bulimia.' *Journal of Personality Assessment*, *50*, 630–9

Slade, P. (1982) 'Towards a functional analysis of anorexia nervosa and bulimia nervosa.' *British Journal of Clinical Psychology*, *21*, 167–80

Yates, A.J. and Sambrailo, F. (1984) 'Bulimia nervosa: a descriptive and therapeutic study.' *Behaviour Research and Therapy*, *22*, 503–17

9

Psychopharmacological Approaches to Anorexia and Bulimia

Janet Treasure

INTRODUCTION

Less than ten years ago, the clinical features of BN were carefully defined (Russell, 1979) and it was suggested that although this disorder was akin to AN (it was originally thought to be a variant of chronic AN), the distinct symptoms and behaviour merited its classification as a separate syndrome. Following this, the classification of patients with eating disorders has been confused with some nosological systems, using weight as a key variable (American Psychiatric Association, 1980), and yet others using the symptom — an overpowering urge to overeat, and the behaviour — periodic consumption of massive amounts of foods, to distinguish the subtypes of eating disorders (Fairburn and Garner, 1986). The validity of the last-mentioned mode of division has been substantiated by research from several centres (Garner, Garfinkel and Shaughnessy, 1983; Garner, Olmsted and Garfinkel, 1985; Fairburn and Cooper, 1984; Fairburn and Garner, 1986).

In this chapter, the term 'restricting AN' will be used to describe patients who fulfil Russell's (1983) criteria of: (a) self-induced starvation; (b) a morbid fear of fatness; and (c) an abnormality in reproductive hormone functioning, indicated by amenorrhea in females or decreased sexual drive and function in males. The subgroup who periodically overeat, but who share, in common with restricting AN, all of the criteria outlined above and who are markedly underweight, will be classified as bulimic AN. Bulimia nervosa will be used to describe patients who: (a) have episodes of gross overeating; (b) attempt to counteract the 'fattening' effects of such binges by stringent dieting or by vomiting or abusing laxatives; and (c) have a morbid fear of fatness and an undervalued idea about the importance of body weight. There will be a degree of cross-categorisation in the use of the terms bulimic AN and BN as they are separated merely by an arbitrary weight threshold.

Is anorexia nervosa a distinct psychiatric syndrome?

It has been suggested that AN may be a variant of an affective disorder with the form and content of the illness shaped by the onset of adolescence, when weight-preoccupation and dieting behaviour is common. Marked depressive symptoms commonly occur in AN when starvation is most intense, but they frequently remit after refeeding and it is thought that they are secondary to the severe metabolic disturbance (Halmi, Eckert, LaDu and Cohen, 1986). Moreover, the illness remains distinct in long-term follow-up studies. Nevertheless, the proportion of affective disorders in the family members of probands with AN almost equals that of probands with affective disorders (Winokur, March and Mendels, 1980) but the converse, i.e. an increase in the number of cases of eating disorders in the families of probands with affective disorder has never been found (Strober and Katz, 1987). Therefore, the balance of evidence would reject the proposition that AN is an atypical form of depression.

Others have suggested that the overvalued ideas concerning weight and eating, which are characteristic of patients with eating disorders, have the intensity of monosymptomatic delusions in some patients and so raise the possibility that AN is a variant of a paranoid disorder.

Is bulimia nervosa a distinct psychiatric syndrome?

When BN was initially described, it was thought to be a chronic variant of AN. However, it is now considered to be a separate, albeit closely akin, syndrome. Although depressive features such as dysphoria and low self-esteem are common in BN, the clinical profile of depressive symptoms is distinct from that of patients with affective disorder (Cooper and Fairburn, 1986). As has been found in AN, major affective disorder frequently occurs in the first-degree relatives of bulimics (Hudson, Pope, Jonas and Yurgelin-Todd, 1983), but there is no evidence that the converse is true. In addition, the biological features of bulimia (such as sleep electroencephalogram and neurohormonal secretion) are distinct from those found in major depressive disorders.

The similarity between BN and addictive disorders such as alcoholism and drug abuse has also been made (Scott, 1986), as the phenomenology is similar (Szmuckler and Tantum, 1984), the symptoms overlap (Garfinkel, Moldofsky and Garner, 1980; Pyle, Mitchell and Eckert, 1981), and such disorders are common in the families of patients with bulimia (Carroll and Leon, 1981).

What is the rationale for the use of pharmacotherapy in the management of patients with eating disorders?

There are two basic reasons for choosing a pharmacological approach in the management of eating disorders. The first is that a drug might correct the basic biochemical defect underlying the condition and the second is that a drug may provide symptomatic benefit. If a drug is to be used to correct a putative metabolic disorder, it is important to review what is known about the biology of the eating disorders.

What is the evidence for biological factors contributing to the aetiology of anorexia nervosa?

The regulation of feeding behaviour in animals is a result of a complicated interplay between peptide, amino acid, prostaglandin and amine neurotransmitters. Food-seeking and ingestive behaviour is probably the dominant system, but this is modulated by a cascade of inhibitory neurotransmitters, some of which arise from central satiety centres and others from the periphery, for example, the stomach. Such a model would explain why the number of substances that have been found to inhibit feeding greatly exceeds the number of stimulatory substances.

The stimulation of feeding

Many of the neurotransmitters which have been found to increase feeding in animals show a degree of specificity in the macronutrient content of the food preferred. Neuropeptide Y and peptide YY (the most potent of the substances that increase feeding) stimulate carbohydrate intake (Morley and Mitchell, 1986); the opiates increase fat intake and, to a lesser extent, that of protein (Marks-Kaufman and Lipetes, 1982); and noradrenaline increases carbohydrate intake directly, by reducing the firing rate of the penultimate inhibitory neuron. These three substances appear to act in concert to increase feeding behaviour and the macronutrients chosen can be finely tuned.

Is there any evidence for a reduction in the substances that increase feeding in anorexia nervosa?

Theoretically, it would be possible for AN to result from a deficiency in one or all of the neurotransmitter systems found to increase feeding. However, preliminary reports have found increased opiate activity within the cerebro-spinal fluid (CSF) in patients with AN (Kaye, Pickar, Naker and Ebert, 1982) and one unconfirmed report found increased levels of pancreatic polypeptide after a test meal (Alderdice, Dinsmore, Buchanan and Admas, 1985). Also, there is evidence for an increase in central noradrenergic turnover (Gerner *et al.*, 1984; Kaye, Ebert, Raleigh and Lake, 1984) with an increase in hypothalamic alpha-2-adrenoreceptors (Kaye *et al.*, 1985). Thus all these reports are consistent in finding an increase, rather than a decrease, in the neurotransmitters that increase feeding in animals, implying that the central control of feeding is responding appropriately to starvation.

The inhibition of feeding

Morley, Levine and Billington (1984) produced a tentative model to explain feeding behaviour in which serotonin (5-HT) and corticotrophin-releasing hormone (CRH) were the terminal neurotransmitters controlling satiation. The list of other substances that have been found to inhibit feeding is long and includes the monoamines, dopamine and noradrenaline; GABA; prostaglandins; and peptides such as cholecystokinin (CCK), neurotensin, calcitonin, vasointestinal peptide, etc. However, the specificity of many of these substances has yet to be established.

Is there any evidence for an increase in the substances which decrease feeding in anorexia nervosa?

Central 5-HT turnover is increased in patients with restricting AN after recovery (Kaye *et al.*, 1984) and elevated levels of CRH have been found in the CSF of patients with AN (Kaye *et al.*, 1987). Thus it is possible that patients with AN are extremely sensitive to satiating stimuli as a result of increased levels of central 5-HT and CRH; and the latter may increase as a result of stress.

Is there any evidence for an increase in the substances which decrease feeding in animals being elevated in bulimia nervosa?

Peripheral noradrenergic activity appears to be reduced in BN (Kaye, Gwirtsman and Lake, 1986), but this may bear no relationship to central levels. Similarly, the sustained elevation of plasma beta-endorphin found in patients with bulimia may not reflect central activity (Fullerton, Swift and Getto, 1986), but it is possible that the craving for food may develop as a result of increased opiate activity.

Is there any evidence that substances which decrease feeding in animals are reduced in bulimia nervosa?

Indirect measure of central serotonin turnover has revealed that patients with the restricting type of AN have higher turnover than those with bulimic AN (Kaye *et al.*, 1984). Further indirect studies of central serotonergic activity using L-tryptophan and m-clorophenylpiperazine also suggest that patients with bulimia have reduced central serotonergic activity (Brewerton *et al.*, 1986). The same group have also measured the tryptophan ratio (the ratio of plasma tryptophan over the plasma concentrations of other large neutral amino acids) in bulimic patients whilst they were binging, finding that those patients who voluntarily stopped binging and vomiting had an early increase in this ratio, but those who continued to feel unsatisfied did not. This is important as tryptophan is a precursor of serotonin and the amount of tryptophan that passes through the blood–brain barrier is dependent upon this ratio. Taken together, these findings suggest that a reduction in central serotonin activity may account for the reduced experience of satiety in bulimia.

Are there alternative, non-pharmacological models of anorexia nervosa?

It has been difficult to find an animal model that incorporates all the clinical features of AN (Beumont, 1984; Mrosovsky, 1984). Animals lesioned in the lateral hypothalamus do lose weight after the operation. However, they then maintain their weight at a new lower level, suggesting that their weight set-point has been lowered by this intervention. Although some patients with AN do maintain a stable, but low weight, in others weight loss falls precipitously to dangerous levels. One animal model that encompasses this inability is that described by Epling, Pierce and Stefan (1983), in which a combination of exercise and limited access to food has been used. Hyperactivity is a notable feature of AN and it is not (as are so many of the other clinical features) a result of starvation and so this model has some face validity.

Are there alternative, non-pharmacological models of bulimia nervosa?

There are some animal models that closely correspond to the clinical picture of BN. One of the most simple is that of rats with a gastric fistula so that any food eaten is drained away. The eating of such animals is excessive (Deutsch, 1987). A rather different model is that of rats chronically exposed to foods of high palatability. Rats develop hyperphagia when exposed to such a regimen, and when such animals are given naloxone, an exaggerated morphine-withdrawal syndrome develops as if they were morphine-dependent (Le Magnen, 1987). It is possible that food of high palatability results in the release of endogenous opiates in the rat. A similar phenomenon could explain the craving for sweet and highly palatable food that many patients with BN describe. A further model is that of stress-induced eating in animals, which is thought to be mediated by endogenous opiates (Morley and Levine, 1980; Lowly, Maickel and Yim, 1980). Such a mechanism may be analogous to binge eating under conditions of stress.

What other evidence is there for a biological propensity to develop an eating disorder?

Several family studies have shown an increased rate of eating disorders amongst female relatives of patients with AN (Gershon *et al.*, 1984; Strober *et al.*, 1985), and the latter authors have some evidence that suggests that restricting and bulimic forms of AN segregate between families. Preliminary findings from twin studies suggest that the genetic component of liability is high in restricting AN (Holland *et al.*, 1984).

What evidence is there that pharmacotherapy is effective in restricting anorexia nervosa?

Both Gull (1874) and Laseque in 1873 suggested that the basic abnormality in AN was an abnormality in the central control of appetite. Following from the basic biological knowledge about the control of feeding referred to previously, such a defect in central appetite control may result from excessive levels of serotonin or CRH, which are thought to mediate the satiety response. Theoretically, drugs that either increase the concentration of those neurotransmitters that stimulate feeding in animals or decrease the concentration of the inhibitory transmitters should be effective in the management of patients with eating disorders.

A wide range of drugs interact with central monoaminergic systems, including the antidepressants. This group of drugs effect the re-uptake of noradrenalin and serotonin into nerve terminals but these neurotransmitters act in opposition in the central control of feeding. The tricyclic antidepressants such as amitriptyline are recognised to have an effect upon appetite and their long-term administration in the management of depression can lead to weight gain (Paykel, Mueller and De La Vergue, 1973). This had led to the use of antidepressants for AN, based both upon a symptomatic and theoretical rationale. Amitriptyline has equipotent effects on the serotoninergic and noradrenergic neuronal activity (Dressé and Scuvée-Moreau, 1984) and appeared promising in open trials (Mills, 1976), but was not superior to placebo when tested under double-blind conditions (Bierderman *et al.*, 1985; Halmi *et al.*, 1986). Clomipramine (with a predominant effect upon serotoninergic uptake, which is thought to increase serotoninergic transmission) increased self-reported hunger and appetite (such an effect would not be predicted on the basis of the animal models), but this did not improve on the weight gain achieved by standard inpatient management (Lacey and Crisp, 1980; Crisp, Lacey and Crutchfield, 1987). However, cyproheptadine, a serotonin antagonist (which theoretically should increase appetite) has been found to slightly increase the weight gain achieved by standard inpatient management (Halmi *et al.*, 1986).

The chronic administration of neuroleptics to patients with schizophrenia results in weight gain and Barry and Klawans (1976) hypothesised that hyperfunctioning of the cerebral dopaminergic system may account for some of the symptoms of AN. Neuroleptics are central dopaminergic antagonists. A double-blind trial of pimozide in combination with an inpatient behavioural regime for bulimic and restricting patients with AN failed to show any marked benefit (Vandereycken and Pierloot, 1983). Nevertheless, in practice, phenothiazines may, on occasions, be used symptomatically to allay severe anxiety and agitation or to treat the rare psychotic episode that may occur after hospitalisation (Grounds, 1982).

What evidence is there for the efficacy of pharmacotherapy in bulimia nervosa?

Patients with BN, in contrast to those with restricting AN, have a marked preoccupation with food and are subject to powerful urges to overeat, to which they periodically succumb. Thus the expected physiological or psychological disturbance would be either a reduction in the normal satiety mechanisms or an increase in the activity of those systems that stimulate feeding and the trials using empirically derived drugs will be described initially.

In acute studies, fenfluramine (which acts to increase serotonin and should theoretically produce satiety) and the opioid antagonist naloxone (which would theoretically be expected to decrease feeding) have been found to decrease the calorific content of a binge (Robinson, Checkley and Russell, 1985; Mitchell, Laine and Morley, 1987). The neuropeptide CCK (which in some animal models produces satiety) did not reduce the content of a binge in similar acute studies (Mitchell *et al.*, 1987).

Similar compounds have also been given in chronic studies. The opioid antagonist naltrexone reduced bulimic behaviour (Jonas and Gold, 1986) but the abnormal liver-function tests, which have occasionally arisen when this drug has been used to treat obesity, will prevent this drug having widespread acceptability (Atkinson, 1985; Maggio, Presla and Bracco, 1985). D-Fenfluramine has also been used in a relatively large (42 patients) double-blind trial and produced a significant decrease in the amount of binging and vomiting (Russell *et al.*, 1987). However, compliance was poor; a large proportion of the patients evaluated declined to enter the study and 42 per cent failed to complete the twelve weeks of the study. These dropouts were not the result of unpleasant side effects.

The depressive symptoms that commonly present in bulimia provide the rationale for a symptomatic approach to the management of this disorder with antidepressants. Nevertheless, antidepressants also interact with monoaminergic systems and so may effect the central or peripheral aspects of feeding.

The definitions of BN used in studies of antidepressants have varied. The majority have used DSM-III criteria in, which overvalued ideas about body weight and stringent weight-control methods such as vomiting and laxative abuse are not necessary. Others have used this definition, but have excluded patients who would also fulfil the DSM-III criteria for major affective disorder (Hughes, Wells, Cunningham and Ilstrup, 1986) whereas Sabine *et al.* (1983) used the more exacting criteria defined by Russell (1983). Therefore, the interpretation and comparison of these trials is fraught with difficulty.

The tricyclic antidepressant imipramine (which has a predominant effect upon noradrenergic transmission) has been used in double-blind trials in patients with eating disorders. In a small six-week study, Pope, Hudson, Jonas and Yurgelun-Todd (1983) found that imipramine decreased the number of episodes of binge eating. This study has been replicated (Agras *et al.*, 1987) but although they found that there was a quantitative reduction in abnormal eating behaviour, only four of the 22 patients became abstinent and there was little change in abnormal eating attitudes. Desipramine was also of symptomatic benefit when given to patients with BN (excluding those with features of major depressive disorders, (Hughes *et al.*, 1986). This study was of interest because plasma levels of the drug were estimated and some non-responders were effectively treated when the dose of antidepressant was increased to produce therapeutic plasma levels. In all of these trials, side effects caused a proportion of patients to drop out of treatment.

The two-year follow-up data on the patients treated with imipramine by Pope *et al.* (1983) are disappointing, as relapses occurred in the majority and considerable experimentation with a variety of drugs (up to five different drugs in some cases) was necessary to maintain improvement. Other antidepressants such as amitriptyline (with effects on noradrenergic and serotonergic transmissions) and mianserin (a so-called atypical or second-generation antidepressant) did not improve on the response to general psychotherapeutic measures (Mitchell and Groat, 1984; Sabine *et al.*, 1983). Although it could be argued that the drug level used in these negative trials may not have been adequate, it is also possible that the psychotherapeutic interventions in the placebo groups may not have been equivalent.

Trials of monoamine oxidase inhibitors have also taken place. However, the risk of dietary indiscretion in these patients, whose basic psychopathology involves a lack of control over eating, means that careful patient selection and detailed education are essential before such treatment is begun. Walsh, Stewart and Roose (1984) found that phenelzine reduced the bulimic symptoms in those patients who completed the trial. However, there was a 58 per cent (20 patients) dropout rate; three of these had violated the dietary restrictions, and five had intolerable side effects. Kennedy, Pira and Garfinkel (1985) in their open trial of another monoamine oxidase inhibitor, isocarboxazid, also had a high dropout rate amongst the patients with BN.

CONCLUSIONS

Overall, for restricting AN, the benefits of drug treatment are small and need to be balanced by the finding that a significant proportion of the mortality found in AN is a result of an overdose of antidepressant medication (Patton, 1987). Thus pharmacotherapy at the present time has little to add to the inpatient regimes of specialised units for the management of restricting AN. However, it is possible that once the biology of AN is more fully understood, then drug treatment may enable recovery to occur in some patients without the need for inpatient treatment.

There does appear to be a place for drug treatment in BN and several drugs have produced interesting and beneficial results. However, our knowledge about the 'disease' BN is still in its infancy and it will probably be necessary to clearly define the subgroup of patients who respond best to the treatment approaches that are currently being evaluated. Although distinct forms of psychotherapy, such as cognitive–behavioural treatment (see Chapter 8), were thought to produce specific benefits, it is now apparent that beneficial results can occur from diverse psychotherapeutic methods (Kirkley, Schneider, Agras and Backman, 1985; Fairburn, Kirk, O'Connor and Cooper, 1986). It is possible that pharmacotherapy will also be found to be non-specific in its effects. Certainly, there is a place for drug trials using operationalised definitions of the disorder and with a large enough group of patients to produce statistically reliable results, even when the seemingly inevitable high dropout rate occurs.

ACKNOWLEDGEMENT

This manuscript was prepared when the author was a Medical Research Council research fellow.

REFERENCES

Agras, W.S., Dorian, B., Kirkley, B.G., Arnow, B. and Bachman, J. (1987) 'Imipramine in the treatment of bulimia: a double-blind controlled study.' *International Journal of Eating Disorders*, *6*, 29–38

Alderdice, J.A., Dinsmore, W.W., Buchanan, K.D. and Admas, C. (1985) 'Gastrointestinal hormones in anorexia nervosa.' *Journal of Psychiatric Research*, *19*, 207–14

American Psychiatric Association (1980) *Diagnostic and Statistical Manual of Mental Disorders*, 3rd edn, American Medical Association

Atkinson, R.L. (1985) 'Naloxone decreases food intake in obese humans.' *Journal of Clinical Endocrinology and Metabolism*, *55*, 196–8

Barry, V.C. and Klawans, H.L. (1976) 'On the role of DA in the pathophysiology of anorexia nervosa.' *Journal of Neural Transmission*, *38*, 107–22

Beumont, P.J.V. (1984) 'A clinician looks at animal models of anorexia nervosa.' In P.J.V. Beumont (ed), *Animal models in psychopathology*, pp. 177–210, Academic Press, Australia

Bierderman, J., Herzog, D.B., Rivinus, T.M., Ferber, R.A., Rosenbaum, J.F., Harmatz, J.S., Tondorf, R., Orsulan, P.J. and Schildkrantz, J. (1985) 'Amitriptyline in the treatment of anorexia nervosa: a double-blind, placebo-controlled study.' *Journal of Clinical Psychopharmacology*, *5*, 10–16

Brewerton, T.D., Mueller, E., George, T., Brandt, H., Lesem, M., Navang, P., Jimerson, D. and Murphy, D. (1986) *Blunted prolactin response to the serotonin agonist imchlorophenylpiparazine (m-CPP) in bulimia.* Colligium Internationale Neuro-Psychopharmacologium, Puerto Rico

Carroll, K. and Leon, G. (1981) 'The bulimic-vomiting disorder within a generalised substance abuse pattern.' Paper presented at the *Annual Meeting of the Association for the Advancement of Behavior Therapy*, Toronto, Canada

Cooper, P.J. and Fairburn, C.G. (1986) 'The depressive symptoms of bulimia nervosa.' *British Journal of Psychiatry*, *148*, 268–74

Crisp, A.H., Lacey, J.H. and Crutchfield, M. (1987) 'Clomipramine and 'drive' in people with anorexia nervosa: an inpatient study.' *British Journal of Psychiatry*, *150*, 355–8

Deutsch, J.A. (1987) 'Signals determining meal size.' In R.A. Boakes, D.A. Popplewell and

M.J. Burton (eds), *Eating habits, food, physiology and learned behaviour*, Wiley, New York, pp. 155–74

Dresse, A. and Scuvee-Moreau, J. (1984) 'The effects of various antidepressants on the spontaneous firing rates of noradrenergic and serotonergic neurones.' *Clinical Neuropharmacology*, *7*, suppl., 572–3

Epling, W.F., Pierce, W.D. and Stefan, C. (1983) 'A theory of activity-based anorexia.' *International Journal of Eating Disorders*, *3*, 27–46

Fairburn, C.G. and Cooper, P.J. (1984) 'Binge eating, self-induced vomiting and laxative abuse: a community study.' *Psychological Medicine*, *14*, 401–10

——, and Garner, D.M. (1986) 'The diagnosis of bulimia nervosa.' *International Journal of Eating Disorders*, *5*, 403–19

——, Kirk, J., O'Connor, M. and Cooper, P.J. (1986) 'A comparison of two psychological treatments for bulimia nervosa.' *Behaviour Research and Therapy*, *24*, 629–43

Fullerton, D.T., Swift, N.V. and Getto, W. (1986) 'Plasma immunoreactive B endorphin in bulimia.' *Psychological Medicine*, *16*, 59–63

Garfinkel, P.E., Moldofsky, H. and Garner, D.M. (1980) 'The heterogeneity of anorexia nervosa: bulimia as a distinct subgroup.' *Archives of General Psychiatry*, *37*, 1037–40

Garner, D.M., Garfinkel, P.E. and Shaughnessy, M. (1983) 'Clinical and psychometric comparison between bulimia in anorexia nervosa and bulimia in normal weight women.' In *Understanding anorexia nervosa and bulimia*, report of the 4th Ross Conference on Medical Research, Ross Laboratories, Columbus

——, Olmsted, M.P. and Garfinkel, P.E. (1985) 'Similarities among bulimic groups selected by weight and weight history.' *Journal of Psychiatric Research*, *19*, 129-34

Gerner, R.H., Cohen, D.J., Farbanks, L., Anderson, G.M., Young, J.G., Scheinin, M., Linnoil, M., Shayiotz, B.A. and Hare, T.A. (1984) 'CSF neurochemistry of women with anorexia nervosa and normal women.' *American Journal of Psychiatry*, *141*, 1441–4

Gershon, E.S., Schreiber, J.L., Hamont, J.R., Dibble, E.D., Kaye, W., Nurnberger, J.I., Anderson, A. and Ebert, M. (1984) 'Clinical findings in patients with anorexia nervosa and affective illness in their relatives.' *American Journal of Psychiatry*, *141*, 1419–22

Grounds, A. (1982) 'Transient psychosis in anorexia nervosa: a report of seven cases.' *Psychological Medicine*, *12*, 107–15

Gull, W.W. (1874) 'Anorexia nervosa (apepsia hysterica, anorexia hysterica).' *Transcript of the Clinical Society*, *7*, 22–8

Halmi, K.A., Eckert, E., LaDu, T. and Cohen, J. (1986) 'Anorexia nervosa: treatment efficacy of cyproheptadine and amitriptyline.' *Archives of General Psychiatry*, *43*, 177–81

Holland, A.J., Hall, A., Murray, R., Russell, G.F.M. and Crisp, A.H. (1984) 'Anorexia nervosa: a study of 34 twin pairs and one set of triplets.' *British Journal of Psychiatry*, *145*, 414–9

Hudson, J.I., Pope, H.G., Jonas, J.M. and Yurgelin-Todd, D. (1983) 'Family history study of anorexia nervosa and bulimia.' *British Journal of Psychiatry*, *142*, 133–8

Hughes, P.L., Wells, L.A., Cunningham, O. and Ilstrup, D.M. (1986) Treating bulimia with desimipramine: a double-blind placebo controlled study. *Archives of General Psychiatry*, *43*, 182–6

Jonas, J.M. and Gold, M.S. (1986) 'Treatment of antidepressant-resistant bulimia with naltrexone.' *International Journal of Psychiatry in Medicine*, *16*, 305–9

Kaye, W.H., Ebert, M.H., Raleigh, M. and Lake, R. (1984) 'Abnormalities in CNS monoamine metabolism in anorexia nervosa.' *Archives of General Psychiatry*, *41*, 350–5

—— Gwirtsman, H.E., George, D.T., Ebert, M.H., Jimerson, D.C., Tomai, T.P., Chrousos, G.P. and Gold, P.W. (1987) 'Elevated cerebrospinal fluid levels of immunoreactive corticotropin-releasing hormone in anorexia nervosa in relation to state of nutrition, adrenal function and intensity of depression.' *Journal of Clinical Endocrinology and*

Metabolism, *64*, 203–8

—— —— and Lake, C.R. (1986) 'Noradrenergic disturbances in normal weight bulimics.' *Proceedings of the American Psychiatric Association*, *139*, NR30

—— —— ——, Suver, L.J., Jimerson, D.C., Ebert, M.H. and Murphy, D.L. (1985) 'Disturbances of norepinephrine metabolism and adrenergic receptor activity in anorexia nervosa: relationship to normal state.' *Psychopharmacology Bulletin*, *21*, 419–23

——, Pickar, D., Naker, D. and Ebert, M.H. (1982) 'Cerebrospinal fluid opioid activity in anorexia nervosa.' *American Journal of Psychiatry*, *139*, 643–5

Kennedy, S.H., Pira, N. and Garfinkel, P.E. (1985) 'Monoamine oxidase inhibitor therapy for anorexia nervosa and bulimia: a preliminary trial of isocarboxaside.' *Journal of Clinical Psychopharmacology*, *5*, 279–85

Kirkley, B.G., Schneider, J.A., Agras, W.S. and Bachman, J.A. (1985) 'A comparison of two group treatments for bulimia.' *Journal of Consulting and Clinical Psychology*, *53*, 43–8

Lacey, J.H. and Crisp, A.H. (1980) 'Hunger, food intake and weight: the impact of clomipramine on a refeeding anorexia nervosa population.' *Postgraduate Medical Journal*, *56*, 79–85

Laseque, E.C. (1873) 'On hysterical anorexia.' *Medical Times Gazette*, *265*, 367–9. Translated in R.M. Kaufman and M. Heiman (eds), *Evolution of psychosomatic concepts*, Hogarth Press, London (1965), pp. 141-55

Le Magnen, J. (1987) 'Palatability: concept, terminology and mechanism.' In R.A. Boakes, D.A. Popplewell and M.J. Burton (eds), *Eating habits, food, physiology and learned behaviour*, John Wiley, New York

Lowly, M.T., Maickel, R.P. and Yim, G.K.W. (1980) 'Naloxone reduction of stress related feeding.' *Life Sciences*, *26*, 2113–18

Maggio, C.A., Presla, E. and Bracco, E.F. (1985) 'Naltrexone and human eating behaviour: a dose ranging inpatient trial in moderately obese men.' *Brain Research Bulletin*, *14*, 657–64

Marks-Kaufman, R. and Lipetes, B.J. (1982) 'Patterns of nutrient selection in rats orally self-administering morphine.' *Nutrition and Behaviour*, *1*, 33–46

Mills, I.H. (1976) 'Amitriptyline therapy in anorexia nervosa.' *Lancet*, *25*, 687

Mitchell, J.E. and Groat, R. (1984) 'A placebo-controlled double-blind trial of amitriptyline in bulimia.' *Journal of Clinical Psychopharmacology*, *4*, 186–93

—— Laine, D.E. and Morley, J.E. (1987) 'Naloxone but not CCK attenuates binge eating in patients with bulimia nervosa'. (in press)

Morley, J.E. and Levine, A.S. (1980) 'Stress-induced eating is mediated through endogenous opiates.' *Science*, *209*, 1259–61

—— —— and Billington, C.J. (1984) 'Neuropeptides and appetite: contribution of neuropharmacological modelling.' *Federation Proceedings*, *43*, 2903–7

—— and Mitchell, J.E. (1986) 'Neurotransmitter/neuromodulator influences on eating.' In E. Ferrari and F. Brambilla (eds), *Advances in the Neurosciences*, *Vol. 60*, pp. 11–20, Pergamon Press, London

Mrosovsky, N. (1984) 'Animal models: anorexia yes, nervosa no.' In K.M. Pirke and D. Ploog (eds), *The psychobiology of anorexia nervosa*, pp. 22–34, Springer Verlag, Berlin.

*Patton, G.C. (1987) 'Mortality in eating disorders.' *British Journal of Psychiatry*, (in press)

Paykel, E.S., Mueller, P.S. and DeLa Vergue, P.M. (1973) 'Amitriptyline, weight gain and carbohydrate craving — a side effect.' *British Journal of Psychiatry*, *123*, 501-7

Pope, H.G., Hudson, J., Jonas, J.M. and Yurgelun-Todd, D. (1983) 'Antidepressant treatment of bulimia: a two year follow-up study. *Journal of Clinical Psychopharmacology*, *5*, 320–7

Pyle, R.L., Mitchell, J.R. and Eckert, E.D. (1981). 'Bulimia: a report of 34 cases.' *Journal of Clinical Psychiatry*, *42*, 60–4

Robinson, P.H., Checkley, S.A. and Russell, G.F.M. (1985) 'Suppression of eating by fenfluramine in patients with bulimia nervosa.' *British Journal of Psychiatry, 146*, 169–76

Russell, G.F.M. (1979) 'Bulimia nervosa: an ominous variant of anorexia nervosa.' *Psychological Medicine, 9*, 1–20

—— (1983) 'Anorexia nervosa and bulimia nervosa.' In G.F.M. Russell and L.A. Hersov (eds), *Handbook of psychiatry, vol. 4: the neuroses and personality disorders.* Plenum Press, New York

—— Checkley, S.A., Feldman, J. and Eisler, I. (1987) 'A controlled trial of d-fenfluramine in bulimia nervosa.' *Journal of Psychopharmacology* (in press)

Sabine, E.J., Yonace, A., Farrington, A.J., Barratt, K.H. and Wakeling, A. (1983) 'Bulimia nervosa: a placebo controlled double-blind therapeutic trial of mianserin.' *British Journal of Clinical Pharmacology, 15*, 1955–2025

Scott, D.W. (1986) 'Anorexia nervosa: a review of possible genetic factors.' *International Journal of Eating Disorders, 5*, 1–20

Strober, M. and Katz, J.L. (1987) 'Do eating disorders share a common aetiology? A dissenting opinion.' *International Journal of Eating Disorders, 6*, 171–80

—— Morrell, W., Bulrough, S., Salkin, B. and Jacobs, C. (1985) 'A controlled family study of anorexia nervosa.' *Journal of Psychiatric Research, 19*, 239–46

Szmuckler, G.I. and Tantum, D. (1984) 'Anorexia nervosa: starvation dependence.' *British Journal of Medical Psychology, 57*, 303–10

Vandereycken, W. and Pierloot, R. (1983) 'Combining drugs and behaviour therapy in anorexia nervosa: a double-blind placebo/pimozide study.' In P.L. Darby, P.E. Garfinkel, D.M. Garner and D.V. Coscina (eds), *Anorexia nervosa: recent developments in research*, Alan Liss, New York

Walsh, B.I., Stewart, J.W. and Roose, S.P. (1984) 'Treatment of bulimia with phenelzine: a double-blind placebo controlled study.' *Archives of General Psychiatry, 41*, 1105–9

Winokur, A., March, V. and Mendels, J. (1980) 'Primary affective disorder in relatives of patients with anorexia nervosa.' *American Journal of Psychiatry, 137*, 695–8

Part Three
Individual Roles

10

The Role of the Nurse in Eating Disorders

Francis Biley and Sally Savage

INTRODUCTION

Much has been written about eating disorders in the nursing press. However, most articles have been concerned with specific case histories, or describe the aetiology, signs and symptoms and possible methods of treatment (e.g. Biley and Savage, 1984). Whilst undeniably valuable, these articles almost invariably follow the 'medical model' philosophy of disease identification and application of appropriate treatment. Despite this, the role of the nurse in caring and treating those with eating disorders is of 'prime psychological importance' (Crisp, 1980) and the development of the nursing model of care should be seen as an integral part of this.

With the increased incidence of AN, the nurse is now likely to encounter these patients in many different settings. In the community, the district nurse, health visitor or community psychiatric nurse (CPN) may be in an ideal position to first recognise disordered eating patterns, and in some instances, in collaboration with other health-care professionals, may be able to supply appropriate support and treatment. In the hospital setting, the nurse may encounter such patients in the outpatients department, medical wards and psychiatric wards. Potentially, the nurse is often the person to have the greatest amount of contact with the patient, and they will be in a position to ensure continuity of care. The primary role of the nurse in any of these areas, therefore, is to act as co-ordinator between the potentially high number of health-care professionals, for example, other nurses, the dietician, psychologist or physician, who might be involved in the care of a particular patient.

This continuity of care, between the nurses themselves and other health-care professionals could more effectively be achieved by employing the current British trend of using the nursing process (the systematic assessment, planning, implementing and evaluation of nursing care), a holistic and patient-centred (rather than task-oriented) style of care. This has been shown to be of great benefit to various groups of patients (e.g. Miller, 1984), and could equally apply to eating disorders, although this has yet to be proven empirically. Furthermore, the effectiveness of this method and philosophy of care could be extended even further if it was employed by all members of the multidisciplinary team. In the meantime, using the nursing process could help the problem that so often occurs — of the patient being regarded as an anonymous disease entity, e.g. 'bed number six must gain ten pounds in weight', and a reasonable understanding of the patient as an individual with specific problems may be gained. For readers interested in finding out more about the nursing process, Kratz (1979) and Roper, Logan and Tierney (1980) can be regarded as important basic introductory texts.

The most essential part of the nursing process is the initial assessment. If performed either on an *ad hoc* basis, or as a series of pre-set questions (such as 'Eating habits?' or 'Hobbies?') delivered in all cases with little deviation, then it is unlikely to be an effective or useful assessment. Particularly over the last fifteen years, theoretical definitions of nursing have been formulated. These 'models of nursing' provide frameworks that can be employed to provide comprehensive, holistic, patient-centred assessments, and their use will contribute to the success of the nursing process. With eating disorders, the need for a comprehensive assessment is of utmost importance in order for the nurse to gain an accurate understanding of the individual and his/her specific problems.

There are several models of nursing that could be employed in the care of patients with eating disorders. For example, Roy's adaptation model (Roy, 1974) views health

> as a continuum (between maximum wellness and maximum illness)... it is the physician's goal to move the patient along the line from illness to health, the nurse's role is to promote adaptation in terms of physiological functioning, self-concept, role-performance and interdependence.
>
> (Chapman, 1985).

Neuman, on the other hand, in her health-care systems model (Neuman, 1974) views an individual (or even a group of individuals or a whole community) as a central core surrounded by various lines of defence and resistance that act as protection for this central core. These lines may be breached by 'stressors' causing different degrees of illness. It is the nurse's function to strengthen or rebuild these lines, using either primary, secondary or tertiary intervention. Nurses could even formulate their own models specifically for use with eating disorders.

ACTIVITIES OF DAILY LIVING

The model employed here to explain the nature of the nurse's role in relation to eating disorders will be a model based on Henderson's (1960) definition of nursing and the 'activities of daily living' (ADL) concept formulated by Roper (1976) and later developed further by Roper, Logan and Tierney (1980). This 'model for nursing' is, so far, the most significant model generated in Britain and has since gained wide acceptance.

Roper identified twelve activities of living that are related to either biological or social and cultural human needs. These are (a) maintaining a safe environment; (b) communicating; (c) breathing; (d) eating and drinking; (e) eliminating; (f) personal cleansing and dressing; (g) controlling body temperature; (h) mobilising; (i) working and playing; (j) expressing sexuality; (k) sleeping and (l) dying. The activities are not independent, but rely to a varying degree on one or more of the others. The degree of importance, and level of ability to perform each ADL, either adequately or skilfully, will vary from one individual to another. For example, a patient with AN will need greater assistance with the 'eating and drinking' activity than a person with a fractured femur, whose main priority may be 'mobilising'. The patient's ability to carry out the twelve ADLs is expressed as the degree of independence or dependence present. An important part of this model of living is assessing where the patient lies on the continuum between independence and dependence for each of the activities. An anorexic could be regarded as being towards the dependent end of the continuum for eating and drinking, but towards the independent end for mobility. For the patient with a fractured femur, the opposite is more likely to be the case.

The model of living describes different components of nursing assistance or intervention. These are dependent on the patient's ability to carry out the twelve ADLs and the 'activities of living' component includes all nursing carried out in relation to the patient's activities of living. It would attempt to preserve, as far as possible, all the patient's usual habits and routines, unless they were contributing to the patient's illness, which they may well be doing in the case of eating disorders. In this case, nursing intervention would be aimed at attempting to modify the patient's attitudes and habits. The prevention component of nursing is concerned with preventing illness and potential health problems from occurring. The comforting component of nursing is concerned with attempting to achieve physical comfort and to enhance the patient's ability to cope with their situation. This is perhaps the aspect most relevant to the care of the patient with eating disorders. Finally, the dependent component of nursing describes the nurse's role in helping the patient adhere to any treatment regimes that may have been prescribed, either by nurses or by other health-care professionals.

As this chapter is primarily concerned with the role of the nurse in caring for patients with eating disorders, the model of nursing has only been described briefly. For those readers interested in finding out more about the model, perhaps wishing to implement it on their own ward or area of work, it is suggested that they read Roper *et al.* (1980).

The following paragraphs will cover each ADL, mentioning the problems that a nurse may encounter when looking after patients with AN. Whilst attempting to mention most of the major problems/needs that may be encountered, it should be noted that no two patients are alike, and very few are likely to express all the problems, behaviours and habits that are going to be described. It is also not possible to mention all the problems that may be encountered and is therefore not fully comprehensive. These paragraphs should therefore not be treated as a standard care plan, which deviates from the philosophy of individualised care, but as a list of potential problems, all of which a nurse is likely to encounter only after spending a considerable length of time caring for a number of different anorexic patients.

Activities of living may best be used in conjunction with an individual assessment that could be based on the model of nursing, but specifically adapted for eating disorders. Obtaining a detailed eating/dietary history should be seen as paramount. Despite commonalities, individuals differ extensively in their eating patterns and associated emotions, behaviours, thoughts and relationships. In addition, by gaining an understanding and acknowledging the idiosyncracies of an individual's difficulties, the foundations of a therapeutic relationship will be laid.

A good individual assessment will need to cover all aspects of the individual's difficulties, i.e. physical, psychosocial and environmental, but it is important that a global assessment does not negate a personal and functional approach. Although it is likely that assessments will be carried out by most of the health-care professionals involved in the care of an individual, the nurse is in a unique and prime position to facilitate an understanding of personal and psychological difficulties and to observe, monitor and report the changes in performance and behaviour of an individual. Several empirically tested aides to assessment have been developed that may assist in this task removing, as far as possible, subjective bias (see Chapter 3). Such assessments may be used to obtain a standard 'scale', with which progress or otherwise may be monitored. They could also be used as the basis for a structured interview situation. Assessment and monitoring of food and drink intake and weight is also of great importance and is best attempted in a discrete (but not secretive) manner, using more traditional methods such as keeping weight and fluid-balance charts.

Even though no two patients are alike, there are several commonalities that the nurse will be able to recognise in most of the patients she looks after. These have been described by Garner and Garfinkel (1982) and are as follows: (a) Difficulty in feeding and control of her body and her life, impaired recognition of internal bodily states and revulsion at physical bodily functions; (b) difficulty in autonomous functioning and in emotional separation from the family or particular individuals; (c) a sense of personal mistrust; (d) feelings of self-worth that are closely bound to external standards for appearance and performance; and (e) starvation perpetuates many of the psychological symptoms and enhances the urge to diet by increasing concerns with self-esteem and self-control.

These commonalities generate aims that are appropriate to the care and treatment of most anorexics. Emphasis on the importance of physical and psychological aspects of treatment vary with the different approaches to treatment and the requirements of an individual (see Biley and Savage, 1984), but a successful treatment plan should be based on two conditions or aims (Palmer, 1980): (a) restoration of a healthy body weight and adequate eating habits in order to maintain that weight; and (b) psychological adjustment involving a reduction of weight phobia and adaptation of methods of coping with emotional conflicts. Commonly, the means to achieve these aims are as follows (Garner and Garfinkel, 1982): (a) If the person is to benefit from psychotherapy, then the effects of starvation must be reversed; (b) even though most of her behaviour may appear to be stubbornly defiant or mistrusting, the patient must always be dealt with openly and honestly with particular attention to her disordered self-esteem; (c) psychotherapies must be directed at the specific predisposing factors operating within an individual to prevent occurrences and to minimise sequelae; and (d) for facilitating the aforementioned, a relationship type of therapy with a slowly evolving sense of trust is a useful context.

Activities of daily living related to the patient with disordered eating

The activities of living are presented as brief statements of actual or potential problems/needs that might be found either on the initial assessment or on assessment at a later date. Problems/needs will vary from one individual to another, and at differing stages of treatment. Brevity has necessitated the need to combine all of these problems into one list. Possible interventions have also been given, which reflect an appropriate treatment or style of care for the particular problems. Again, in the interests of brevity, they have been confined to perhaps too-global statements. However, the list should have importance in supplying broad guidelines for care.

Maintaining a safe environment. Hospital admission may be necessary to prevent suicide, family crisis intervention, restrict availability of food and alcohol if binging, structure daily living, provide a non-threatening environment and restrict access to kitchen, toilets and bathroom. Nursing intervention also enables the assessment of psychological functioning, weight, signs and symptoms, TPR (temperature, pulse, respiration) and BP (blood pressure), and family and peer interaction.

Communication. Problems in this area may include difficulties in communicating, and being distrustful of nursing staff and other team members. Intervention would include: establishing a therapeutic relationship based on warmth, empathy and trust (see Chapter 13); promoting an environment in which the patient can talk openly; and also, including items concerning communication (e.g. social-skills training).

Breathing. Nursing problems include electrolyte imbalance, inhalation of vomit and a potential risk of choking. Intervention includes being aware of and observing physical signs of electrolyte imbalance, unobtrusive observation of vomiting or choking during and after mealtimes and teaching and encouraging the use of breathing exercises (relaxation).

Eating and drinking. Nursing problems include undernourishment, emaciation, alcohol abuse, binging and social problems such as difficulty with eating in company, coping with aversive comments and traumatic family meals. Behavioural problems include those behaviours that function in order to avoid weight gain or in order to lose weight, such as avoidance of carbohydrate intake, self-induced vomiting, laxative abuse and self-imposed fluid restriction. Cognitive problems include dysfunctional beliefs regarding the food, eating and weight-gain relationship (e.g. metabolism), irrational thoughts regarding body size and shape, distortion of body image and negative mood states associated with eating and feeling fat.

Involved in intervention are dietary education, a slow introduction of 'normal' (mutually arranged but reasonable) diet, initial dietary supplements if required by low weight, the formulation of a 'contract', cognitive-behaviour therapy to modify thought patterns (see Chapter 8), a slow introduction to social eating with family, etc. and observation for food disposal, water-loading, binging and manipulation. A section highlighting the problems of manipulation is included later.

Eliminating. Nursing problems include abnormal bowel patterns, amenorrhea and the commencement or recommencement of menstruation. Intervention involves observation for constipation (following the stopping of laxative abuse), loose stools (may indicate continued laxative abuse or constipation), measuring urine (concentration may reveal dehydration) and menstruation. Support and guidance will be needed during the onset or recommencement of menstruation, as this may be a traumatic time for the patient.

Cleansing and dressing. Nursing problems centre around the patient's obsessive–compulsive, self-cleaning behaviour. Intervention involves the observation of frequency, and a behavioural-treatment programme in conjunction with the clinical psychologist.

Body temperature. Control of this may be poor due to circulatory defects, and lack of subcutaneous tissue and body fat. Basic intervention entails a warm environment and adequate but light bedclothes.

Mobilising. Nursing problems include overexercising, especially following a period of bedrest. Intervention may be a mutually agreed exercise programme, which discourages excessive exercise.

Working and playing. Nursing problems include social isolation, boredom and rumination, obsessive–compulsive studying, and obsessive competitiveness and a desire to be successful and liked. Interventions will include vocational guidance, a relaxed ward atmosphere, diversional therapy, an agreed or contracted study programme, cognitive therapy, concentrating on the subject of competitiveness and encouraging engagement in less-favoured tasks.

Expressing sexuality. Problems include avoidance of menstruation (which may have caused the initial abnormal dietary behaviour), lack of sexual knowledge and changing body shape and image. Intervention will involve sex education at a level indicated by the individual's specific needs and support during menstruation and whilst body image/shape changes.

Sleeping. Problems include altered or poor sleeping patterns and tiredness (potential avoidance behaviour) following meals. Interventions will cover the observation of sleeping patterns, administration of prescribed hypnotics, mental and physical activities during the day, which will help the patient sleep soundly at the correct time, and teaching alternative coping strategies to sleeping following meals.

Dying. Problems here include the need to acknowledge and accept the serious life-threatening nature of the disorder/behaviour, support for relatives and helping the patient towards peaceful death (if appropriate). Interventions would include educating the patient regarding the seriousness of the disorder, counselling patients (and relatives of those) who are about to die, and the breaking of the mutually arranged therapeutic contract in order to allow life-saving medical interventions.

It has now become obvious from this list of ADLs (covering only the main aspects of care and by no means being totally comprehensive) that the nurse caring for patients with eating disorders is in a challenging position. At first, she will not be trusted by the patient. Later on, as the therapeutic relationship develops, the patient will come to depend on the nurse to such a degree that this also becomes challenging and even threatening. As many nurses are young and female, although this may be something of an advantage to the anorexic as they should be able to show empathy, they may find themselves identifying closely with the plight of the anorexic and may be at risk of developing similar thought patterns and eating behaviour. This is to be avoided at all costs. For this reason, it is necessary to supply support and guidance, perhaps in the form of regular meetings, where members can openly discuss their fears and thoughts in strict confidentiality.

It is not generally considered necessary, and sometimes may even be detrimental, for sufferers to be admitted to hospital, usually for some kind of crisis intervention following the failure of treatment as an outpatient or late recognition of the disorder in an individual. Hospitalisation can therefore be regarded as having a life-saving value (Bruch, 1973). Garner and Garfinkel (1982) state that hospital admission should be considered for the following reasons: (a) When weight loss is considerable. Exactly how much depends on several variables, although if more than twenty-five per cent of previous weight, the anorexic will find it difficult to gain weight by herself. If more than forty per cent, emergency action is indicated (Mayer, 1963). (b) To break cycles of starvation and binging–vomiting in normal weight individuals; and (c) for diagnostic investigations, treating complications, short-term crises, confronting denial, and initiation of therapies.

Patients' needs not specific to anorexia nervosa

When hospital admission occurs because of extremely low weight, this causes severe additional nursing problems/patient's needs that have not been included in the previous list of ADLs. This is because these problems are not specific to AN, and the solutions/nursing care can be found in general nursing textbooks (e.g. Brunner and Suddarth, 1980). However, because of their importance, a chapter on the role of the nurse in caring for AN would not be complete without briefly mentioning them. They are as follows.

Extreme emaciation. This may lead to the development of decubitus ulcers whilst on bed-rest. Bed-rest is often prescribed during the early stages of treatment and may continue for as long as two or three months in order to facilitate weight gain. In addition, other complications of bed-rest such as infections of the urinary tract, muscle wasting and boredom may occur. Because of these risks, and in order to minimise their occurrence, it is preferable for patients to be on modified bed-rest, where they are encouraged to get out of bed regularly for short periods of time, e.g. to go to the toilet. If the patient's condition does not allow this, then all the usual nursing care such as two-hourly turning in bed, passive muscle exercises, light bed clothes and the use of certain aids such as bed cradles, sheepskins, etc. should be initiated in order to minimise these risks.

Refeeding. An intensive refeeding programme may be needed when indicated by poor physical condition due to extreme emaciation. It is not uncommon for anorexics to lose so much weight that they find themselves in a life-threatening position. When this occurs, it is necessary to implement a programme of increased carbohydrate intake, often in greater amounts than can be taken orally, even when the patient is willing or physically able to eat. This means that either nasogastric-tube feeding or parenteral hyperalimentation will be indicated. It should be noted, however, that this form of treatment should only be prescribed by a physician or psychiatrist as a last resort, but may be necessary as weight restoration must occur before psychotherapy can become effective (Crisp, 1980). It should be avoided if possible, because of the following reasons: (a) it is a direct intrusion into the gastrointestinal tract; (b) it may be seen as an assault or act of hostility; (c) increased mistrust may follow minimal co-operation; (d) there may be significant (negative) psychological effects; and (e) 'It is almost always unnecessary' (Garfinkel and Garner, 1982). In addition to the negative psychological effects that this treatment may cause, it may also cause the physical dangers present with any patient on such a regime. Incorrect techniques when introducing a nasogastric tube may result in the introduction of foodstuffs into the respiratory tract, obviously with devastating effects. Fluid and electrolyte imbalance could occur if the dietary regime is not followed closely and accurately. Strict asepsis with all aspects of hyperalimentation, particularly with the anorexic, is called for. Significant changes in blood composition, with leukopenia leading to an increased risk of septicemia, and neutropenia, which can increase the probability of bacterial infection (Rieger, 1978), must also be avoided.

Once treatment has reversed critical weight loss, emphasis changes to the psychological side of care. Within the heading 'working and playing', the patient may have unrealistic perfectionist aims and tendencies. A desire to be 'first rate' is almost always met by failure, as targets are not fixed and are moved to higher standards as previously set goals are reached.

MANIPULATION

As well as the aforementioned areas that might cause great problems, there is a final series of situations that the nurse will find herself facing, which will present the greatest challenge. Most, if not all, anorexics will take opportunities to manipulate the whole variety of situations in which they find themselves. This may be in order to maintain a low calorific intake, dispose of unwanted food (either uneaten, ingested or digested), or, if a power struggle has developed, to manipulate a situation just in order to win and maintain power over whoever is concerned, i.e. the carer or relative. Manipulation should not be seen as a defiance, but as a manifestation of an extreme fear of becoming 'fat'.

In order to minimise feelings of the need to manipulate others, it is important for the nurse to be able to facilitate high levels of communication based on a relationship founded on warmth, empathy and trust. This has already been stated but cannot really be stressed enough. The formation of a contract, whether it be formal (written) or informal (verbal), thereby establishing mutually agreed aims, objectives and means of treatment early on will help to establish the boundaries and limitations of the therapeutic relationship and patient/staff behaviour. An explicit detailed contract, outlining the expectations of both the patient and carer, can ease communication by avoiding the tendency to debate and negotiate, for example, over food quantities or access to exercise. If the contract is rigidly adhered to by staff (the only alterations occurring after consultation with the patient and other relevant health-care professionals), distrust of staff should diminish and the patient will feel increasingly safe.

Despite this, the anorexic might still feel the need to manipulate a certain situation, for instance, ways of disposing of food, and they will always find an opportunity to do this. More commonly found situations are outlined in the next part of the chapter (Biley and Savage, 1984). However, the nurse should always be aware of the possibility that they or their colleagues are being manipulated (even when a sound, open relationship with free channels of communication exists). If they do suspect some kind of manipulation, then it is always best to approach the patient at as convenient a time as possible after the event, preferably in a manner as least threatening as possible. It should be noted that manipulation, when it occurs, is a symptom of the disorder. The patient is often confused and ashamed of their behaviour, even to the point of experiencing extreme self-disgust if self-induced vomiting or laxative abuse has become regular and has been kept secret. The nurse must reassure the patient that she understands the problem and is not shocked by the behaviour. It may be useful to explain that the patient is not alone and that others experience similar problems. A non-judgemental, empathic relationship will help the patient to be open and honest about her current problems and avoidance behaviours. Difficulties in communication will arise if the patient is openly challenged, if she fears that she will be punished or accused of manipulation. She will then attempt to return to her previous secrecy and further devious methods of food disposal.

Commonly encountered manipulation

1. Disposal of food into wastepaper bins, handkerchiefs or out of the windows.
2. Self-induced vomiting into toilets, washbasins, tissues or clothing. The patient may attempt to justify this by citing physical illness.
3. Patients may obtain laxatives from visitors or other patients, or attempt to conceal them on admission.
4. Binging may occur in patients as a means of rapid weight gain in order to accelerate a potential discharge date. Visitors, who may interpret the wish to eat as a healthy sign, should be discouraged from bringing food into the hospital unless this is part of the carefully controlled contract. Binging may be indicated by the patient sweating excessively or appearing flushed.
5. If excessive water intake is observed, this may be to facilitate vomiting, or (if prior to being weighed) as a means to manipulate perceived weight gain.
6. Wearing multiple layers of clothes, jewellery and 'weights taped to the insides of fingers' (Sanger and Cassino, 1984), books hidden around the waist under a gown (McNamara, 1982) are attempts to falsely increase body weight.

REFERENCES

Biley, F.C. and Savage, S.A. (1984) 'Anorexia nervosa.' *Nursing Times*, 1 August 227–330

Bruch, H. (1973) *Eating disorders: obesity, anorexia nervosa, and the person within.* Routledge and Kegan Paul, London

Brunner, L.S. and Suddarth, D.S. (1975) *Textbook of medical–surgical nursing.* Lippincott, New York

Chapman, C.M. (1985) *Theory of nursing: practical applications.* Harper and Row, London

Crisp, A.H. (1980) *Anorexia nervosa: let me be.* Academic Press, London

Garfinkel, P.E. and Garner, D.M. (1982) *Anorexia nervosa: a multi-dimensional perspective.* Brunner/Mazel, New York

Garner, D.M. and Garfinkel, P.E. (1979) 'The eating attitudes test: an index of the symptoms of anorexia nervosa.' *Psychological Medicine*, *9*, 273–9

—— —— (1982) 'Sociocultural factors in the development of anorexia nervosa'. *Psychological Medicine*, *10*, 647–56

Henderson, V. (1960) *Basic principles of nursing care.* International Council of Nurses, Geneva
Kratz, C. (1979) *The nursing process.* Ballière Tindall, London
McNamara, R.J. (1982) 'The challenge of treating eating disorders: the role of the nurse at the bedside. *The Canadian Nurse,* November, 34–6
Mayer, J. (1963) 'Anorexia nervosa'. *Postgraduate Medicine, 34,* 529–34
Miller, A. (1984) 'Nursing process and patient care.' *Nursing Times, 80,* occasional paper
Neuman, B.A. (1974) 'The Betty Neuman health-care systems model: a total approach to patient's problems.' In J. Riehl and C. Roy (eds), *Conceptual models for nursing practice,* Appleton-Century Crofts, New York
Palmer, R.L. (1980) *Anorexia nervosa: a guide for sufferers and their families.* Pelican, Harmondsworth
Rieger, W.L. (1978) 'Hematologic changes in anorexia nervosa.' *American Journal of Psychiatry, 135,* 984–5
Roper, N. (1976) 'A model for nursing and nursology.' *Journal of Advanced Nursing, 1,* 219–27
—— Logan, W. and Tierney, A. (1980) *The elements of nursing,* Churchill Livingstone, Edinburgh
Roy, C. (1974) 'Adaptation: a conceptual framework for nursing.' *Nursing Outlook, 18,* 42–5
Sanger, E. and Cassino, T. (1984) 'Eating disorders: avoiding the power struggle. *American Journal of Nursing,* January, 20–2

11

Occupational Therapy in the Rehabilitation of the Eating Disordered Patient

Mary Elizabeth Allen, Gordon Giles and Derek Scott

INTRODUCTION

The first part of this chapter develops a rehabilitative viewpoint for the occupational therapist (OT) in relation to the eating-disordered patient. Maximising the individual's level of psychosocial functioning is seen as the primary goal of treatment. A model for addressing the patient's needs is described, which examines environmental factors, the use of contracts and the importance of assessment and follow-up. A cognitive-behavioural approach is discussed and suggestions are made for adapting it to the therapist's practical approach. In the second part of the chapter, suggestions for therapy are discussed.

Eating disorders may be severe and potentially life-threatening, with a current mortality rate of 0 to 5 per cent (Hsu, 1980; Wooley and Wooley, 1980). Unfortunately, individuals with the disorder are invariably reluctant to seek help. As reviewed by Hsu (1980), treatment methods are varied and outcome studies have not been properly designed to assess treatment effects. Less severe cases continue to be followed by individual physicians and psychotherapists. However, in recent years, multidisciplinary teams have been developed in order to better manage the more resistant examples of these psychosomatic disorders.

Despite the prevalence of the condition, AN has received minimal attention from OTs. It is only over the last five to ten years that formal treatment programmes for eating disorders have been developed. Prior to this, the anorexic patient was either hospitalised on a medical unit and then seen individually by a psychiatrist, or treated among the general psychiatric population (Martin, 1978). In the former case, the anorexic patient was often not referred for OT at all, or at best, only referred for strengthening exercises just prior to discharge. Occasionally, referrals were made to 'give them something to do'.

When trying to develop a treatment programme on a psychiatric unit, therapists would have to treat the anorexic against a background of often seriously disturbed and psychotic patients. The needs of anorexics were typically ignored. However, with the advent of eating-disorders units (EDUs), therapists have been able to develop specialised treatment programmes to meet the complex demands of this patient population.

The multidisciplinary team approach

Most researchers advocate a multidisciplinary team approach to treatment (e.g. Andersen, Hedblom and Hubbard, 1983). Individual psychotherapy (Bruch, 1973), group treatment (Roybyrne, Leebenne and Yager, 1984), family intervention (Chng and Giles, 1984; White, 1983) and the adjunctive use of drugs (Halmi, Owen, Lasley and Stokes, 1983) are also employed. Therapists should work in close co-operation with other members of the treatment team, contributing expertise in assessment and treatment planning, as well as the practice of realistic life skills to the team. An effective treatment team requires the participation of a consultant psychiatrist, a clinical psychologist, a physician, a dietician, an OT, a social worker and skilled nursing staff. One appropriately qualified member of the treatment team should be designated as primary psychotherapist for each patient.

With the current emphasis on inpatient care, treatment of the eating-disordered patient will usually fall into two phases. Initially, the medical intervention is primary and is directed towards stabilising the patient's physical condition and helping her to work through her acute and potentially life-threatening, physiological reaction to weight gain. The second part of the treatment will involve an attempt to help the patient to stabilise her weight and to work on her problems through psychotherapy. It is in this latter stage that the OT's rehabilitative approach is most useful.

The overall treatment approach on any individual EDU or other treatment setting is likely to reflect prevailing theories of causation. Current treatment approaches include the medical (Russell, 1977), psychoanalytic (Sours, 1969), family therapy (Minuchin, Rosman and Baker, 1978), behavioural (Agras and Werne, 1977) and more recently, the cognitive-behavioural approaches (Garner and Bemis, 1982). These approaches have been more fully described elsewhere (Giles, 1985). The type of treatment approach will also affect the likelihood, length and quality of hospitalisation. Most patients will, however, receive inpatient/hospital treatment at one time or another, and most will receive some form of therapy.

In our view, the potential role of the OT is underestimated by other professionals and indeed, by themselves. Such workers are trained in rehabilitation, with particular attention to aspects of functional ability. With this population, as with any other, the aim of these therapists is to help the patient achieve the highest attainable level of psychological, physical and social competence.

REHABILITATIVE AND ENVIRONMENTAL MODELS

Treatment planning

The first step in the course of treatment can be summarised as 'manipulating the environment'. The therapist creates an environment that is conducive to learning and change. The next step in treatment is *assessment.* All relevant factors need to be included if an assessment is to be effective. Biological, social and psychological factors must all be considered. The purpose of assessment is to identify the problems in order to determine an effective strategy. Kanfer and Saslow (1964) recommend viewing behaviour in terms of (a) behavioural excesses; (b) behavioural deficits; and (c) behavioural assets. It is important, therefore, for the therapist to examine strengths as well as deficits because the former can often be used to overcome the latter.

Once assessment is completed and the areas of deficit are isolated, *performance* can be practised. Learning can be seen to have taken place through a decreasing variability in performance and an increasing smoothness and accuracy in execution. Once performance is adequate, one can *integrate* this change into the patient's everyday activities. Follow-ups should be initially frequent, and then gradually curtailed, although the patient should understand that the therapist is ready to assist should problems arise.

The anorexic and bulimic roles

Any individual's life can be conceptualised in terms of the roles that they play. The roles that the anorexic or bulimic have assumed, for whatever reason, are severely limiting, particularly with respect to opportunities for self-development. Although in the *short term*, anorexic or bulimic behaviour may help the individual to cope with life, in the *long term*, these coping mechanisms are self-destructive, both physically and psychologically (Slade, 1982; Donohoe, 1984). However, because the dieting behaviour has been powerfully reinforced by both internal (biological and cognitive self-reward) and external (social) factors, it may be necessary to establish some form of positive reinforcement other than dieting.

Therapists can help the patient develop new and more adaptive roles. They can give the patient the opportunity for accepting increased responsibility for their behaviour and help them cope without the roles of sickness and dependency. Occupational therapy can provide patients with a more realistic environment than that of the relatively insulated life on the ward, where the attention of nursing staff will frequently be directed towards bodily functions. Disruptive behaviour on the ward is often not continued in therapy areas.

The therapist's approach to the eating-disordered patient can be 'activity oriented' (Giles and Chng, 1984). The patient is never a passive recipient of treatment as she may be initially on the ward. So, for example, if a patient shows extreme anxiety over eating and weight gain, rather than placing the patient under pressure to conform, a problem-solving approach may be preferable. The patient is encouraged to use coping techniques to reduce anxiety, with such activities as yoga, relaxation, or preferred diversional activities or to examine her own inappropriate thoughts and catastrophic expectations (see section on therapeutic activities).

Creating the environment

Occupational therapy considers one of its main tools to be the 'therapeutic use of self'. It is through the patient–therapist relationship that the patient's development will be fostered. Thus, a main concern of the therapist is to establish a good rapport with the patient. As their relationship develops, the therapist must be constantly aware of the effect her behaviour has on the patient. This does not mean that they are constantly trying to ensnare the patient into 'mini-psychotherapy' sessions. Certain types of interventions, particularly with manipulative patients, can disrupt individual psychotherapy.

The therapists not only gear their response to the changing needs of the patient and the treatment goals, but also help the patient to test reality. In addition, they serve as a good role model for healthy interpersonal dealings. Furthermore, they address the problem of independence of the family from the perspective of independence in daily living skills. As the patient experiences competence in these daily living tasks, she then feels more prepared to assume emotional independence. The therapist can encourage younger patients to do their own washing, cooking and self-care activities, whilst actively discouraging family overinvolvement.

Establishing a contract

Owing to the nature of eating disorders, most patients have a limited degree of insight into their problems. Many patients also have difficulty in talking about themselves and their own feelings, especially those feelings that are not socially acceptable (Bruch, 1973). The negotiation of a contract is often a great help in establishing a basis for treatment and in helping the patient to keep constantly in mind her own individual aims (Giles and Chng, 1984). Individual contracts might include those such as 'I want to be more assertive with others', or 'I want to be able to express my feelings more'. Other contracts might include aspects more specifically concerned with eating behaviour such as 'I want to feel comfortable eating with others'. It should be remembered, however, that the more general the wording of the contract, the less likely it is to provoke any behavioural change. To be effective, the contract should be *specific* to the needs of the patient. The contract makes clear that the patient herself is responsible for change and that her success will often depend upon her degree of motivation. A contract also reminds the therapist of the importance of an initial and continuing assessment.

In the early stages of treatment, the patient will vacillate between accepting her problems and denying them. At one moment, she may claim that she is not ill and does not have an eating problem, and at another moment that, if only her eating problem could be sorted out, everything would be fine. It is essential that the patient be encouraged to take responsibility for her own progress. By the use of a contract and problem-solving approach, many activities can be rendered relevant to the patient's individual aims of self-development and change.

A final aspect to the discussion of contracts is that of setbacks. A transient, though often severe, exacerbation of symptoms is not an infrequent feature of therapy. Lapses or setbacks can, however, if used correctly, be of great benefit in highlighting awareness of specific problem areas; the therapist should alert the patient to the possibility of fluctuations in symptoms and encourage her to use such changes to further her progress. The issue of 'relapse' and coping strategies will be discussed later.

THE COGNITIVE-BEHAVIOURAL APPROACH

The tendency to choose either a psychotherapeutic or a behavioural approach leads to a failure to recognise the link between cognitive and behavioural factors. Those approaches that exclusively address *either* cognition *or* behaviour are likely to prove ineffective as a result. For instance, certain authorities regard some form of psychotherapy as an essential part of treatment (e.g. Garner and Bemis, 1982; Palmer, 1982). However, a psychodynamic approach used in isolation from other intervention strategies may not enable the patient to overcome all her practical difficulties. It is one thing for the patient to gain insight into her eating pattern through psychotherapy, and quite another for her to behave appropriately when faced with the task of preparing food for herself and others. The cognitive-behavioural approach will now be examined to see what use this may have to the OT (see also Chapter 8).

Cognitive therapy emphasises the role of negative cognitive distortion in many forms of mental disorder. Although it was originally designed by Beck and his co-workers (e.g. Beck, 1976) for use with depressive, neurotic and obsessive–compulsive subjects, many now consider cognitive therapy appropriate in the treatment of AN and bulimia (Garner and Bemis, 1982; Fairburn, 1983). Faulty construction of reality is considered to have a detrimental effect on the individual's behaviour and emotions. Although the patient's behaviour appears illogical, it may be quite logically based on certain fundamental premisses and beliefs about thinness and weight loss. The main form of therapy is, therefore, the examination of the patient's thoughts and ideas about herself in relation to food and eating. Within cognitive therapy, certain techniques are used to identify, test and correct distorted conceptualisations. These techniques include 'prospective hypothesis-testing', 'what if' techniques, and decentering. These are described more fully elsewhere (Garner and Bemis, 1982; Garner and Garfinkel, 1982; Fairburn, 1983). The individual is taught to monitor him/herself for negative automatic thoughts and to recognise the connection between cognition and behaviour. The patient is encouraged to examine evidence for and against 'automatic thoughts' e.g. 'this food is bad and instantly converted to fat', and can be taught to identify and replace beliefs that lead to inappropriate behaviour.

Scott (1983) has recently described some commonalities between food and alcohol abuse and called for a cross-fertilisation of ideas for treatment. For instance, adaptive strategies from Marlatt's (1978) 'abstinence violation effect' may be usefully applied to binge eating. From his cognitive-behavioural analysis, Marlatt concludes that the most important determinants of relapse are environmental/situational factors and the individual's reactions to them. Marlatt has suggested a common denominator across different consummatory disorders, the 'abstinence violation effect'. This consists of two cognitive components; a cognitive dissonance effect and a personal attribution effect. According to the former, the first drink (or 'forbidden' food) following a period of abstinence arouses conflict or guilt that is reduced by subsequent drinking (binging) and the realignment of self-image with renewed binging. In terms of the latter, a return to drinking (binging) is attributed to personal failings. This sense of personal inability to control subsequent intake lowers resistance to additional temptation. Suggestions are given for overcoming this 'all is lost' phenomenon.

Despite the many advantages of a cognitive-behavioural approach, practical activity has been inadequately stressed. Particular negative thoughts will arise and be dealt with more spontaneously in the relevant situations, e.g. helping a patient work through her inappropriate thoughts about cooking and eating a meal would be most effectively done while cooking and eating (although see Chapter 14 for a different view). Once the area of difficulty is isolated, the patient must practise alternative ways of behaving. When this link has been made, cognitive therapy becomes well suited to the functional problem-solving skills of a practical therapist.

THERAPEUTIC ACTIVITIES

No activity is, in itself, therapeutic for the eating-disordered patient. For an activity to become therapeutic, it is important that both the therapist and the patient be committed to designing activities that will help the patient to change. In order to do this, the patient and therapist should try to establish concrete goals for each session. Before the patient can decide about how she wants to change, she needs first to find out about herself as she currently is. This idea of self-discovery may also be set up in the form of a contract.

The activities used by the therapist can be classified under two headings. Under the first can be grouped those activities where the emphasis is clearly on the practice of skills for independent living or the overcoming of physical deficits. Here, examples might include cooking and shopping for clothes. These activities can also be used to help the patient produce adaptive behavioural and cognitive change. Under the second heading are grouped those activities that are not directly relevant to the individual's normal life outside the treatment setting, but are used because of their ability to provoke adaptive changes in the way the patient interacts with and thinks about her environment and herself. Examples of this second type of activity are movement and expressive art groups. A description of various therapeutic activities that can be used in the treatment of the anorexic patient are as follows.

Functional approaches

Cooking assessment and practice. Central to the patient's problems are her inappropriate behaviour around food and her reluctance to eat. The patient's preoccupation with calorie content often hinders her from being able to produce a well-balanced, 'ordinary' meal. Therapists need to de-emphasise caloric intake and help establish normal eating patterns.

In the later stages of treatment, when the patient may be shopping for herself, the therapist should determine whether the patient is able to: prepare a shopping list, estimate quantities of food to be purchased, cook what is generally regarded as a nutritionally balanced meal and dispose of unused food and waste correctly (i.e. without binging). Therapists should be present during the shopping, cooking, and eating of the meal to provide moral support and prompt the use of coping techniques to resolve conflicts precipitated by the cooking practice. From a cognitive standpoint, the opportunity of cooking practice can be used to examine faulty information-processing and thinking 'styles'.

Holmgrens *et al.* (1984) describe a programme run by the OTs at Uppsala University Hospital in Sweden. Initially, the patient prepares her own meals, starting with exact amounts of basic ingredients. Next, she is expected to plan her meal, shop and cook for herself. Later, she will be expected to cook for a group and to help herself to food without calculating the exact amount. Previously, 'forbidden' foods, the consumption of which in the past would have inevitably led to a binge, are also included in this later phase. Snack foods eaten with coffee in the cafeteria are also included in the programme. This is done to make the subsequent eating of such foods less 'catastrophic' (Scott, 1985) for the patient and less likely to lead to a binge.

For the eating-disordered individual, food may have become associated with anxiety. Visiting restaurants may be a particularly important activity. Research into the eating behaviour of normal subjects has consistently shown there to be a facilitatory effect on eating by groups, particularly mixed-gender groups (Klesges *et al.*, 1984). The patient should be encouraged to eat out frequently; initially this should be with the therapist, but later with family and friends.

Clothes shopping. The trying on of new clothes for the first time after weight gain may be traumatic for the patient. If the therapist accompanies the patient on her first trip to buy clothes, this is an opportunity for examining how the patient tries to select clothing, and for observing any signs of panic over her new size. As this may be the first trip out of the hospital for some time, the patient will have to deal with presenting a new 'fat' self in public. The patient will often feel that people are watching her and the therapist can be on hand to help the patient examine the validity of these thoughts.

Teaching behavioural strategies. Even when the teaching of behavioural strategies is undertaken by a psychologist, other therapists should be aware of and facilitate the use of these strategies in the patient's daily life. Examples of possible strategies for use with bulimics are 'Don't eat or drink except in the company of others', 'only eat set meals', and 'decide what is to be eaten before beginning to eat'. The most useful forms of coping strategies that can be taught appear to be those that either directly or indirectly reduce the availability of food. In addition, engaging in behaviour incompatible with binging may also be useful, particularly at difficult times of the day such as in the evening. Other useful strategies include: (a) encouraging the patient to keep a food diary; (b) encouraging the patient to write a daily record of 'intrusive' thoughts; and (c) teaching the patient stress-management techniques.

Therapists may also make a domiciliary visit in order to help patients work out a particular problem, e.g. storing food or cooking meals. The learning of coping strategies in the patient's own home has obvious advantages for generalisation.

Social skills. There are a number of indications for the use of social-skills training (SST) or assertiveness training (AT) with this population. One of the most consistent findings of follow-up studies on AN are the social anxiety and isolation experienced by patients (Schwartz and Thompson, 1981). However, despite the apparent theoretical justification for SST with these patients, little research has actually been done into its efficacy. Most reports are limited to the single-case study design which, though valid in itself, cannot substitute for controlled trials (Lang, 1965; Argyle, Trower and Bryant, 1974). In one of the few controlled trials known in this area, Pillay and Crisp (1981) looked into the impact of SST on an established, inpatient, AN treatment programme. Unfortunately, this study is so beset by methodological problems that it is impossible to draw any firm conclusions from it. We believe that SST and AT are justified on theoretical and practical grounds, though empirical validation is clearly needed.

Many individuals who suffer from AN and bulimia appear socially adept. However, closer examination invariably reveals that these patients are not fulfilling their needs in social relationships (Eason, 1984). The improvement of social skills is an aim of many therapy groups. Nevertheless, it is useful to have a group specifically designed to deal with more problematic areas of social functioning, such as going to a party or being asked out by the opposite sex (Martin, 1978). The goals of the social-skills group include the expression of clear, congruent messages and the examination of thinking. Techniques of assertion, self-awareness, clarification of values and role-playing are used. Video equipment is often useful in this setting.

Relaxation. The possible advantages of relaxation-training are numerous. Various relaxation techniques can be used and patients can select the one they find to be most effective. Relaxation techniques include deep breathing, visualisation and contract–relax methods (Jacobson, 1938; Shultz and Luthe, 1969). The most important benefits that might be derived from relaxation-training by eating-disordered patients are briefly summarised as follows: (a) reducing anxiety levels; (b) increasing competency in dealing with stress; (c) avoiding unwanted behaviours that appear to depend (at least in part) on stress, e.g. binging; (d) increasing self-esteem as a result of increased control over stress reactions; and (e) improved interpersonal relationships.

Many patients are hyperactive and unable to relax. Generally, they seem to have difficulty in understanding and responding to the messages they receive from their bodies (Bruch, 1973). Biofeedback can be used to help the patient become more aware of her body and develop an awareness of internal stimuli. Patients may be under considerable stress and are often in an almost perpetual state of overarousal. Biofeedback helps the patient gain healthy control by providing precise and easily understandable information about bodily functioning (McKee and Kiffer, 1982). Some patients may object to becoming relaxed because of a fear of losing control. The therapist must be prepared to discuss this and deal with issues that arise for the patient when relaxed. As patients are often at their most anxious before and after meals, it may be appropriate to schedule relaxation sessions at these times.

Exercise. Exercise sessions are helpful in teaching patients how to moderate their level of activity, as well as providing an opportunity for toning, strengthening and cardiac reconditioning. The therapist can assist the patient in noting bodily changes and sensations that signal sufficient exercise (Holmgrens *et al.*, 1984). The therapist also helps the patient examine her normal daily routines in relation to an exercise programme. The more exercise the patient's general activities involve, the less she will need to engage in additional exercises of any sort. The patient can also practise adjusting her food intake to maintain a constant weight. As the anorexic is typically hospitalised in a depleted and tense state, her general endurance and overall strength may be low. Cardiac performance should be monitored at all times. This is especially important for patients with metabolic abnormalities, particularly those with hypokalaemia associated with chronic vomiting, as they are known to be prone to severe arrhythmias, including ventricular fibrillation.

Body-image distortion. From the recent research on body-image distortion (e.g. Freeman, Thomas, Solyom and Miles, 1983), at least three avenues are available to the therapist. The first is to continue to present the patient with information on her actual body size by, for example, the use of video equipment, in order to help generate a more realistic appraisal of body size. The second strategy is to concentrate on examining the subjective meaning of body size for the patient. Gottheil, Backup and Cornelison (1969) reported successful treatment of an anorexic's denial of thinness by repeatedly confronting her with motion pictures of her emaciated body. Many therapists, however, prefer to approach the problem indirectly (Lucas, Duncan and Piens, 1976). Garner and Bemis (1982) and Garner and Garfinkel (1982), among others, suggest that rather than attempting to alter misperceptions directly, the therapist should help the patient change how she interprets them. The patient may, for example, be taught that they are manifestations of illness and that they should be ignored in favour of other more objective criteria, such as the opinion of a trusted friend.

Expressive techniques

The following brief discussion of creative and expressive techniques is selective. The exclusion of such approaches as music, dance, and drama therapy is not intended as a comment on their value, although the appropriateness of different techniques will vary between treatment settings.

Art therapy. When using art as an expressive media, the quality of the artwork is much less important than the act of production, and the way the art helps the patient see herself and her ideas in concrete form. Art can be used in a number of different ways, from the encouragement of emotional expression to being used as a more structured expressive medium. For example, a therapist may employ hand and finger painting, and colour collages early in treatment in order to help the patient express moods and emotions. Later, more threatening material may be dealt with by the therapist suggesting such titles as 'How I feel at target weight' or 'How I see my family', in order to tap more complex ideas and feelings (Martin, 1978).

Creative movement. The goals of a creative-movement group are to help the eating-disordered patient increase self-awareness through movement, and to identify and express feelings (Garner and Bemis, 1982; Garner and Garfinkel, 1982). Many psychotherapeutic approaches have stressed the integration of mind and body. Patients may be thought of as repressing feelings by muscular tensions. These psychological repressions may restrict personal growth and development. In many ways, a person's sense of self is perceived through their body. Patients are encouraged to use their bodies as a means of self-expression. Many patients report hating their bodies and are disgusted by them. This sort of group focuses on trying to help the patient feel good about their body by experiencing it. Creative movement helps the patient develop a simultaneous awareness of self and environment. It has also been proposed that movement helps the individual to integrate various aspects of the self including various levels of awareness, memory, sensations, and emotions (Morgan, Purgold and Welbourne, 1983; Van Deussen and Allen, 1985).

OUTCOME

Only one recent outcome study has included a discussion of practical therapies such as OT in any depth (Holmgrens *et al.*, 1984). Although the results of this study were encouraging, it is not possible to assess the effect of practical therapy because of the many treatment approaches used. We can currently base our intervention strategies only on evidence that seems suggestive of good outcome from other sources, and on the generalisation of approaches that have been used effectively elsewhere. Current research is needed in this area and, indeed, many of the areas previously referred to.

CONCLUSION

This chapter has presented a model for the treatment of AN and bulimia. Special attention has been paid to the importance of continuing assessment involving the participation of both the therapist and the patient. The OT needs to gain a rapport with the patient and by manipulating the patient's environment, can invite the anorexic to assume new and more adaptive roles. We have discussed how contracts can be used to help the patient establish, and be constantly aware of, her own treatment goals. Such an approach helps her both to maintain her commitment and to assume responsibility for her own behaviour and progress.

REFERENCES

Agras, S. and Werne, J. (1977) 'Behavior modification in anorexia nervosa: research foundations.' In R.A. Vigersky (ed), *Anorexia nervosa*, Raven Press, New York

Andersen, A.E., Hedblom, J.E. and Hubbard, F.A. (1983) 'A multidisciplinary team-treatment for patients with anorexia nervosa and their families.' *International Journal of Eating Disorders, 2,* 181–92

Argyle, M., Trower, P.E., and Bryant, B.M. (1974) 'Explorations in the treatment of neurosis and personality disorders by social skills training.' *British Journal of Medical Psychology, 47,* 63–72

Beck, A.T. (1976) *Cognitive therapy and the emotional disorders by social skills training.* International Universities Press, New York

Bruch, H. (1973) *Eating disorders: obesity, anorexia nervosa, and the person within.* Basic Books, New York

Chng, C.L. and Giles, G.M. (1984) 'Anorexia nervosa and the family: etiology and treatment.' *Family Perspective, 18,* 3–10.

Donohoe, T.P. (1984) 'Stress-induced anorexia: implications for anorexia nervosa.' *Life Sciences, 34,* 201–18

Eason, B.J. (1984) 'Social competence and problem-solving abilities in anorexic, bulimic, and non-eating disordered females: empirical investigation of a role-playing instrument.' *Dissertatations Abstracts International, 44 (10)*

Fairburn, C. (1983) 'The place of the cognitive behavioural approach in the management of bulimia.' In P.L. Darby, P.E. Garfinkel, D.M. Garner, and D.Y. Coscina (eds), *Anorexia nervosa: recent developments in research,* Alan Liss, New York, pp. 393–402

Freeman, R.J., Thomas, C.D., Solyom, L. and Miles, J.M. (1983) 'Body image disturbances in anorexia nervosa: a re-examination and a new technique.' In P.L. Darby, P.E. Garfinkel, D.M. Garner and D.Y. Coscina (eds) *Anorexia nervosa: recent developments in research,* Alan Liss, New York

Garner, D.M. and Bemis, K.M. (1982) 'A cognitive–behavioral approach to anorexia nervosa.' *Cognitive Therapy and Research, 6,* 123–50

—— and Garfinkel, P.E. (1982) A multidimensional psychotherapy for anorexia nervosa. *International Journal of Eating Disorders, 1,* 3–46

—— —— and Olmsted, M.P. (1983) 'An overview of sociocultural factors in the development of anorexia nervosa.' In P.L. Darby, P.E. Garfinkel, D.M. Garner and D.Y. Coscina (eds), *Anorexia nervosa: recent developments in research,* Alan Liss, New York

Giles. G.M. (1985) 'Anorexia nervosa and bulimia: an activity oriented approach.' *American Journal of Occupational Therapy, 39,* 510–17

—— and Chng, C.L. (1984) 'Occupational therapy in the treatment of anorexia nervosa: a contractual-coping approach. *British Journal of Occupational Therapy, 47,* 134–41

Gottheil, E., Backup, C.E., and Cornelison, F.S. (1969) 'Denial and self-image confrontation in a case of anorexia nervosa.' *Journal of Nervous and Mental Disease, 148,* 238–50

Halmi, K.A., Owen, W.P., Lasley, E. and Stokes, P. (1983) 'Dopaminergic regulation in anorexia nervosa.' *International Journal of Eating Disorders, 2,* 129-33

Holmgrens, S., Sohlberg, S., Berg, E., Johanson, B.M., Norring, C. and Rosmark, B. (1984) 'Phase I treatment of the chronic and previously treated anorexia bulimia patient.' *International Journal of Eating Disorders, 3,* 17–36

Hsu, L.K.G. (1980) 'Outcome of anorexia nervosa. A review of the literature (1954-1978).' *Archives of General Psychiatry, 37,* 1041–46

Jacobson, E. (1938) *Progressive Relaxation.* University of Chicago Press, Chicago

Kanfer, F.H. and Saslow, G. (1964) *Behavioral diagnosis in behavior therapy: appraisal and Status.* In C.M. Franks (ed), McGraw-Hill, New York

Klesges, R.C., Bartsch, D., Norwood, J.D., Kautzman, D. and Haugrud, S. (1984) 'The effects of selected social and environmental variables on the eating behaviors of adults in the natural environment.' *International Journal of Eating Disorders, 3,* 35–41

Lang, P.J. (1965) 'Behavior therapy with a case of anorexia.' In L.P. Ullman and L. Krasner (eds), *Case studies in behavior modification* Holt, Rinehart and Winston, New York

Lucas, A.R., Duncan, J.W. and Piens, V. (1976) 'The treatment of anorexia nervosa.' *American Journal of Psychiatry, 133,* 1034–8

Marlatt, G.A. (1978) 'Craving for alcohol, loss of control and relapse: a cognitive analysis.' In P.E. Nathan, G. Marlatt and S. Loberg (eds) *Alcoholism: new directions in behavioral research and treatment,* Plenum, New York

Martin, J.E. (1978) 'Anorexia nervosa: a disorder of weight.' *British Journal of Occupational Therapy, 41,* 304–9

McKee, M.G. and Kiffer, J.F. (1982) 'Clinical biofeedback therapy in the treatment of anorexia.' In M. Gross (ed), *Anorexia nervosa,* Callamore Press, New York

Minuchin, S., Rosman, B.L. and Baker, L. (1978) *Psychosomatic families: anorexia nervosa in context.* Harvard University Press, Cambridge, Mass

Morgan, H.G., Purgold, J. and Welbourne, J. (1983) 'Management and outcome in anorexia nervosa: a standardised prognostic study.' *British Journal of Psychology, 143,* 282–7

Palmer, R.L. (1982) 'Anorexia nervosa.' In K. Granville-Grossman (ed), *Recent advances in clinical psychiatry: vol. 4,* Churchill-Livingstone, Edinburgh

Pillay, M. and Crisp, A.H. (1981) 'The impact of social skills training within an established in-patient treatment programme for anorexia nervosa.' *British Journal of Psychiatry, 139,* 553–8

Roybyrne, P., Leebenne, K. and Yager, J. (1984) 'Group therapy for bulimia - a year's experience.' *International Journal of Eating Disorders, 3,* 97–116

Russell, G.F. (1977) 'General management of anorexia nervosa and difficulties in assessing the efficacy of treatment.' In R.A. Vigersky (ed), *Anorexia nervosa,* Raven Press, New York

Schwartz, D.M. and Thompson, M.G. (1981) 'Do anorexics get well? Current research and future needs.' *American Journal of Psychiatry, 138,* 319–23

Scott, D.W. (1983) 'Alcohol and food abuse: some comparisons.' *British Journal of Addiction, 78*, 339–49
—— (1985) 'Catastrophe theory applications in clinical psychology: a review.' *Current Psychological Research and Reviews, 4*, 69–86
Shultz, J.M. and Luthe, W. (1969) *Autogenic therapy, vol. I: autogenic methods.* Grune and Stratton, New York
Slade, P.D. (1982) 'Towards a functional analysis of anorexia nervosa and bulimia nervosa.' *British Journal of Clinical Psychology, 21*, 167–79
Sours, J. (1969) 'The anorexia nervosa syndrome: phenomenologic and psychodynamic components.' *Psychiatric Quarterly, 43*, 240–56
Van Duessen, J. and Allen, M.E. (1985) 'Is there a perceptual-motor function in anorexia? Suggestions for research by therapists.' *Physical and Occupational Therapy in Pediatrics, 5*, 200–3
White, M. (1983) 'Anorexia nervosa: a transgenerational system perspective.' *Family Processes, 2*, 255–73
Wooley, S.C. and Wooley, O.W. (1980) 'Eating disorders: obesity and anorexia.' In A. Brodsky and R. Hare-Mustin (eds), *Women and psychotherapy: an assessment of research and practice.* Guildford Press, New York

12

Dietary Factors in Eating Disorders

Carol Bowyer

INTRODUCTION

Losing weight

There is no typical profile for the dietary pattern of the eating-disordered patient. Avoidance of carbohydrate has largely been regarded as the distinctive feature of diets chosen by anorexics to lose weight. Crisp (1967) describes them as suffering from 'carbohydrate starvation' and Russell (1967) states that 'they show a studied avoidance of fattening foods and particularly of carbohydrates'. Beumont (1981), however, showed in a retrospective study of a typical 24-hour intake of 17 anorexics that their diets 'were significantly lower in energy and in all major nutrients than those of control subjects. The proportion of energy derived from protein was significantly higher, from fats significantly lower and from carbohydrates not significantly different from that of controls.'

The differences between the observations of the first two authors and those of Beumont may lie within methodology and also within the age of the study. Crisp and Russell's statements were made in the late-1960s and it may be that the differences are related to changes in nutritional recommendations. The high protein/low carbohydrate slimming diets, at one time so popular when bread and potatoes were regarded as 'fattening' foods, have been replaced by slimming diets where a high starch-intake, particularly high-fibre starch, for example, eating wholemeal bread, jacket potatoes, etc. is encouraged. Taking dietary histories in the 1980s, it does seem that foods most commonly avoided are high-energy dense foods and these are highest in fat and/or sugar, in preference to the classical avoidance of carbohydrate in the forms of starch and sugar.

Dietary fat has recently been branded the 'baddie' in nutrition, both in relation to calories and slimming as well as to heart disease. There is enormous media and commercial interest in alternative, low-fat products as advertised in womens' magazines and present in all supermarkets. It is therefore not suprising that changes made in nutritional recommendations are being reflected in the eating patterns of anorexics, and in the experience of the author, carbohydrate certainly continues to be avoided but it is in the form of sugar, rather than starch, and often in association with fat.

Foods that continue to be consumed, often in abnormally large quantities, are fruit and vegetables; low-fat-containing protein foods such as fish, chicken, cottage cheese and yogurt will be chosen and if milk is drunk, it is now likely to be skimmed. Foods will be categorised into 'good' and 'bad', 'allowed' and 'forbidden' or 'non-fattening' and 'fattening' depending on whether they are eaten or avoided. Alcohol is commonly avoided.

Rather than eliminating certain foods from their diet, some anorexics may begin by following planned calorie-controlled regimes, limiting the daily calories allowed further and further. For those who do count calories, their knowledge of calorie values of foods can be extremely extensive, certainly exceeding many a dietitian's mental list!

For those still at school, and therefore living at home with parents, there may be no obvious evidence of missing food initially as the schoolgirl opts out of eating school dinner, and throws or gives away her packed lunch. If the household is busy in the mornings, with everyone getting their own breakfast, this meal is also easily avoided, enabling her to lose weight whilst continuing to eat normally with the family in the evenings.

Vegetarianism

Eating a vegetarian diet has become increasingly popular within the general population and particularly with young people; reasons for the change being health, finance and issues of morality. Whereas at one time, vegetarians were seen as people on a 'health kick' or 'going through a phase', nowadays many establishments do offer a vegetarian choice on their menus, frequently due to pressure from the consumers. Recently, Kadambari, Gowers and Crisp (1986) reported, in a retrospective study of 180 anorexics, that 77 (45 per cent) were vegetarian. They went on to say that this group were more likely to be abstainers, hyperactive, vegans and to consume large quantities of noncalorific fluid. Most commonly, red meat is the first animal protein to be avoided.

Many teenagers become vegetarian and a girl wanting to lose weight and try to gain control over her food intake at home may announce that she is going to stop eating meat. For the mother of a meat-eating family, the arrangement may be that her daughter provides her own alternative at meal times, much to her delight, and small portions of carefully grilled fish devoid of fat and cottage cheese are added to the meal, hence decreasing the calorie intake. Alternatively, a meal can appear adequate and acceptable to the parents' eyes when her plate is filled as normal but it is easily filled with vegetables only and without a meat substitute, decreasing calorie intake further.

Coffee

Frequently, large quantities of coffee, particularly black coffee, are drunk. Sometimes this is taken very strong and it is not unknown for anorexics to use three or four spoonfuls of instant coffee per cupful. This is likely to be the cause of frequent headaches. Coffee acts as a stimulant and also attempts to fill a stomach crying out for food. Fluids are generally drunk very hot; hot fluids being more effective in counteracting hunger sensations than cold fluids.

EFFECTS OF LOSING WEIGHT

As someone settles down to starving themselves, there are many physiological and psychological changes due to the decrease in body weight through the effects of starvation itself. For the majority, this is semi-starvation as opposed to complete starvation, although some will decide to stop eating and/or drinking completely.

It is important for those professionals working with anorexics at low body weights to understand the effects of starvation. Many of the symptoms and behaviours of an anorexic, which are so frequently described as characteristic of AN are, in fact, symptoms that she shares with a starving person. The anorexic 'attitude' to weight, shape and food distinguishes the condition from simply starvation alone the anorexic's subsequent terror of regaining the lost weight. A low body weight, in physiological terms is a very fragile state for the body to be in, as there is a very powerful urge in the body to eat and survive.

PHYSIOLOGICAL EFFECTS

Reduced metabolic rate

As the anorexic restricts her food intake and her body weight falls, her body attempts to protect itself and utilises its resources as best as it can. The metabolic processes are slowed down and the amount of heat produced by the body is reduced. With the most important organs of the body in its trunk, blood flow is diverted to these organs and the brain at the expense of the extremities, i.e. the hands and feet, where the circulation to small blood vessels near the surface of the skin closes down. Symptoms of these metabolic changes include slow heart beat (bradycardia), low blood pressure (hypotension), reduced body temperature (hypothermia) and bluish-mauve extremities (acrocyanosis). Anorexics at low body weight are continually cold.

Hair and skin changes

Downy hair, or lanugo, may grow on parts of the body that would normally be quite hairless. Lanugo is thought to help the body with its thermoregulation. Anorexics also report that their hair falls out and feels very dry in texture.

PSYCHOLOGICAL EFFECTS

Some of the most detailed observations of semi-starvation are described by Ancel Keys (Keys *et al.*, 1950) in *The biology of human starvation.* He headed a research team at the University of Minnesota where 36 young male volunteers were fed a diet containing 1,570 calories a day for a period of 24 weeks, inducing average weight losses of 24 per cent of their original weights within the group. A practical goal of the Minnesota experiment, as it was called, was in an effort to throw light on problems of famine and food shortage. The team examined both the effects of prolonged undernutrition and various refeeding regimes. The young men were of high intellectual capacity and educational level, and had made a good social and occupational adjustment to life, but all developed symptoms of psychological disturbance as the semi-starvation progressed. They became apathetic, irritable and obsessed by thoughts of hunger, food and body weight.

The following are extracts from this very important research, which illustrates the similarities in thoughts and behaviours between an anorexic that the reader may be working with and the semi-starved volunteer. This, hopefully, will increase the reader's understanding of the anorexic as a starved person.

> Anticipation of eating heightened the craving for food... For the most part they ate silently and deliberately and gave total attention to the food and its consumption. Many ingenious devices were used to make the food seem to go further... As the starvation progressed the number of men who toyed with their food increased. They made what under normal conditions would be weird and distasteful concoctions. There was a marked increase in the uses of spice and salt... Towards the end of starvation some of the men would dawdle for almost two hours over a meal... They did much planning as to how they would handle their day's allotment of food... Food in all its ramifications became the principle topic of conversation, reading and daydreams for almost all... Various techniques were developed to approximate a substitute for the satisfactions normally derived from eating.

CONSTIPATION AND LAXATIVES

Stool formation and bowel movements are directly related to the type and quantity of food eaten. It is therefore not suprising that for someone whose intake is minimal that their output is minimal too. Anorexics frequently complain of constipation, giving that as the reason to only eat wholegrain cereals, products such as natural bran or eating large quantities of fresh fruit and vegetables and dried fruits. Some are constipated in the medical definition of the term, i.e. the infrequent and difficult passage of small, hard stools leading to discomfort — this being due to inadequate intake. Others connect frequency of bowel movements with 'a cleansing of the system' wanting to 'push the food through quicker' and even though they are not constipated, want to expel food from the body as quickly as possible.

Laxatives may be bought with the belief that their action has an effect on intestinal absorption of food, therefore helping to control body weight. There is good evidence, however, that use of laxatives is a relatively ineffective means of controlling body weight (Lacey and Gibson, 1985). This study compared the food intakes of normal weight bulimics who either vomited only or purged only. Results showed that the calorie intakes of the vomiters far exceeded that of the purgers, whose intakes were within normal range even though their eating patterns were bulimic. The purgers were slightly above their desirable weight range and above that of the vomiters, despite lower calorie intakes. This showed that their weight control was due to dietary restraint (binging and starving) and this controlled their energy intake rather than any intestinal malabsorption caused by the laxatives.

Those who abuse laxatives should be made aware that purging does not control body weight. However, it does cause excessive faecal loss of water and continued habitual use can lead to dehydration and loss of electrolytes, with the risk of hypokalemia.

REGURGITATION

From the author's experience, there are a number of anorexics who report regurgitation. They regurgitate their food, either during a meal or just after it, chew it for a long period and swallow it down again. It is not a behaviour readily talked about as they feel so ashamed and disgusted about doing it. After a while, the regurgitated food tastes foul because of the hydrochloric acid from the stomach. A young anorexic woman, when asked why she regurgitated when on a refeeding programme in hospital, said that if she was at home she would be binging (and vomiting) all day, so she would have food in her mouth constantly. Although she hated herself for doing this, she said that it was the only way she could continually taste food. Additionally, it prolongs and delays the end of a meal.

The small number of anorexics who regurgitate, whom the author has known, have desperately wanted to stop but have found it difficult to do so. Apart from feeling so ashamed, they have recognised how antisocial it is and how it would prevent them from eating normally with others.

GAINING WEIGHT

This section deals with the practicalities of refeeding, assuming that alongside the weight gain there is psychotherapeutic support. There is no question of force-feeding.

How many calories?

The choice of calorie content of the diet must reflect the need not to prolong the time necessary for weight restoration unduly, but at the same time, should not be totally unacceptable to the anorexic. Whatever the quantity prescribed, there will be anxiety as the anorexic faces weight gain. From the literature, intakes vary from 1,600 to 5,500 kcal per day. Russell (1962) increases the calorie intake gradually to a maximum of 3,500 to 5,500 calories per day. Dally and Sargant (1966) also suggests an increase over the first week or two of admission until an intake of 4,000 calories per day is reached. Marshall (1978) showed a mean daily intake of 3,800 calories for a small number of anorexics treated in a teaching hospital metabolic unit on enforced bedrest with a mean weekly increase of 1.6 kg.

To reach these high levels of intake, nutritional supplements in the form of high-calorie drinks are used, in addition to normal food or as the sole calorie intake. Alternatively, normal foods may be fortified with e.g. sugar (sucrose), glucose, skimmed milk powder, cream or commercially prepared glucose polymers, which are isocaloric to glucose but tasteless. It is totally unnecessary and dishonest to 'lace' a diet with extra calories. It serves no purpose other than to reinforce an anorexic's fear that a small amount of food makes her fat!

Crisp (1980), on the other hand, prescribes a 3,000 calorie diet 'with normal amounts of carbohydrates' using normal hospital food, expecting a weight gain of approximately 1.5 kg per week with the anorexic on bedrest. This is achieved by three main meals a day of average-sized portion sizes and three mid-meal snacks. Lucas, Duncan and Piens (1976) have a different approach, advocating a diet initially containing sufficient calories 'calculated to maintain the admission weight' with small caloric increments added to achieve gradual weight gain in line with the anorexic's progress.

Whilst opinions vary as to the optimum caloric intake of the diet prescribed and rate of weight gain expected, most authors agree that there is no need for nasoenteric tube feeding or intravenous feeding. However, in a life-threatening situation in which a severely emaciated anorexic is admitted as an emergency into a general hospital, this may be considered necessary by those involved.

The nutritional content of the diet, irrespective of the calorie load can be based on proportions of nutrients eaten by the general population, without the need for increasing body-building constituents. Forbes, Kreipe, Lipinski and Hodgman (1984) have compared two dietary regimes; a high-protein diet (20 per cent protein/energy) and a low-protein diet (10 per cent protein/energy) on the effect of body composition changes during weight gain, and concluded that 'satisfactory nutritional rehabilitation of patients with AN does not require a high-protein diet'.

Immediate reactions to high-calorie refeeding programmes in hospital vary from being totally unnecessary to barbaric, most certainly by anorexics, through fear of a very rapid weight gain and of becoming fat, but also by professionals involved in their care. A programme incorporating initial stabilisation of the admission weight must give an anorexic confidence that her carers are not solely committed to feeding her up. It also allows rehydration either caused by vomiting, purging or self-imposed fluid restriction prior to admission. Inclusion of carbohydrates to a diet depleted of such also results in fluid retention as the glycogen stores of liver and muscle are replenished. Depending on the severity of the dehydration, initial weight gain, due to fluid retention, even on very low-calorie intakes, may be substantially high and it is important to discuss the probability of this happening with the anorexic *before* she is weighed. Otherwise, she may stop eating as she experiences a very rapid initial weight gain, fearing that it will continue at the same rate. There may be excessive fluid retention with the body overhydrating, resulting in very little urine output and possibly ankle oedema, particularly if activity is restricted. She should be reassured that this will resolve as her body's fluid balance becomes normal and her urine output increases, with the disappearance of her swollen ankles.

As previously stated, whatever the rate of weight gain, refeeding alone will not promote recovery from AN. However, due to the anorexic's starved state, the low metabolic requirements mean that weight gain can be expected on unusually low-calorie intakes, which are more likely to meet the desires of the anorexic. More outcome studies are needed to determine whether a slow, steady weight gain, perhaps in a step-like manner, individually prescribed according to the patient's progress, facilitates long-term psychological and physiological health when compared with more aggressive refeeding. When looking at purely reversing the effects of starvation, it is of interest to note that Keys *et al.* (1950) observed that those volunteers who were refed very slowly ate more when allowed to choose their own food and gained more weight as a result. It may be speculated that the hunger of the body is actually heightened by receiving only a small amount of extra food.

At all levels of caloric refeeding, the volunteers of Keys *et al.* (1950) were always 'hungry'. Many anorexics whilst gaining weight express fears of their appetite; they are frightened of the feelings of hunger that they experience after a 'huge three-course meal'. They fear being unable to stop eating once they have started and of therefore becoming obese. How will they control themselves eating when it is not being controlled for them? They must be reassured that staff are just as concerned that they do not become obese as they are about them not starving themselves. Dietary treatment must be directed at helping each anorexic to relearn her own level of food intake to maintain a healthy weight and be responsible for feeding herself. As the body's needs are fully replenished, and as lost tissue is regained, the constant sensation of hunger will diminish.

LEARNING TO MAINTAIN A HEALTHY WEIGHT

Research has shown that in the weeks after just achieving a healthy weight and terminating refeeding, that anorexics have a greater caloric requirement than normal controls (Kaye, Gwirtsman, Ebert and Peterson, 1986). There is some evidence that resting metabolic rate (RMR) rises disproportionately to body weight increase during refeeding (Obarzanek, Lesem, Kaye and Jimerson, 1987) and it may be that an elevated RMR is maintained during these early weeks. Kaye *et al.* (1986) have also reported that non-bulimic anorexics have a greater caloric requirement than bulimic anorexics at both low weight and after weight restoration. It is likely that anorexics will have difficulty in maintaining a healthy weight anyway. In the light of research showing greater caloric needs at such an important time, this is an added problem.

If refeeding has been in the hands of the carers, responsibility should be given back slowly, perhaps a meal at a time, whilst the diet is being adjusted to ensure that sufficient calories are provided for the healthy weight to be maintained, bearing in mind this is a time when activity will also increase. Some anorexics voice a feeling of being deprived when the weight-gaining diet is reduced. This may be a consideration for gradually increasing the calorie intake of a diet during weight gain rather than eventually having to decrease a very high-calorie one.

It should not be assumed that having reached a healthy weight, anorexics will know how much to eat — they will not. For those who prepared and cooked meals for the family, they are likely to have only fed the family and deprived themselves. Also, the quantities that they *did* feed themselves whilst at a low body weight are now not appropriate at a higher weight.

It is very much a process of relearning about 'eating normally' and to enable them to eat according to their nutritional needs. Recognising that they have needs is an important part of recovery, and fulfilling them is a difficult task. Initially, they will be unable to rely on feelings of hunger and satiety. Instead, anorexics require education, structure and guidance, enabling them to take on the responsibility of feeding themselves at a healthy weight.

It is in the author's opinion that the dietitian, as a member of a multidisciplinary team, should be the person responsible for ensuring the nutritional needs of the anorexic during refeeding. Subsequent dietary management and nutrition-counselling at a healthy weight should be an integral part of any programme if anorexics are to begin 'eating normally' again. This can be achieved individually and within a group.

A structured eating plan

It is important to have a knowledge and to be familiar with the anorexic's previous eating patterns, both during and prior to the AN — family eating patterns; her list of 'forbidden' or 'fattening' foods; her feelings, ideas and beliefs about exercise and energy expenditure; body-weight fluctuation and body processes; her family's attitudes towards food, weight and dieting, and the situation to which she is being discharged — home, hostel, flat-share, etc.

Dietary management for anorexics is based on building up a structured pattern of eating. The pattern of eating can be seen as a 'prescribed eating plan', which is a vital part of their continuing recovery. With the anorexic's involvement, the plan should be based on three meals a day plus in-between snacks, according to the individual calorie requirements for weight maintenance.

By using food-exchange lists, meals can be planned in a structured way, providing variety to meet the nutritional needs of each individual. The extent to which an anorexic will vary her diet depends on her continued need for rigid control and unfamiliar foods provoke a great deal of anxiety. The eating plan may need to include defined times for eating, particularly when eating away from the hospital, at weekends and at discharge. It may be that the anorexic, whilst eating strictly in accordance with the agreed plan, gains confidence that she can maintain her weight (without gaining), which will enable her to continue at discharge. It must be remembered that ultimately, the responsibility for eating and not resorting to anorexic behaviour can only be with the anorexic herself.

The food-exchange lists are based on average-sized portions. By way of an example, to plan a meal it would need to consist of foods from each of the following groups, 1 to 4, and for each group, there would be an exchange list.

1. Meat or equivalent foods;
2. Starchy foods;
3. Vegetables or salads; and
4. Fruit and/or desert.

The lists enable meals that seem very different, to be planned adequately.

It is because of the vast choice of foods available that anorexics are so unsure of what to choose and on what basis to make the choice. Decision-making over food becomes a painful task and going to a supermarket can be a paralysing prospect because of the extensive choice available. Exchange lists relieve some of the anxiety over this decision-making. A structured eating plan also fills the need to ensure an individual eats sufficient when they cannot rely on hunger and satiety cues.

'Forbidden' or 'fattening' foods can slowly be incorporated into the plan. These may be foods previously avoided or only ever eaten in a binge. Some of them may have been included in the weight-gaining diet, which was then felt to be acceptable, but because of the idea that they are fattening are now not allowed within a weight-maintenance diet. There are misconceptions surrounding particular foods that can be tackled. It may involve an anorexic going out to buy one bar of chocolate, the first in a long time, and eating it as a dessert in company, without compensating for it (eating less at the next meal) or vomiting. Chocolates, cakes, etc. are particularly difficult foods. Many anorexics worry that once they have a taste for these foods they will binge on them and doing that is likely to have been their previous experience. If they starved all day to eat a bar of chocolate, then one bar is not likely to have satisfied either a craving for that food or a starved body. Now their bodies are not starving and these foods are not disallowed.

Calorie-counting as such should be discouraged as should be buying 'diet' foods. As food is sold increasingly with calorie values stated on the labels, it becomes difficult, as anorexics are drawn to reading the labels. Calorie-counting like this bears no relation to their total needs; it just has to be the item with the lowest caloric value that is bought.

CONCLUSIONS

In the long term

Recovery from AN is a long and slow process and sufferers need support from someone whom they can relate to and trust for a long time. Many treatment centres recognise the value of prolonged psychotherapeutic support.

The question: 'Do anorexics ever eat normally or have a normal relationship with food?' begs the question: 'How normal is normal eating?' How many times are comments like the following heard in restaurants?: 'I skipped my lunch to eat tonight', 'Tomorrow I'll diet to make up for this', ' I shouldn't be eating this; it's fattening' These are predomminantly comments made by or directed towards women.

From the author's experience of taking dietary histories from anorexics who are managing to maintain a healthy weight out of hospital, they show continuing anxieties about food of varying degrees. There is a definite strictness about food choices and variation within their diets and calorie-counting does remain. There is still a fear of overeating and 'going out of control' and compensatory undereating after meals eaten outside of their normal pattern. Dally (1967) reports that 'fear of eating or weight increase, or food fads, persist in about one-third of recovered patients' and of the 100 female anorexics followed up four to eight years after initial presentation by Hsu, Crisp and Harding (1979), only 37 had a normal food intake and 33 had persistent anxiety on eating with others. It may be that with time, the fears and anxieties of these people do eventually lessen.

REFERENCES

Beumont, P.J.V., Chambers, T.L., Rouse, L. and Abraham, S.F. (1981) 'The diet, composition and nutritional knowledge of patients with anorexia nervosa.' *Journal of Human Nutrition, 35*, 265–73

Crisp, A.H. (1967) 'The possible significance of some behavioral correlates of weight and carbohydrate intake.' *Journal of Psychosomatic Research, 11*, 117–131

—— (1980) *Anorexia nervosa: let me be.* Academic Press, London

Dally, P.J. (1967) 'Anorexia nervosa — long-term follow-up and effects of treatment.' *Journal of Psychosomatic Research, 11*, 151–5

—— and Sargant, W. (1966) 'Treatment and outcome of anorexia nervosa.' *British Medical Journal, 2*, 793–5

Forbes, G.B., Kreipe, R.E., Lipinski, B.A. and Hodgman, C.H. (1984) 'Body composition changes during recovery from anorexia nervosa: Comparison of two dietary regimes.' *American Journal of Clinical Nutrition, 40*, 1137–45

Hsu, L.K.G., Crisp, A.H. and Harding, B. (1979) 'Outcome of anorexia nervosa.' *Lancet, i*, 62–5

Kadambari, R., Gowers, S. and Crisp, A.H. (1986) 'Some correlates of vegetarianism in anorexia nervosa.' *International Journal of Eating Disorders, 5*, 539–44

Kaye, W.H., Gwirtsman, G., Ebert, M.H. and Peterson, R. (1986) 'Calorie consumption and activity levels after weight recovery in anorexia nervosa: a prolongued delay in normalisation' *International Journal of Eating Disorders, 5*, 489–502

Keys, A., Brozek, J., Henchel, A., Mickelso, O. and Taylor, H.L. (1950) *The biology of human starvation, vols. 1 and 2*, University of Minnesota Press, Minneapolis

Lacey, J.H. and Gibson, E. (1985) 'Does laxative abuse control body weight? A comparative study of purging and vomiting bulimics.' *Human Nutrition: Applied Nutrition, 39A*, 36–42

Lucas, A.R., Duncan, J.W. and Piens, V. (1976) 'The treatment of anorexia nervosa.' *American Journal of Psychiatry, 133, 9*, 1034–8

Marshall, M.H. (1978) 'Anorexia nervosa: dietary treatment and re-establishment of body weight in 20 cases studied on a metabolic unit.' *Journal of Human Nutrition, 32*, 349–57

Obarzanek, E., Lesem, M.D., Kaye, W.H. and Jimerson, D.C. (1987) 'Resting metabolic rate of anorexic patients during weight gain.' *International Journal of Obesity, 11*, Suppl. 2, 24

Russell, G.F.M. (1967) 'The nutritional disorder in anorexia nervosa.' *Journal of Psychosomatic Research, II*, 141–9

—— and Mezey, A.G. (1962) 'An analysis of weight gain in patients with anorexia nervosa treated with high calorie diets.' *Clinical Science, 23*, 449–61

13

Counselling the Eating-Disordered Person

Phillip Proctor

INTRODUCTION

The provision of counselling for those with eating disorders could, in itself, provide sufficient material for another book. Within this chapter I will briefly explore the role that Rogerian therapy can play within those situations that have to deal with eating-disordered people.

In the 1950s, Carl Rogers began to develop a type of counselling now known as 'client centred therapy'. The name of the approach itself gives clues to the framework. Rogers suggests very strongly that all individuals have the ability and responsibility to bring about their own change in their growth as a person and that the counsellor is there to facilitate that change rather than give direction to the change. Successful client-centred therapy conducted under optimum conditions would imply that the therapist was able to enter into an intensely personal and subjective relationship with the client. The relationship is neither as a scientist to an object of study nor as a physician expecting to diagnose and cure, but rather as person to person. This necessitates the therapist being genuine and meeting the client with the feelings that he/she is experiencing, and not hiding behind a defensive facade. It also means that the therapist is able to 'let go' in understanding the client, that no inner barriers prevent sensing what it feels like to be the client at each moment of the relationship, and that something of this empathic understanding can be conveyed to the client. Implicitly, the therapist must be comfortable in fully entering into this relationship, without cognitively knowing where it will lead, but satisfied in providing a climate that permits the utmost freedom for a client to be him/herself.

From the client's perspective, this would involve an exploration of increasingly unknown and dangerous feelings within herself, and may be possible only because she realises her unconditional acceptance. She thus becomes acquainted with elements of her experience that have previously been denied awareness as threatening and too damaging to the structure of the self. She finds herself experiencing these feelings so completely within this relationship that for the present moment she *is* her fear, anger, tenderness, strength, or whatever. As these widely varied feelings are lived in all their degrees of intensity, she discovers that she has experienced herself; that she is all those feelings. She will find that her behaviour is changing in a constructive way and in accordance with the newly experienced self. She then approaches the realisation that she no longer needs to fear what experience may hold, but indeed can welcome it freely as part of her changing and developing self (Rogers, 1961).

REQUIREMENTS OF THE THERAPIST

Rogers identifies the following characteristics for a competent facilitator: empathic, genuine, congruent, real, and confrontative.

1. *Empathy.* This is the ability to get inside the other person's experiential field and feel what that person is feeling, rather than to stand alongside showing non-purposeful sympathy.
2. *Genuine.* This refers to the ability to communicate warmth, respect, acceptance and positive regard for others, no matter what the others are going through.
3. *Congruent.* This implies the ability to tie together in harmony what one does and what all one says and is. Rogers uses the term 'whole person' in this context.
4. *Real.* This is the ability to be in touch with and express all which makes us human, particularly in the area of expressing feelings.

These four qualities in themselves would easily make a counsellor into a 'sponge' type of person who merely takes what is given to them by a client and holds it for the client, but Rogers also recognises the need for the fifth element.

5. *Confrontative.* This refers to the ability to gently point out inconsistensies in what is said in a non-threatening, non-judgemental way, enabling the client to choose to make congruent the communications.

Rogers described this type of therapy as being non-directive and that in the counselling situation, the client chooses what areas to look at and the facilitator thus becomes a sounding board for the client to identify the feelings inherent in that situation. The facilitator then helps the client to get in touch with those feelings, helps to make them real, and helps the client to 'own' them. This may then require the client to change, as the consequences of the identification and owning of feelings is made more real to her. The client thus brings about her own change and growth. There is, of course, much more to what Rogers says in terms of a theory of personality, self-concept theory and the experiencing of being, and the reader is referred to Rogers' various works (1942, 1959, 1961, 1969, 1970, 1973, 1978).

COMPONENTS OF THE THERAPY

Most of what happens to those with eating disorders occurs within themselves. 'Internal dialogues' about self, self-image, eating, family or personal problems all occur within the experiencing person, and the counsellor needs the skills to release these internal dialogues. There are several major problems that need to be dealt with by a counsellor at any point, even when a client presents themselves for counselling. These will be presented next.

Confidentiality and the building up of trust

Eating disorders themselves can create patterns of reality that cause people to act in different ways in public, in the family and in private so that lying, evasion of truth, hiding of food, purging and binging, in different patterns, are part of the anorexic's and bulimic's 'normal' experience. It will require much time to build up trust with eating-disordered people, and Rogers argues that the trust grows as the facilitator puts into action those abilities listed previously and that as the client experiences these non-judgemental, non-threatening patterns of behaviour a person-to-person relationship is built up and trust grows. In an early counselling session, I clearly indicate that I will not break trust and discuss with anyone at all which areas are covered in any counselling session without the person's permission. Furthermore, I also give an idea of the institutional setting and how it is structured and to whom I am accountable, so that the impression can be created of order and protection (particularly necessary as a male dealing mainly with teenage females and its attendant risks).

The need to describe the style of counselling

It should be stated that it is not directive and that one does not have the answers to any of the problems, but that together, facilitator and client can work at identifying what is and what is not happening and then begin together to find ways through the situation. This again is very difficult because no matter what the stage of the eating problems, the person is looking at the counsellor to have the answers to their problem. This requires gently helping the person to begin to describe their experiences and showing the empathy that one genuinely has as a share in their experiential field. This requires great listening skills, but is more than that because as one is listening, one needs to be identifying the feelings that the person is clearly giving out and also being in touch with one's own feelings. By reflecting back, using other words than those used by the person, the counsellor can show that they are understanding what the person is saying verbally and what feelings they are expressing emotionally.

The difficulty the person has in expressing their feelings

Many eating-disorder problems occur within the minds of the person, and they may have constant conflicts within themselves over what to eat, what not to eat, what to do if you have eaten, etc. Recently, this was expressed as 'If only I could have peace of mind'. Most anorexics whom I have dealt with are fairly vocal and express themselves and this in itself would suggest an active, thought-invoking mind. However, the mind in all its power can take over the person in such a way that to ask questions such as 'How do you feel at the moment?' and 'What did it feel like when you did that?' elicit responses about the person's state of illness and not about their state of being. In all of Rogers' work the ability to be in touch with one's feelings, to be able to recognise them and claim them as your own is fundamental to any change or growth.

AIMS OF LONG-TERM COUNSELLING

Any long-term counselling would then be aiming towards helping the person to become aware of what they were feeling moment by moment, event by event, situation by situation. This becomes vital in helping the person deal with their food problem because it then becomes much easier to identify the pattern of action, thought and feelings that trigger off 'problem-food' situations. By understanding the triggers, the person can begin to develop alternative strategies to delay, switch off, or avoid those triggers.

Secondly, long-term counselling would aim to move the person's mind away from itself and into other consuming activities, challenging work, meaningful hobbies and interests. By occupying the mind with other activity the attention of the person is distracted away from the 'food problems' and lessens the pressure on the person. Satisfying activity and intellectual pursuits begin to create an alternative experiential field that can give meaning, purpose and security to the person and, coupled with a greater emotional awareness of oneself, careful discipline over eating and improved relationships can begin to help the person create a new life style and future.

Beware, nevertheless! The mind is very powerful and it takes a long time for its power to be broken. It may be necessary to go over the same material many times with the person. It may also be necessary at times to point out the avoidance of doing certain things that make it safer to stay with a food disorder than to begin to venture out into a new self. Such confrontation in itself, if arising out of a carefully built-up trust, respect, acceptance and positive regard can be the key(s) to helping the person move forward. Rogers pointed out that there could be those people who counsel others but who turn people off rather than set them free. They could never reach the previous stage because they have lost the person a long time ago. Confronting the person can be very difficult on the counsellor as it raises all kinds of questions about fully appreciating where the person is, or thought to be. There is always a risk that it may not result in growth but a regression. This can only be checked by the counsellor being aware of what they are feeling and why they need to confront gently.

Although this client-centred approach helps the person find themselves, particularly in terms of coping with their feelings, as a process it uses external reality to challenge the eating-disordered person's view of reality. The counsellor may not have to say anything about this external reality, but one of the most basic assumptions of this therapy is that the individual has some idea of what it is to be a normal human being and that in some way they want to go back to being that person. Subsequently, if they have little experience in their early life of being human (not 'normal') then they would have much greater difficulty in coming to terms with themselves and their eating patterns.

CONCLUSIONS

Rogerian counselling offers a person with eating disorders the chance to explore with another person what it is to be really human, and together, to work through a range of issues, largely connected with an identification and ownership of feelings, to grow towards change and greater humanness. As we see more and more people experience problems with food (as with drink), this approach of dealing with these people as people will become more used and developed.

Finally, this article is my tribute to Carl Rogers who died earlier this year and I beg his forgiveness for any misrepresentation of his ideas, life and work.

REFERENCES

Rogers, C.R. (1942) *Counseling and Psychotherapy*. Houghton Mifflin, Boston, Mass.

—— (1959) 'A theory of therapy, personality and interpersonal relationships.' In S. Koch (ed), *Psychology: a study of a science, vol. III*, McGraw-Hill, New York and London

—— (1961) *On becoming a person*. Houghton Mifflin, Boston, Mass.

—— (1969) *Freedom to learn: a view of what education might become*. Charles E. Merril, Columbus

—— (1970) *Carl Rogers on encounter groups*. Harper and Row, New York

—— (1973) *Becoming partners: marriage and its alternatives*. Constable, London

—— (1978) *Carl Rogers on personal power*. Constable, London

14

The Role of Self-help Groups in Eating Disorders

Pat Hartley

INTRODUCTION

Support groups, in spite of their growth in recent years, have received little systematic attention, either in conceptual or methodological terms. Such groups, involving both self-help and mutual support, exist amidst a variety of peer-group helping networks and associations. According to Vickers (1971) such groups involve a search for 'an appreciative system, sufficiently widely shared to mediate communication, sufficiently apt to guide action and sufficiently acceptable to make personal experience bearable'. Vickers maintains that systems may involve face-to-face encounters, letters, phone-lines and printed information. Caplan (1974a) drew on his own experience to suggest that 'the quality of emotional support and task-oriented assistance provided by a social network' is the critical intervention in mental health. He wrote:

> The characteristic attribute of these social aggregates that act as a buffer against disease is that in such relationships the person is dealt with as a unique individual. The other people are interested in him in a personalised way. They speak his language. They tell him what is expected of him and guide him in what to do... Above all, they are sensitive to his personal needs which they deem worthy of respect and satisfaction.

This statement provides a precise and succinct account of the essence of the self-help approach.

The emergence of such groups, involving a wide range of interests, was seen as a factor in evolution by the 19th-century Russian scientist, Prince Petr Kropotkin (1914), who maintained that man as a social animal could survive the evolutionary process only within a form of group life. In his book, *Mutual aid*, he suggests that groups could include tribes, families and mutual-benefit groups, in all of which mutual aid is the dominating influence.

During the 20th-century development of sociology and psychology, various theorists suggested not only that the group influenced the individual, but also that the growth of self was, in fact, contingent upon the group and particularly upon specific individuals within the group. The concept of the 'looking-glass self' was postulated both by Horton Cooley (1982) and by Meade (1952), and within his interpersonal theory, Harry Stack Sullivan (1956) stated that 'We are the sum of the reflected appraisals of others'. Erickson (1963) stressed the role of 'significant others' in his psychosocial development theory. To some extent, Carl Rogers' (1961) work also reflects similar concepts, with its emphasis on unconditional acceptance and positive regard. If one accepts, then, that the growth of self is dependent to some extent on the group, it may well follow that change, either positive or negative, may also be effected within the group.

PRINCIPLES AND FEATURES OF GROUPS

As the type of group exerting influence upon the individual may vary considerably, the structure and principles of groups should be examined. In general, a group consists of two or more individuals coming together as a result of common interests and/or shared goals. The earliest experience of groups is, for most people, the family. Schools, peers, work and leisure widen the individual's experience of group activity and set his/her place within society as a whole. Groups vary in terms of their structure, which may involve an emphasis, for example, on work, leisure, religion or politics. The common interests and shared goals contribute to the group's cohesiveness and strength. In minority groups, perhaps involving specific creeds or nationalities, this cohesiveness affords protection from perceived threat and thereby reduces, to some extent, any felt anxiety.

As groups increase in membership and number of branches, the structure will usually change. Greater size may well result in a more formal structure involving more complex organisation and role-allocation. Communication between groups and within groups may also be affected by increased size. Provided that communication is efficient and effective, increased membership in groups may well lead to increased strength and power to achieve group goals.

Self-help and mutual-aid groups reflect such structure and principles. They may be seen as alternative care-giving systems and adjuncts to the professionals. They are felt to be growth-promoting and helpful support systems and even agencies of social control. These groups, in common with all groups, involve: (a) common experience of their members; (b) mutual help and support; (c) the helper principle; (d) collective willpower and belief; (e) shared information; and (f) constructive action towards shared goals.

SELF-HELP GROUPS AND MUTUAL-AID SOCIETIES

Relevant literature

In an overview of the literature on mutual-help groups in the United States, Killilea

(1976) refers to Caplan's definition of the role of many groups of this type. Caplan (1974b) maintains that:

> Support systems are attachments among individuals or between individuals and groups that serve to improve adaptive competence in dealing with short-term crises and life transitions, as well as long-term challenges, stresses and privations through (a) promoting emotional mastery (b) offering guidance regarding the field of relevant forces involved in expectable problems and methods of dealing with them and (c) providing feedback about an individual's behaviour that validates his conception of his own identity and fosters improved performance based on adequate self-evaluation.

Toch (1965) sees groups such as TOPS (Take Off Pounds Sensibly) and Alcoholics Anonomous (AA) as social movements aiming to produce changes within their members rather than in society, and in which 'community of membership is the chief means to the movement's goals'. He suggests that each individual's efforts to solve his own problems become part of his efforts to solve a social problem with which he is intimately familiar and personally concerned. Efforts towards change can be directed both at the particular and at the universal goal.

While acknowledging the increase in the number of self-help groups in recent years, the possible reasons for such an increase must be addressed. Gussow and Tracy (1972), in a study of such organisations, state that 'the emergence of such consumer-initiated services constitutes a social movement. Such phenomena arise when a hiatus exists between felt need and the existence of available services, representation or social benefits adequate to meet such needs.'

Vattano (1972) maintains that self-help groups are a 'power-to-the-people' social movement with clinical applications. He suggests that groups such as AA have caused non-professional self-help groups to emerge as a potent force in the design and delivery of health and welfare services. Mowrer (1971) claims that to some extent, these groups may largely replace the established church, commenting that Christianity started as a small-group movement with therapeutic powers. Although religion has become irrelevant for many modern men and women, self-help groups may provide similar support in terms of human reintegration, reconciliation and *reconnection* (the true definition of religion). Murray and Adeline Levine (1970) suggest that:

> Social and economic conditions and the intellectual and political spirit of the times exert profound influences upon the particular mental health problems which concern us and upon the particular forms of help which develop and flourish... One can argue that changes in the forms of help are shaped at least as much by the predominant social forces of the times as they are by thoroughly supported developments in the science of human behaviour.

Glasser (1971), on the development of Gaudenzia, a self-help addiction-treatment programme, suggests that:

> Self-help programs such as Gaudenzia... have a definable... theoretical background... there are basic similarities between their basic principles and the thought of such men as Alfred Adler and Kurt Lewin... It appears that there are close similarities between the basic ideas of these programs [AA and Gaudenzia] and current thought in at least the areas of existential philosophy and learning theory.

Stunkard (1972), reporting on TOPS, sees the organisation as an adjunct or potential adjunct to the formal care-giving systems and as solutions to the shortage of professional personnel. He suggests that:

> If the family physician or internist could confidently turn over to TOPS the jobs of weight monitoring and psychological support for obese patients his efforts at controlling obesity could be confined to periodic assessments of their diet and weight goals. We believe such a plan is feasible and that it would result in larger weight losses for obese patients and in conservation of the physician's time and energy.

Gellman (1964), in an analysis of AA, relies on Parson's (1961) sociological model of organisations to demonstrate the effectiveness of the association. He suggests that AA is essentially a circular system in which the organisation is the therapeutic agency, which, in turn, is moulded and shaped by the activities and accomplishments of its members. This, he believes, amounts to a socialisation process that becomes a way of life: 'In effect, a sub-culture is created in which the status of alcoholic has positive connotations'.

Adler and Hammett (1973) view self-help groups as extensions of the concept of the therapeutic community in its broadest sense, making use of the social milieu as a major instrument of change. According to their view, all therapeutic systems build on the individual's need for attachment to a group system and the change process can be generically stated as 'progression from "disease" through "cure", involving first crisis, then conversation and finally cult formation'. They believe that this process may be a common therapeutic pattern for significant attitude change. Similarly, Hurvitz (1970) perceives the ideal self-help group as a fellowship or movement that attempts to foster maximum interaction and mutual assistance between peers, that requires complete self-revelation and which affords the members the opportunity for mobility within their fellowship or movement as they overcome their common problems or inappropriate behaviour. Zusman (1969), however, proposes that 'no-therapy' describes the activities occurring in groups like AA, which are not labelled therapeutic but which help people cope with problems. He suggests that 'no-therapy' is a way of suppressing symptoms and encouraging conformity.

SELF-HELP GROUPS IN THE MANAGEMENT OF EATING DISORDERS

The origin of the movement

In spite of a long-established tradition of mutual-aid groups (AA was formed in 1935), the first support group for people with eating disorders was not formed until 1974. Anorexic Aid was launched by the author in May of that year with an inaugural meeting in the Department of Psychology at Manchester University, UK. This initiative was triggered off partly by the public response to an article published by the *Observer* newspaper, 24th February, 1974. A journalist wrote of the difficulties that she experienced during her daughter's struggle with AN. Readers' comments were invited and approximately 200 letters were received, the largest response for any article to date. The major theme common to these letters was a sense of isolation, accompanied by feelings of guilt and helplessness. The paper published a further request for interested sufferers or relatives to contact me with a view to setting up a self-help/mutual-support organisation specifically for those involved with eating disorders, either personally as a patient or as a relative or friend. Within two weeks, a further 535 letters were received and Anorexic Aid was formed. Within a year there were over 1,000 members and 33 active groups. The movement spread rapidly to the United States, where there are now several hundred similar groups. A list of headquarters is given at the end of this chapter.

The philosophy of self-help groups

The rationale underlying the formation of Anorexic Aid was similar to that which instigated groups such as AA. Katz (1970) states that 'the fact of sharing a central problem... defines membership status in self-help groups despite many individual differences. A peer in a self-help group has a commonality or mutuality with others.' Silverman (1970) believes that among the primary characteristics of self-help groups are:

> that the care-giver has the same disability as the care-receiver; that the recipient of service can change roles to become a care-giver; and all policy and program is decided by a membership whose chief qualification is that they at one time qualified and were recipients of the services of the organisation

Ablon (1974), in her study of the organisation Al–Anon, stated that many came to Al–Anon thinking that they alone have suffered these 'unique' experiences. Recognition of the universality of these problems and the finding of a safe arena in which to talk about their own feelings and modes of handling the problems are of utmost importance in the Al–Anon experience.

This facility is offered by Anorexic Aid and other self-help groups for eating-disorder sufferers. The groups establish a specific role for the member. One aspect of this role is that the individual is a member of a group that meets regularly and within which, each member has certain obligations towards his/her fellow members. In return, he/she has certain expectations about their behaviour towards him/her. Each is expected to show concern about the condition and progress of other members, to provide them with support and acceptance and to help them in the application of the principles of the group. One of the strengths of self-help groups is participation by recovered members. The successful 'ex-patient' may act as a positive and, most importantly, *credible* role model in a way that not all professional care-givers can necessarily achieve. Such members can give reassurance and realistic goals for those at an earlier stage of the illness.

It has been suggested by Riessman (1965) that in 'helper' therapy it may be the helpers who benefit most from the exchange. He suggests transforming recipients of help into dispensers of help, reversing their roles and structuring the situation so that 'helpees' will be placed in roles requiring the giving of assistance. This principle is fundamental to the philosophy of Anorexic Aid but is not necessarily the case in all self-help groups for eating disorders. Skovholt (1974) summarises the benefits of helping as follows: (a) the effective helper often feels an increased level of interpersonal competence as a result of making an impact on another's life; (b) the effective helper often feels a sense of equality in giving and taking between themselves and others; (c) the effective helper is often the recipient of valuable personalised learning acquired while working with a helpee; and (d) the effective helper often receives social approval from the people they help.

Within those groups where sufferers and recovering or recovered members are key figures, these benefits will be described. The view of Bruch (1974) that AN involves a struggle towards autonomy reinforces the notion of involving the client in her own move towards recovery. Self-respect and self-esteem within illness are contingent to some extent on feelings of control and involvement in decision-making. For example, the knowledge of the availability of analgesia during child-birth or dental treatment has been associated with a reduction in the number of requests made for painkillers rather than a dependence on such drugs.

It must be stressed that a good self-help group does not set itself up as a replacement for treatment but as a complement to treatment. Garfinkel and Garner (1982) suggest a multidisciplinary approach to treatment that may include not only medical intervention and medication as necessary, but also assertion training, sessions devoted to body image and accurate perception of internal proprioceptive cues, discussions of sociocultural influences affecting individuals with eating disorders, nutritional counselling and self-help groups.

Rubel (1984) suggests that the definition of self-help groups is difficult, with those in the USA designed for people with eating disorders providing members with support, encouragement and a non-judgemental, safe atmosphere in which to voice problems and concerns as well as joys and triumphs. Goals may include not only symptom reduction, but also increased self-esteem, integrated relationships with others, honesty, self-love and more effective social skills. It is suggested, based on accounts from members of Anorexic Aid, that symptom reduction is concomitant with these aspects of the group and may be viewed as 'secondary' goals.

INFORMATION DISSEMINATION

One very important aspect of self-help and mutual support is the sharing of information. If individual members were simply to pool their own resources, the reservoir of information would be sizeable. Barish (1971) describes how the educational element of self-help groups promotes greater factual understanding of the problem condition. Such education may be directed at the general public but is also on offer to members of the group. This information may take the form of leaflets describing signs and symptoms, the behavioural changes occurring particularly in eating disorders, the dangers of self-starvation, binging and purging and details of the range of treatments available. Reading lists that cover different approaches to anorexia and bulimia are also made available. More specifically, some groups may offer short courses on eating disorders, counselling skills and self-help group organisation to voluntary workers involved in mental health, and in some cases, to relevant professionals. One practical aspect of information-sharing is that members may discover alternative coping strategies that reduce their dependence on starving or binging. Ablon (1974) found that the imparting of information in its own specialised form was the most prominent process element in the Al–Anon experience. The sharing of coping strategies provides alternatives for members to consider, to adopt or reject as desired.

Whereas the aforementioned are goals that are general to all self-help groups, they are also relevant to those groups for sufferers from eating disorders. Inherent within such groups is the emphasis on personal responsibility and effectiveness. Membership implies a common conviction that individuals are neither helpless nor hopeless, but able, with some support, to make positive changes in themselves, their behaviour and their environment. These beliefs coincide with those of Rogers (1961), whose confidence in man's ability to change in the direction of positive self-esteem is fundamental to his supportive, client-centred therapy. Kelly (1955) maintains that man's behaviour is based upon his perception of the world. If the individual misconstrues that world and himself within it, his behaviour will, accordingly, be inappropriate. In order to effect a change in behaviour, the constructs themselves must undergo change. The self-help group, offering mutual support, can provide the matrix for such change.

Many sufferers of AN or bulimia welcome the group-setting as a place in which they feel safe enough to explore their private fears, concerns and possible solutions. As individuals, members are often reticent and embarassed, needing time to listen and observe before reaching a point at which they feel secure enough to contribute. Often, others verbalise the thoughts and feelings that some members cannot initially express in words. Consequently, such members are given the opportunity for self-examination in a non-critical environment. New ways of being are explored and new, self-nourishing behaviours, not necessarily food-related, are discussed. Many group members are receiving professional help and some are referred to the groups by their therapists. This in itself is beneficial as the group can then support individuals who may need treatment in their decision to accept such intervention.

A more general effect of membership of a self-help group is to provide the individual member with the opportunity to reduce social isolation and alienation. The group acts as a bridge from isolation to social and intimate relationships. Although initially, such relationships may involve other members of the group, individuals find the confidence and courage to establish normal, healthy relationships outside the group. Members of Anorexic Aid, for example, have found that the group gave them the support to move from a housebound situation to enrolling on college courses and moving into full-time employment.

Most groups focusing on eating disorders offer support to parents, relatives and friends. Anorexic Aid in the UK, and the American groups also, recognise from the start that in common with other maladaptive behaviours, anorexia and bulimia create difficulties for many in close contact with the sufferer. In some associations, the total membership divides into subgroups; one or even two for sufferers, and one for relatives and friends. Other groups may subdivide intermittently, but meet as a whole more generally. To some extent, the pattern is set by the number attending the meeting. Dividing into subgroups affords the opportunity to express thoughts and feelings that may be painful for family members to witness, but at the same time recognise the validity and relevance of such expression when made by others with whom they are not involved on such a personal and emotional level. Parents and friends also offer and benefit from the support and information-sharing, which is also obtained by the sufferers themselves. Some of the guilt and shame felt may be diminished by recognising the problems experienced by other, apparently 'normal' and caring parents, partners and friends.

Where such subdivisions occur, common features may be observed in each group. These features were described by Kinoy (1985). In the sufferers' group the following observations were made:

1. The group works to reduce isolation, particularly at the severe stage of the disorder.
2. Group members recognise that their sense of 'uniqueness' is misplaced, thus confronting their own defensive behaviour.
3. Self-blame is aired, but guilt and shame discouraged. Members are encouraged to take responsibility for their own action.
4. Myths, fears, bizarre behaviour and thoughts are shared and modulated by interaction.
5. Members act as role models, and can see the progress toward recovery. Although the sufferer's own body image may be distorted, she will recognise the reality of severe emaciation in others. Kinoy comments that competition must be guarded against.
6. Individual members will seek to adopt the health-promoting behaviours of

others within the knowledge that they can work safely towards such responses.
7. The recurring problem of separation and individuation between sufferers and parents may result in low self-esteem. To regard peers as a source of wisdom and help, and to identify with them, may result in an increase in the sense of self-worth. The group also supports the individual in her efforts to understand her own identity in terms of familial and societal expectations.
8. The recovering anorexic or bulimic represents a 'next stage', not so distant as the professional view and having the hallmark of experiential truth.

Similar patterns are observed in the group of family and friends:

1. Isolation is reduced.
2. The opportunity is given to compare themselves and their reactions with members of other families.
3. Information is shared, relating to resources available, successful treatments and coping strategies.
4. Confidence in own judgement is increased after listening to others' experiences, and the right to feelings of anger and frustration may be derived from the group. The stereotype of the 'parent' of an anorexic or bulimic may be examined and evaluated.
5. Parents of recovered anorexics act as role models, giving hope and support as well as the opportunity to share emotions such as anger and fear.
6. An extra-familial support system is available from the group, often outside the meetings. Many families are very isolated, nuclear families or maybe find it impossible to share their problems within the family network.
7. Group members are welcomed as officials, thus focusing attention away from the 'sick' family member and thereby developing greater objectivity.
8. Family members are not always involved in therapy. Some therapists encourage family members to attend groups for the support they offer.

LINKS WITH PROFESSIONALS

The majority of self-help groups involve liaison with professionals. These may be medical practitioners, psychologists, social workers or counsellors from a variety of backgrounds. The level of input varies from group to group, but it is the author's belief that some involvement is crucial for maximum effectiveness of the group, while at the same time preserving the autonomy of group members and the philosophy of self-help. This input may take the form of teaching specific skills, such as assertiveness or peer-counselling, opening sessions, suggesting guidelines for meetings, advising on organisational problems and contributing to the preparation of books, leaflets and other informational material. Such support and advice should ideally contribute to the effectiveness of the group but in no way detract from the control and responsibility of the group members.

POTENTIAL PROBLEMS

Several potential problems have been identified in the self-help group movement. Firstly, group members must be clear about what the group can offer, so that any unrealistic expectations can be dispelled at the outset. Most groups do not offer 'therapy' and members should be discouraged from regarding the group as a replacement for treatment. It is preferable to see group attendance as an adjunct, complementing treatment. If unrealistic expectations are maintained, this could result in self-blame or 'victim-blaming' where individuals not deriving benefit from the group may actually suffer.

Self-help cannot necessarily change society or family dynamics, nor can it affect genetic or biochemical issues. The role of the group is to offer coping strategies and give support. Members should not be deceived on this count.

Overdependence on the group should be discouraged. Initially, the group may provide acceptance and friendship to replace isolation. The group should encourage personal growth towards healthy relationships in the world at large. Self-help groups for people with eating disorders should encourage a belief in recovery, emphasising new attitudes to life, weight and food, stressing that self-nourishment is one's right and not simply self-indulgence. Whereas dependence on a 'higher power' may be useful for some members at some stages, ultimately each individual needs to feel responsible and in control, thus avoiding feelings of inadequacy and self-disgust, especially during a period of relapse.

Poor leadership skills may well be a problem. The facilitator should guard against overcontribution, listening rather than lecturing, and guiding discussions so that more reticent members have the opportunity to contribute should they so wish. A recovered member, though a useful role model, may fail to see that each individual, although sharing many aspects of the condition, is unique and may not find solutions in the way it is suggested that she would. It may be also that a 'recovered' member still has difficulties with relationships, perhaps with a parent, and this difficulty may be presented as a cause of her problem. This may be so, but if its expression is uncontrolled in the group, this may lead to more problems than it solves for other members.

Poor attendance may be experienced and care should be taken against feelings of failure and inadequacy. Group facilitators also benefit from a support network of the type operated by Anorexic Aid. Examination of the structure of the group, the form and content of the meetings and acknowledgment of the 'private' nature of eating disorders may clarify some of the reasons for low attendance. Many groups find an almost 'seasonal' pattern for attendance with post-Christmas and post-holiday periods usually resulting in an increase.

If the group's organisation is dependent on one individual, the level of commitment involved is often too demanding. It is wiser therefore to involve members as much as possible in the organisation and general maintenance of the group, thereby ensuring its continued effective function.

Finances may present a problem, as most self-help groups are funded by voluntary contributions. It is seen as helpful if each attendee pays a small fee, as in this way, individuals feel that they are contributing. In eating disorders particularly, the feeling of 'giving' is easier to tolerate than 'taking'. Fund-raising may form a major activity for some groups.

Finally, poor communication between groups is a problem, especially where vast distances are involved. In the UK, Anorexic Aid circulates members with a quarterly magazine and holds an annual general meeting and weekend 'conference' to which all members have access. The headquarters can be contacted at any time and sends out information on request. Links with other self-help organisations have been forged and will hopefully develop further in the future.

THE FORMAT OF MEETINGS

The format for meetings varies from group to group and it is suggested that no 'best' pattern exists. The following is simply a proposed outline.

1. Self-introduction by facilitators and members, each perhaps declaring the nature of her involvement.
2. Any group business or announcement of future activities.
3. A clear statement of group goals and 'rules', especially if new members are present.
4. A short presentation by a member or invited speaker chosen from topics such as:

    (a) Effective goals and coping strategies.
    (b) Perfectionism.
    (c) Sex-role stereotyping.
    (d) Guilt.
    (e) Pleasurable alternatives to dieting and binging.
    (f) Family dynamics.
    (g) Medical complications of starving, binging and purging.
    (h) Anger and rage. Forms of expression.
    (i) Personal accounts by recovered anorexics or bulimics.

5. A discussion of the presentation, perhaps in subgroups.
6. A feedback session involving the full group.
7. Conclusion — involving opportunity for members to exchange telephone numbers and addresses or to arrange individual meetings; discussion of other issues relevant to members. A selection of leaflets, booklists or books for loan may be available for members before and after the main part of the meeting.

The frequency of meetings will also vary according to the needs of group members. On average in the UK, Anorexic Aid groups meet fortnightly. One London branch holds weekly meetings, but not necessarily for all members, some being exclusively for sufferers and others exclusively for family members. Other meetings will include all those involved. It has been suggested by Kinoy (1985) that monthly meetings meet the needs of the American Anorexia/Bulimia Association, New Jersey, most effectively, as more frequent meetings were felt to be too intense and involved a level of commitment that some members found threatening.

THE EFFECTIVENESS OF SELF-HELP GROUPS

Although there is little evidence as yet to establish the effectiveness of self-help groups, Slade (1983) found that sufferers experience these groups as helpful, providing a meaningful complement to orthodox methods of treatment. Hartley (1983) claims that self-help groups:

> focus the patient's energy on to the more positive areas of helping others in a similar situation and encourage self-growth and self-acceptance... The sense of achievement resulting from being instrumental in one's own recovery is bound to increase self-esteem and self-confidence.

It is widely accepted that control is a central issue in eating disorders (Bruch, 1974) and 'external locus of control' may be experienced as stress (Ferrari, 1962). Self-help and mutual support can actively contribute to a movement towards internal locus of control. In this way, self-esteem, personal power and effectiveness may all be increased.

According to Rubel (1984), a good self-help group will provide members with the following 'services': (a) reinforcement for positive change; (b) programmes for gradual elimination of negative behaviour; (c) information on various ways of controlling behaviour; (d) information on ways of including more pleasant, rewarding and self-nourishing patterns in daily life; (e) role-modelling in stress-coping; (f) role models of successful ways of changing destructive behaviour; (g) advice on patterns for changing stressful environments; (h) alternative ways of considering problems; (i) new ways of thinking about self and others; and (j) new ways of interpreting various critical life events.

As Rubel (1984) points out, people who develop eating disorders are often totally negative in their view of themselves and certain aspects of their lives. Ideally, members of self-help groups learn to see that they do not need to be passive and 'acted upon'; that they do have power that they can begin to use in the safe context of the group. The group may then involve a 'rite of passage', when members develop autonomy and independence, enabling them to feel in control of their own lives.

CONCLUSIONS

The principles involved in peer-group mutual aid, apart from being beneficial in specific conditions, may also have important implications for prevention. In the author's view, based on observations made throughout a career in education at all levels, training in life skills is sadly lacking. This is particularly so in relation to stress-coping strategies. Stressful events are a fact of everyone's life and, in the main, present education and socialisation give little guidance on how to cope with such events. It is hardly suprising that individuals discover various ways of coping, including dependence on drugs and food. If such methods can be acquired within socialisation processes at present, it is logical to assume that through the structured framework of an efficiently organised self-help group, alternatives and more positive coping strategies can be adopted.

APPENDIX

Self-help/mutual support groups

United Kingdom

Anorexic Aid, The Priory Centre, 11 Priory Road, High Wycombe, Bucks.

Anorexic Family Aid, Sachville Place, 44 Magdalen Street, Norwich, Norfolk NR3 1JE

USA

American Anorexia/Bulimia Assoc., Inc. (AABA), 133 Cedar Lane, Teaneck, New Jersey 07666 201/836 – 1800

Anorexia Nervosa and Associated Disorders, Inc. (ANAD), P.O. Box 271, Highland Park, Illinois 60035 312/432 – 8000 (ext. 3307) or 312/831 – 3438

Anorexia Nervosa and Related Eating Disorders, Inc. (ANRED), P.O. Box 5102, Eugene, Oregon 97405 503/344 – 1144

Bulimia, Anorexia Self-help, Inc. (BASH), 522 North New Ballas Road, Suite 206, St Louis, Missouri 63141 314/567 – 4080

National Anorexic Aid Society, Inc. (NAAS), P.O. Box 29461, Columbus, Ohio 43229 614/895 – 2009

Canada

The Anorexia Nervosa and Bulimia Foundation of Canada (ANAB, Canada), c/o Dr Pierre Leichner, Department of Psychiatry, University of Manitoba, Winnipeg, Canada

REFERENCES

Ablon, J. (1974) 'Al–Anon family groups.' *American Journal of Psychotherapy*, *28*, 30–45

Adler, H.M. and Hammett, V.O. (1973) 'Crisis, conversion and cult formation: an examination of a common psychological sequence.' *American Journal of Psychiatry, 130*, 861–4

Barish, H. (1971) 'Self-help groups.' *Encyclopedia of Social Work, vol. II*. pp. 1163–9. National Association of Social Workers, New York

Bruch, H. (1974) *Eating disorders: obesity, anorexia nervosa and the person within.* Routledge and Kegan Paul, London

Caplan, G. (1974a) *Support systems and community mental health: Lectures on concept development.* Behavioral Publications, New York

—— (1974b) *A study of natural support systems* (mimeo). Laboratory of Community Psychiatry, Harvard Medical School

Cooley, C.H. (1982) *Human nature and the social order*. Brunner/Mazel, New York

Erickson, E.H. (1963) *Childhood and society*. Penguin, Harmondsworth

Ferrari, N.A. (1962) 'Institutionalisation and attitude changes in an aged population.' Unpublished PhD thesis, Western Reserve University

Garfinkel, P.E., and Garner, D.N. (1982) *Anorexia nervosa: a multidimensional perspective.*' Brunner/Mazel, New York

Gellman, I.P. (1964) *The sober alcoholic*. College and University Press, New Haven

Glasser, F. (1971) 'Gaudenzia, Incorporated: historical and theoretical background of a self-help addiction treatment program.' *Journal of Addictions, 6*, 615–26

Gussow, Z. and Tracy, G.S. (1972) A prospectus: *voluntary self-help health organisations*: A study in human support systems (mimeo). Louisiana State University, New Orleans

Hartley, P.M. (1983) 'The value of self-help groups in anorexia nervosa.' In E. Karas (ed), *Current issues in clinical psychology, vol. I*, pp. 95–103, Plenum, New York

Hurvitz, N. (1970) 'Peer self-help psychotherapy groups and their implications for psychotherapy.' *Psychotherapy: Theory, Research and Practice, 7*, 41–9

Katz, A.H. (1970) 'Self-help organisations and volunteer participation in social welfare.' *Social Work, 15* 51–60

Kelly, G. (1955) *The psychotherapy of personal constructs, vols I and II*. Norton, New York

Killilea, M. (1976) 'Mutual help organisations: interpretations in the literature. In G. Caplan and M. Killilea (eds), *Support systems and mutual help*. Grune and Stratton, New York

Kinoy, B.P. (1985) 'Self-help groups in the management of anorexia nervosa and bulimia: A theoretical base.' *Transactional Analysis Journal, 15*, 73–8

Kropotkin, P. (1914) *Mutual aid*. Extending Horizons Books, Boston

Levine, M. and Levine, A. (1970) *A social history of the helping services: clinic, court, school and community*. Extending Horizons Books, New York (reprint)

Meade, G.H. (1952) *Mind, self and society from the standpoint of a social behaviourist.* Chicago University Press, Chicago

Mowrer, O.H. (1971) 'Peer groups and medication, the best 'therapy' for professional and laymen alike.' *Psychotherapy: Theory, Research and Pracice, 8*, 44–55

Parsons, T. (1961) *Complex Organisations*. Holt, Reinhart and Winston, New York

Riessman, F. (1965) 'The 'helper' therapy principle.' *Social Work, 10*, 27–32

Rogers, C. (1961) *On becoming a person*. Constable, London

Rubel, J.A. (1984) 'The function of self-help groups in recovery from anorexia nervosa and bulimia: symposium on eating disorders. *Psychiatric Clinics of North America, 7*, 381–94

Silverman, P.R. (1970) 'The widow as a caregiver in a program of preventative intervention with other widows: I know what it is like. Let me help you.' *Mental Hygiene, 54*, 540–7

Skovholt, T.M. (1974) 'The client as helper: a means to promote psychological growth.' *Counselling Psychologist, 4*, 58-64

Slade, P.D. (1983) 'The role of counselling and self-help groups in the management of anorexia nervosa.' In E. Karas (ed), *Current issues in clinical psychology, vol. I*, pp. 73–82, Plenum, New York

Stunkard, A.J. (1972) 'The success of TOPS, a self-help group.' *Postgraduate Medicine*, May, 143–7
Sullivan, H.S. (1956) *Interpersonal theory of psychiatry*. Tavistock, London
Toch, H. (1965) *The social psychology of social movements*. Bobbs-Merrill, New York
Vattano, A.J. (1972) 'Power to the people: self-help groups.' *Social Work*, *17*, 7–15
Vickers, G. (1971) 'Institutional and personal roles.' *Human Relations*, *24*, 433-7
Zusman, J. (1969) '"No Therapy". A method of helping persons with problems.' *Community Mental Health Journal*, *5*, 482–5

15

Dealing with Children and Young Adolescents: Special Considerations

Rachel Bryant-Waugh

INTRODUCTION

Anorexia nervosa is usually associated with adolescent and young adult females, but the disorder is not restricted to females in this particular age group. It can also occur in much older women and in children of both sexes. This chapter is particularly concerned with AN in childhood and early adolescence. It specifically addresses issues involved in the identification and management of the disorder in young people. Children with AN exhibit many of the characteristic clinical symptoms associated with older patients, yet present a number of differences in terms of aetiology, diagnosis and treatment. This chapter aims to highlight some of these. To be of more practical relevance, advice is offered on how to recognise anorexia in children, and recommendations for approaches to therapeutic intervention are outlined. The material presented is based on the author's experience at London's Great Ormond Street Hospital, where the number of children referred for help with eating disorders continues to rise.

FEATURES OF THE EARLY-ONSET ANOREXIA NERVOSA POPULATION

Before describing the 'early-onset' AN population in more detail, some clarification regarding terminology is required. Throughout this chapter, 'early onset' is taken to refer to the development of AN in young people aged between eight and 14. It is possible that children below the age of eight may develop the disorder, although no such case is known to the author. In general, individuals up to the age of about eleven are called 'children' whilst those over the age of eleven or twelve are classed as 'early adolescents'. There can be such a discrepancy in physical and emotional development between individuals of similar age during the 'early-onset' period, that terms based on the criteria of age may not be very helpful in grouping individuals in this context. It seems more appropriate to make a distinction between individuals in the early-onset group on the basis of pubertal status at time of onset of the eating disorder. This may provide clues to factors related to physical development triggering and maintaining AN in the different groups. Thus, in the age range of eight to 14, some individuals will be 'prepubertal' (without secondary sexual characteristics), some will be pubescent (secondary sexual characteristics have begun to develop but the process is incomplete), and some will be 'post-pubertal' (full secondary sexual characteristics are present, and in girls, menstruation has started but has ceased in association with the eating disorder). Early onset, therefore, includes both children and early adolescents, and covers the whole range of pubertal developmental stages.

Very little research has been carried out involving younger subjects with a diagnosis of AN, and consequently there are few 'hard' facts about the early-onset population. There has, for example, been insufficient research to allow any unequivocal statements to be made regarding the presence or absence of clear aetiological factors related to pubertal status as mentioned above. It is evident, however, that the number of patients aged 14 and under referred and receiving specialist treatment, forms a relatively small number of patients referred for treatment of AN. This suggests that AN is less prevalent in those under 14 than in those aged between 14 and 20, certainly as far as females are concerned. One of the reasons why there is, as yet, comparatively little research on series of young patients may therefore be that there are simply fewer of them. Most of the published studies that do include younger subjects have tended to group them together with older adolescents, so that unfortunately, little specific information has emerged.

The true size of the population of all AN sufferers is not known. Estimates of incidence or prevalence are rarely attempted, and no one has anything more than a rough idea of approximate numbers. The few statistics available relate mainly to those individuals receiving NHS inpatient psychiatric treatment. However, many others may be successfully treated by their GPs, or may develop a brief form of AN that is successfully overcome without specialist intervention.

A belief sometimes expressed in the literature, although not based on sound evidence, is that early-onset AN represents a 'milder' variant of the later-onset disorder, so that it is comparatively easy to treat. Experience has shown that there is a similar range in severity of the presenting disorder and in different individuals' response to treatment, to that existing in older patients. Some respond well to treatment and resume problem-free eating habits after one relatively short anorexic episode. Others fare less well, continuing to experience considerable eating problems, and suffer from emotional and physical disturbances until well into adolescence or even adult life. It is inadvisable to construe the disorder in younger patients as somehow less serious simply because of the individual's age, as this may lead to a more complacent attitude towards treatment. It should always be remembered that AN is a potentially fatal disorder and that children can, and do, die from causes directly related to their eating problem.

One striking feature to emerge from the published studies of early-onset AN is the surprisingly high numbers of males (Fossen, Knibbs, Bryant-Waugh and Lask, 1986; Jacobs and Isaacs, 1986). Estimates of the male proportion of the total anorexic population are generally placed at between five and ten per cent, yet in children, this figure appears to be much higher. As many as one quarter of groups of young patients reported in the literature are male (see Chapter 3).

What then, might the factors be that contribute to the development and maintenance of AN in children and young adolescents of both sexes? There is no simple aetiological theory that satisfactorily explains exactly why the disorder should develop in any age group. Most now accept that AN is a multidetermined and multifaceted disorder, with considerable individual differences in contributory factors. Such factors may include psychological, sociocultural, physiological or family issues. Anorexia nervosa can perhaps best be understood as arising out of a particular constellation of triggering factors occurring in the context of a vulnerable individual. The individual's particular situation, combination of illness features and personal resources play some part in determining the course and outcome of the disorder. In younger patients, identified background features (i.e. potential precipitating factors) have included difficulties at school, worries about pubertal development, an older sibling leaving home, an episode of illness resulting in appetite loss, starting a new school, and many such others. In most cases, it would be inappropriate, if not impossible, to ascribe a causal relationship to any one factor.

One very common clinical impression that has been supported to some extent by more formal research studies, is that the families of children with AN often experience considerable interactional difficulties. In some cases, this may be due to a poor marital relationship. The child's anorexia appears to serve a stabilising function in holding together an unstable marital relationship by providing a common focus for both parents. In other families, there may be some difficulty in adjusting to the child's growing need for individuality and independence. In such a situation, AN can serve as a vehicle for making a powerful individual statement and rejecting parental intervention. Some families appear to make very poor use of verbal communication, which may result in unresolved conflicts, or lack of understanding of other members' needs and wishes. In such families, AN can be interpreted as a manifest expression of unhappiness or conflict that cannot be stated verbally.

'Family pathology' is a popular explanation for the development of AN, particularly in younger patients, yet it is by no means the only possible one. As with all other aetiological theories (e.g. sociocultural pressures, pituitary–hypothalamic disturbance, psychodynamic interpretations), family pathology cannot account for the onset of the disorder in all individuals. There will always be exceptions in the form of apparently well-functioning families with a severely anorexic child.

THE IDENTIFICATION OF EARLY ONSET ANOREXIA

Clinical experience often suggests that the longer an eating disorder has had time to become established prior to treatment, the more difficult it is to overcome. Swift intervention, which may prevent the development of a chronic, damaging illness, relies partly on timely recognition. Early identification of eating disorders is thus important in all age groups. How then, can AN be recognised in children?

Many people are familiar with the eating problems of very young children; mealtime tantrums, 'fussy' or 'faddy' eating, and periods of being 'off' food, are all extremely common and not usually a cause for any real concern. There are, however, clear and important differences between food refusal or other unusual eating habits in young children, and with AN. The latter occurs at a later stage of childhood and is potentially much more damaging and dangerous. The formal means of identifying a disorder is to ascertain whether an individual fulfils appropriate diagnostic criteria. The following criteria have been suggested for early-onset AN (Lask and Bryant-Waugh, 1986).

1. Failure to gain weight at the time of expected growth spurt (10–14 years) or an actual loss of weight in the absence of any physical or mental illness.
2. The presence of a determined food avoidance.
3. Two or more of the following: (a) preoccupation with body weight; (b) preoccupation with calories; (c) distorted body image; (d) fear of fatness; (e) vomiting; (f) excessive exercising; and (g) laxative abuse.

Such criteria, although essential in arriving at a formal diagnosis, may not be of most practical use to those in a position to pick up early signs, such as teachers, parents and GPs (see also Chapter 5). It is often of more direct relevance to have a knowledge of the signs and symptoms suggestive of AN, which may alert to the need for clarification of diagnosis allowing appropriate intervention. Some such 'clues' are presented below.

Physical /physiological clues

One of the characteristic and instantly recognisable features of AN is emaciation. Anorexic children who restrict their food intake to a minimum generally look extremely thin. Physical appearance is clearly an obvious pointer towards AN, yet when does a child become 'too thin'? Being thin is associated with being underweight, thus the question could be rephrased as when does a child become 'too underweight'? The first point to establish is that there is no specific healthy weight that any one child should be at any one time, but a range into which weight should fall. This 'normal' range of weight is determined by the child's height, age and sex (there are a number of charts and tables that allow such calculations to be made; e.g. Haslam, 1986), usually by simply marking the relevant height and age and reading off the corresponding weight range on a graph. Although somewhat more complicated than simple weight measurements, it is essential to take account of each particular child's height when determining 'ideal' weight, given that children vary so much in height at similar ages.

Physical appearance provides the most obvious clue to the existence of AN, yet it is not altogether reliable. Children, particularly younger ones, vary enormously in their appearance at similar weight for height measurements. Some children who have very thin arms and legs may fall within the 'normal range' for weight for their height. It is often difficult, therefore, to rely on visual appearance alone when attempting to detemine whether a child is underweight. To do this more reliably, the percentage weight for height should be calculated (e.g. by using the 'Cole Slide Rule Calculator' devised for this purpose and obtainable from Castlemead Publications, Hereford, England). If this results in a figure within the range of 90–110 per cent, this can be considered acceptable. Measurements of 80 per cent or below (the so-called 'wasted' range) signify that the child is dangerously underweight, and should receive help to gain weight as a matter of some medical urgency.

Very low weight for height measurements suggest that the child's body fat levels are low. Body fat serves an essential insulatory function, regulating core temperature. Insufficient fat results in greater heat loss, which in turn may lead to symptoms of hypothermia. Anorexic children tend to feel the cold, suffer from cold extremities and show a variety of other physical features associated with malnutrition and emaciation (e.g lanugo, low pulse rate). Weight loss in children can be particularly serious as it tends not to stem from loss of fat alone. Many children, particularly prepubertal children who have not acquired the increase in fatty tissue that accompanies pubertal development, have a limited amount of fat to lose. Where this is the case, weight loss may, for an important part, be due to wasting of muscle tissue.

A child who is underweight and has insufficient body fat is either taking an inadequate diet or has a medical condition resulting in disturbances in uptake, or use or absorption of nutrients. Weight loss due to a medical condition is relatively rare, and in determining the cause of lost weight, attention should first be directed towards the child's diet to ascertain whether adequate amounts of necessary foodstuffs are being consumed. Medical investigations should be considered only for those children who appear to be consuming a sufficient diet but who remain underweight for their height.

A note of caution should be added at this point; anorexic children, as is so of their older counterparts, are extremely skilled at concealing the true amount that they are eating. Many are experts at disposing of food, either before it has been eaten, or immediately after meals by vomiting. A child who is thought to be eating a normal diet may be investigated for a whole range of relatively obscure medical conditions before AN is diagnosed. It is essential to be certain about a child's eating habits, which may involve a closer degree of observation before a lengthy period of medical investigations is initiated. In many cases, the search for an organic cause for weight loss has served to postpone treatment of AN, which has been identified only at a relatively late stage. A further tendency, which often serves to delay identification, is that children with AN often present with physical complaints such as abdominal pain, nausea, constipation and in the case of post-pubertal girls, amenorrhea. It is very easy to be sidetracked by such symptoms, and to search for underlying physical illnesses or disturbances. This is paticularly a problem in childhood-onset AN, where an eating disorder is not generally placed high on a list of differential diagnoses due to the patient's age.

Behavioural clues

In the early stages, a child may simply seem to be off their food, or become more selective about certain items in the diet. The refusal of foods previously enjoyed (usually foods perceived as fattening) may be attributed to a general loss of appetite or lack of interest in food. In some children, especially those who are mildly overweight or come from families conscious of the importance of healthy eating, the reluctance to eat sweets or cakes may be encouraged. Suspicions should begin to be aroused if relatively large amounts of a few select items are consumed (particularly if these are low-calorie foods), or if large amounts of liquids are drunk. One young girl's eating disorder was not recognised until after many months of refusing most food at home except dry breakfast cereal or copious amounts of diet lemonade. Her plea that she was not hungry was accepted as a genuine loss of appetite.

True appetite loss is not unusual in children and has many potential causes. One of the most common causes is simply illness. Another common, though less directly evident cause of appetite loss, is worry or stress. Children's worries about a whole range of situations, for example worries about something which they may have with their performance at school or difficulties in the family, may lead to a temporary loss of appetite. Although it may, at times, be difficult to distinguish between true appetite loss and the dietary restriction of AN, particularly within the early stages of the disorder, in most cases the restriction accompanying AN is characterised by cutting back on specific items and by a deliberate and consistent change in eating habits and attitudes towards food. Appetite loss tends to involve a passive refusal of food, whereas AN involves an active avoidance of food. True appetite loss in children is, in most cases, short-lived, and tends not to be accompanied by the development of bizarre eating behaviour.

Whilst AN itself is not characterised by loss of appetite, in some cases it may, however, be preceded by a genuine loss of appetite. In some individuals the onset of the disorder appears to be associated with an episode of physical illness involving both appetite and weight loss. It may be that this is in some way experienced as pleasurable, and provides the trigger for a more deliberate refusal of food.

Bulimia nervosa appears to be rare in children. There are no documented series of childhood-onset bulimic patients. In the author's experience, few children indulge in regular binge eating. This may be because it is typically a behaviour carried out in secret; children living with their families generally have less privacy than young adults. Binging is also a very expensive habit, and most children will have limited amounts of available money. Laxative abuse is also relatively uncommon in children, perhaps because they have less access to purgatives, or because many do not understand their action. Vomiting is somewhat more frequently encountered, and usually occurs in the context of restricted food intake and avoidance of weight gain, rather than as a sequel to binging. Children who vomit, tend to do so after eating a meal from which they could find no escape.

There are times when a child may appear to be engaging in binging behaviour by adult standards. Some children can consume prodigious amounts of sweets, biscuits or cake, which, to a weight-conscious adult, may be viewed as a 'binge'. An only too common phenomenon at children's parties is overeating with resultant vomiting. It is important then, to be clear about the differences between binge-eating in the context of BN, and simply overeating. The key features of a binge are that it tends to be a secretive activity, that it is followed by vomiting or the ingestion of large quantities of laxatives and that it is associated with a profound sense of guilt and self-worthlessness. Although a few children may display this constellation of factors, most overeating in children does not appear to be related to true BN.

Further clues related to eating behaviour and attitudes to food include an interest in calories and the 'fattening' qualities of different foods. It is interesting, however, that some of the younger anorexic children appear to be ignorant about the nutritional value of different foods and concern with calories does not form part of their disorder. One child adamantly refused to eat most foods, yet when pressed to eat something, would choose bread thickly spread with butter. This same child was reluctant to drink too much water, as she feared that this would make her fat. In many children, calorie-counting does not appear to be a predominant feature of the disorder.

Another behavioural pointer to the presence of an eating disorder is an increase in physical activity. Excessive exercising is well known as a feature of older-onset AN, and it has certainly been identified in many younger patients. Again, at first, this may appear relatively innocuous, and in many instances will be encouraged. Gradually, however, the child begins to take more and more exercise, and becomes very distressed if prevented from doing so. Anorexics have a remarkable staying capacity, and often drive their bodies to the limits of endurance. In some children, exercising may occur in secret; for example, one young girl spent considerable periods each night doing push-ups in her bedroom.

Of course, these examples do not provide an exhaustive list of the potential behavioural changes that may accompany the development of AN in children. They do perhaps illustrate the often insidious nature of the onset of the disorder, and the fact that many of the changes may at first seem acceptable. Often, behavioural changes will appear age-appropriate, such as a developing interest in appearance and weight, or an interest in cooking. However, where such changes occur against a background of weight loss and increasing rigidity in eating habits, suspicions should be aroused.

Psychological Clues

Psychological changes associated with the development of AN are perhaps the hardest to pick up, as to do so relies on a relationship with a child wherein fears, worries and attitudes are openly expressed. In most instances, psychological changes are initially inferred from observable behaviour. For example, an anorexic child who is restricting food-intake and engaging in excessive exercises will almost certainly have an underlying dread of becoming fat or gaining weight. This fear may not be expressed overtly. When questioned about their eating habits, many children do, however, state that they are afraid of becoming fat.

It is very difficult to determine the extent to which distortion of body image plays a role in childhood-onset AN. Certainly, many children claim that they are fat when they are extremely emaciated, but whether they truly believe this, or whether they suffer from true perceptual distortion, is another matter entirely. It has often been observed that children admitted for treatment of AN are inconsistent in their expressed views regarding their size. Body-image distortion is not always a helpful concept, particularly when discussing clues to early identification. It may be of more value to be alert to an expressed opinion about body size that is at considerable odds with reality. As with so many of the features already discussed, it is partly a question of degree that leads to suspicions about AN, as almost everyone displays some inaccuracy when judging their own body size relative to others.

Finally, many children suffering from AN are depressed. This may be expressed by tearfulness, unhappiness or a lack of interest in activities previously enjoyed. Children with AN may become very 'moody' and difficult, especially in situations involving food. Often, they become acutely distressed when forced to eat something they do not want. Many suffer from low self-esteem and experience an overwhelming lack of control over their life. Restriction of food-intake may represent a means of regaining some sense of control, and the right to do so becomes central to the child's existence. It is a sad fact that the battles that ensue from feeding difficulties, and the lying and deceit that anorexics so often engage in, may detract from the child's deep underlying distress. It takes much patience and perseverance to break through the rigid barriers erected around food, and to be able to reach and help the unhappy child inside.

THE MANAGEMENT OF EARLY ONSET ANOREXIA NERVOSA

The management of AN in children is often difficult and distressing for all concerned. Patients may arrive for specialists' help after many months of thwarted attempts to encourage more normal eating habits. General practitioners may feel that they can offer no further advice or suggestions to break the course of the disorder, and even in specialist centres, there are a relatively high number of relapses and 'treatment failures' in young adolescent and child anorexics admitted to hospital. On the other hand, there are, of course, successful recoveries. Some children recover with the help of their parents and GP. Others, whose physical state has deteriorated to such an extent that they require hospitalisation, respond well to inpatient treatment and return to problem-free eating behaviour. In between these two extremes, are those who achieve a precarious improvement that allows them to function satisfactorily in everyday life, but who tend to slide back into anorexic episodes on a number of occasions in the years following the initial episode. Such patients generally succeed in keeping their AN in check, but cannot be said to have made a good recovery.

Given that AN is a highly complex and multifaceted disorder, and the constellation of factors contributing to its development and maintenance differs between individuals, there are no easy solutions in terms of treatment. What proves successful or useful in one case may not do so in another. Having said this, there are a number of basic rules in attempting to help children with AN. Amongst the most essential are those related to the management of mealtimes, and the involvement of the parents.

The management of mealtime behaviour

A useful way to approach mealtimes with an anorexic child is to expect a battle. Having started from this premiss, one can be prepared for a struggle and means of dealing with it can be worked out in advance. If mealtimes are approached with a 'fingers crossed' attitude, the adult supervising may become unsure of how far the child should be pushed to eat. It is essential to have a clear plan before entering the situation. So often anorexics will complain that a plate is too full, that they don't like a particular type of food that has been served, or that it is unfair that they have to eat what they don't want when others don't have to. Arguments about the amounts that a child is expected to eat once the food has been presented can escalate into major rows, with much screaming, shouting or crying. This is obviously distressing, not only to the child and the adult trying to encourage them to eat, but also to any others who may be present; at home, siblings, friends or relatives, and in hospital, other patients, staff and visitors. The 'feeder' begins to feel that they are being too hard, or becomes so exasperated that they can stand it no longer, and the child eventually wins. It is extremely difficult to be consistent with such children, particularly as a parent, when the situation requires one to be so seemingly cruel to be kind.

Especially in the early stages of managing AN in children, a 'non-negotiable' stance should be adopted. Food should be served in non-negotiable amounts, and discussions about mealtimes and eating should not be allowed to take place at the table. A child should be served reasonable, but not excessive amounts, and under no circumstances should any compromises be struck once the plate is on the table. The time for negotiation is not at mealtimes, but between meals. In general though, it is preferable to keep all discussion about amounts of food to a minimum.

It is important to take care with the amounts and types of food offered if the refeeding of an emaciated child is to be successful. Many anorexic children complain that they feel full after a few mouthfuls, or that they suffer from severe abdominal pain after eating. This can make it very difficult for the adult to remain firm about how much the child is expected to eat, as worries about physically damaging the child may be aroused.

Any emaciated individual, whether child or adult, needs gradual refeeding. If excessively large quantities of food are consumed after a prolonged period of starvation, serious medical complications can result. A useful and safe way to begin refeeding is to serve, initially, small amounts of food, supplemented by high-calorie drinks. Gradually, the amount of solid food should be increased to normal amounts. An anorexic child should never be forced to eat an enormous plateful of food. Where anorexic children are refed at home, the advice of a dietician or GP regarding acceptable amounts may serve to allay parental anxieties about overfeeding.

The above suggestions for the management of mealtime behaviour involve the adult or adults taking control of the child's eating. It has already been stated that in many cases, AN seems to be associated with a pervasive sense of loss of control, and it could be argued that the above merely serves to intensify this. Clinical experience suggests, however, that once an eating disorder has become established, it is extremely difficult for the child to exert anything other than a destructive form of self-control regarding eating. By initially relieving the child of the burden of controlling food intake (which will almost certainly be met with resistance), the way can be laid open for more appropriate means of addressing issues of control. It is of course possible, once the child has gained weight, to enter a more negotiable phase regarding eating. This can be an important step in increasing the child's sense of independence.

Parents can clearly play a vital therapeutic role in the context of mealtimes as described above. There are, however, a number of other issues involving parents that need to be addressed in order to maximise the anorexic child's potential for recovery. It has been our experience time and time again that children whose parents act as a 'team' are more likely to improve than children whose parents do not act together. Parental consistency in the management of mealtime behaviour is paramount. It is essential that both parents are in agreement about amounts to be eaten, what should be done in the event of persistent refusal, etc. They must also be seen to be supporting each other in their management of the situation. For some parents, the discussion and negotiation required to reach this common stance may prove very difficult. Parents experiencing some marital problems, or couples in which food and eating has always been the mother's concern may need help; firstly in understanding the importance of their united action to the health of their child, and secondly in the process of reaching agreement and carrying this through in practice. Where parents are unable to act together, an anorexic child may play one off against the other or an alliance between one parent and the child may serve to thwart the other parent's efforts.

Parents must be made to understand the potential seriousness of AN, and the reasons why it must not be allowed to develop any further. In some cases, the professional dealing with the family may sense collusion on the part of the parents. In many instances, this will not be intentional, and may occur through the parents' desire to minimise their child's distress. For whatever reasons, as long as parents collude with avoidant eating behaviour, recovery will be hampered. It is extremely important to be as clear as possible with parents about their role in maintaining the disorder without creating the unhelpful impression that they are to blame.

It may also be important to help parents accept that their child will go through a period of expressing hostile feelings towards them, and that they will be required to stand up to very difficult tantrums and scenes. Many anorexic children display behaviour that worries and concerns parents, as they have not seen it before. If there are other siblings in the family, they too may need to be helped to understand what is happening. Anorexia in children affects all members of the family and therefore all must be involved in the process of recovery.

Direct professional involvement

In some cases, attempts to overcome a child's eating disorder at home are met with failure. The child may continue to lose weight, and the rest of the family become exhausted and hopeless. Parents who have tried to help their child but eventually seek professional help are likely to feel defeated. Many will have struggled through months of difficult mealtimes, uncomfortable rows and frequent visits to the GP for monthly or weekly weighings. By the time they arrive at a hospital to see a specialist, many are ready to hand over the problem to someone who can make things better or take the problem away from them. It is important to be aware of what such families may have already been through before their initial presentation for direct professional involvement. For the hospital-based treatment team, a new referral is a fresh case, yet for the child and the family it is often seen as the next step in a continuing battle. For some, it is a final resort. Parents may place unrealistic hopes in the abilities of the hospital staff to 'cure' the problem and their attitude towards the person conducting an initial interview may be coloured by the amount of help and understanding that they have received from their own family doctor.

Where a child's weight has slipped to a very low level, inpatient admission may be necessary in extreme cases in order to save the child's life. The inpatient treatment of anorexic children is not easy. Parents and siblings may be required from the start to take an active part in the therapeutic process by attending for regular family-therapy sessions. Such sessions also take place when the treatment is offered on an outpatient basis. Family work forms only a part of the total treatment package; other techniques used include weight restoration, social-skills training and, in some children, individual psychotherapy. The use of these techniques with children does not differ significantly from their use with older patients, and more detailed descriptions can be found elsewhere in this volume.

Clearly, some alterations in therapeutic style may be necessary in view of the child's age.

CONCLUSIONS

Anorexia nervosa in children and young adolescents is a complex and, as yet, poorly documented disorder. The presenting symptoms are similar to those identified in older patients, with the exception of age-related differences such as menstrual disturbances. Outcome appears to cover a similar range to that existing in the older age group; some patients recover completely, whereas others remain severely troubled for many years. Published studies of early-onset patients reveal a relatively high proportion of boys in the group of children referred for treatment of AN. The disorder is multidetermined and follows no set pattern of presentation or course. Although family difficulties are a popular explanation for the development of AN in children, this cannot be considered an adequate aetiological theory in every instance. Physical, behavioural and psychological indicators have been outlined as a means of addressing the importance of early identification. This is particularly important in children, as AN is often not suspected in view of the patient's age. Manageable advice regarding mealtime behaviour and the involvement of parents has been presented, together with some brief comments on the nature of professional involvement. Finally, it is concluded that the central issues of low self-esteem, lack of sense of control and the destructive expression of conflict and distress can be identified, even in the youngest of patients. These issues must be addressed, if necessary, after initial weight gain has been achieved, in order to ensure complete and lasting recovery.

REFERENCES

Fossen, A., Knibbs, J., Bryant-Waugh, R. and Lask, B. (1986) 'Early onset anorexia nervosa.' *Archives of Diseases in Childhood, 62*, 114–18

Haslam, D. (1986) *Eat it up*. MacDonald, London

Jacobs, B.W. and Isaacs, S. (1986) 'Pre-pubertal anorexia nervosa: a retrospective controlled study.' *Journal of Child Psychology and Psychiatry, 27*, 237–50

Lask, B. and Bryant-Waugh, R. (1986) 'Childhood onset anorexia nervosa.' In R. Meadow (ed), *Recent advances in pediatrics, No. 8*, Churchill Livingstone, London

16

Ethical Considerations

Mark Strasser and Gordon Giles

INTRODUCTION

Most authorities agree that involuntary treatment of anorexics should occur only as a last resort because such interventions tend not to promote the patient's long-term recovery. Some authorities go a step further and suggest that involuntary interventions should never occur because they violate patient autonomy. The former claim seems relatively uncontroversial and hence will not be discussed here. However, the suggestion that patient's rights are violated by compulsory treatment is quite controversial. Furthermore, as the way in which this issue is settled may have important implications for how other instances involving autonomy issues that the practical therapist may encounter ought also to be settled, this chapter is primarily devoted to exploring this autonomy issue. It is also hoped that this chapter will foster critical examination of controversial issues surrounding eating disorders generally.

The problem may be stated relatively simply. If the anorexic is not mentally 'competent' (i.e. irrational), then treatment (e.g. forced feedings) against her will is, perhaps, appropriately called 'involuntary treatment' but is not a violation of her autonomy. For, the patient's true (or 'rational') will would not have been defied by such a procedure; i.e. had the patient been well, she would not have objected to such a procedure. However, if the anorexic is mentally competent (i.e rational), then forced feedings would indeed be against her 'rational' will and we would not be able to justify such procedures by appealing to what an autonomous agent would have wanted — indeed, we may not be able to justify such a procedure at all. We shall see that the criteria for competence (and thus for autonomy) are not sufficiently robust to provide a useful, non-question-begging standard by which to determine when a patient is not competent.

Actions as providing grounds for establishing incompetence

One might be tempted to argue that there should be no difficulty in establishing the incompetence of an anorexic. After all, the anorexic starves herself, sometimes to the point of extreme emaciation. However, such behaviour may not be sufficient to establish the anorexic's incompetence. Dresser (1984), for instance, implies that anorexics may be analogues to hunger strikers. She notes that the 'hunger striker engages in behaviour that looks substantially similar to that of the anorexic. Beyond the typically more public declaration of purpose by the hunger striker, there are no apparent behavioural differences between the two actions' (p. 331). Fost (1984) objects to such an analogy:

> Unlike the hunger striker, who welcomes thinness as a means to achieve a chosen and articulated end, the anorexic cannot appreciate the instrumental value of her thinness because she, in fact, believes she is fat. In response to the question, 'Why are you fasting?', the hunger striker responds: 'To become thin, or dead if necessary, so people will feel constrained to change their policies'. The anorexic's reply would be: 'To remove this excess fat'. (p. 379)

Fost may be correct, in that some anorexics cannot appreciate the instrumental value of their *thinness* because they do not perceive themselves as thin. However, he is incorrect in that anorexics cannot appreciate the instrumental value of their behaviour and its results. For instance, the anorexic may appreciate that she has discovered a way of exercising power and control over her family. Or, she might appreciate that she has found a way to arrest some of the natural processes of maturation (see Dresser, 1984, p. 335). Thus, even if anorexics do have a body-distortion problem (i.e. perceive themselves to be much fatter than they really are), we should not therefore conclude that anorexics cannot engage in means–end reasoning and cannot realise the 'benefits' of their apparently self-destructive behaviour.

Fost's comments illustrate a further point. When medical professionals look at an anorexic, they may be visibly struck by the anorexic's overall emaciation. However, when the anorexic looks at herself, she may not be looking at her overall appearance but rather, for instance, at her 'huge' hips. Of course, the anorexic may still be misperceiving (e.g. see her hips as larger than they actually are), but she may also be correctly perceiving that some part of her anatomy does not meet the aesthetic 'ideal'.

Often enough, non-anorexics also overemphasise certain 'less-than-ideal' parts of their anatomies, both in terms of the part's overall size, and, in terms of the importance that part has for the individual's overall appearance. Dresser points to studies that suggest that there is no significant difference between the extent of body distortion in anorexic and in non-anorexic women (Dresser, 1984, p. 335).

Of course, even if we cannot distinguish between anorexics and non-anorexics by looking at differences in body distortion, we can distinguish between them in absolute terms (e.g. by looking at average weights relative to given heights). However, that method of differentiation will be unhelpful if we want to distinguish between the two groups mentioned by Dresser (i.e. hunger strikers and anorexics).

One way to distinguish between these two groups would be to look at their respective goals. One might claim, for example, that the anorexic's goal of achieving some aesthetic ideal is much less serious than is the religious ascetic's goal of achieving some sort of spiritual communion (see Crisp, 1980, p. 10).

Yet, this method of distinguishing would be suspect for a few reasons. First, we would need some account to show why the pursuit of beauty is not a 'worthy' goal. Secondly, we would need to show that the pursuit of beauty is indeed the goal of the anorexic. Suppose, for instance, that Bruch (e.g. 1977) is correct in that anorexics are seeking autonomy. On that account, the anorexic is not merely seeking to attain beauty but to establish her autonomy and individuality. Certainly,. those goals are quite worthy.

Admittedly, part of the problem here is that we cannot quite be sure exactly what the anorexic's motives are. Fost points out that 'Discussion of the anorexic's motives is entirely speculative, because her stated motive — "to get rid of her fat body" — makes no sense at all and forces us to guess about her real motives' (1984, p. 379). Of course, if Fost were correct that the anorexic 'in fact believes that she is fat' perhaps because she is likely 'delusional concerning her body size and shape' (p. 378), then the anorexic's motivation would be quite understandable (at least prima facie). Fost argues that the 'martyr's motives may be questioned, but we are at least clear on what she thinks she is doing' (p. 379). Yet, our problem is precisely that we do not know what either the anorexic or the hunger striker think they are doing. The hunger striker's stated motives seem much more plausible than do the anorexic's. However, if we really believed that the anorexic's body image was extremely distorted, then her actions would seem much more understandable. We might have some difficulty in understanding *why* her body image was so severely distorted (e.g. in figuring out which neurochemical imbalances were responsible), but that would be a different sort of puzzle.

Part of the reason that we have difficulty in determining the anorexic's motivation is that she *does* seem to appreciate that she is quite thin. Dresser, for instance, reports a conversation between two anorexics in which one claims that others (i.e. non-anorexics) are jealous because they are unable to achieve what the anorexics can achieve weight loss (see Dresser, 1984, p. 326). The point here is not that the anorexic is correct that others are jealous of her 'accomplishment', but only that her comment presupposes her recognition that she is indeed much thinner than many other people in the population.

Means – end reasoning

Fost argues that the:

> pursuit of moderate thinness is not irrational, either in the sense of being illogical or dysfunctional. Being underweight, compared to overweight, is associated with reduced morbidity and mortality from common causes of premature death

and disability. It may also have psycholog...
stating that thinness is a widely shared and admired goal. Th...
served, however, when weight falls into the anorexic range, and at t...
continued pursuit of thinness becomes irrational.

(Fost, 1984, p. 383)

Yet, Fost's analysis of why anorexic behaviour is irrational is a bit surprising.

Suppose that Jo, who is rather obese, loses weight because she believes that her doing so will cause the President of the United States to resign. Certainly, we would be hesitant to call her action 'rational', despite her actions being likely to promote her health. Or, suppose that a woman decides to starve herself because she sees that by so doing she will be able to save her family or country. Just as we might call the hunger striker's action rational, we might call this person's action rational, at least, if there were some reason to believe that this person's assessment of the situation was a reasonable one. We must not assume that actions that promote one's health are somehow intrinsically reasonable, nor that actions which promote one's lack of health are somehow intrinsically unreasonable.

The point here is *not* to claim that the anorexic is acting rationally. Rather, the point here is to claim that the anorexic's action is not *necessarily* irrational, even if it is associated with increased morbidity and mortality. To evaluate the rationality of the anorexic's refusal to eat, we must examine her goals and see whether the chosen behaviour is an effective means of achieving those ends.

Fost argues that:

> The justification...for interfering with anorexic behavior, particularly when death is imminent, is precisely because the behaviour does not result from free choice and, in fact, is likely to result in an outcome that is contrary to the real desires of the patient. Most anorexic patients apparently do not want to die. The great majority remain in the hospital voluntarily. The ones who die often do so out of miscalculation, not by choice.
>
> (Fost, 1984, p. 383)

Fost is correct in that sometimes the anorexic's behaviour is (or at least seems to be) not freely chosen. Bruch (1978) describes patients who talk as if some person inside them forces them not to eat. Yet, often enough, the anorexic feels that one of the few things that she can control is her own eating. Insofar as she improves her own self-image because of her ability to control her own food-intake, the anorexic's behaviour looks to be quite 'free'. While Fost is correct to claim that the anorexic usually does not desire to die, she does not desire to put on any weight and that desire may accurately be labelled as one of her present, 'true' desires. Fost is misleading insofar as he implies that the anorexic is necessarily acting against her own true desires.

Suppose, for instance, that the anorexic's desire not to gain weight is stronger than is her desire to continue living. Should the anorexic be force-fed? Fost seems somewhat ambivalent. He suggests that:

> We interfere because there is a reasonable probability that forced treatment will not only save a life, but also that the person will be restored to a life that is worth living by her own standards. If, at some point, despite the availability of treatment, the person wilfully refuses help, and consciously chooses to die, it can be argued that she should be left alone.
>
> (Fost, 1984, p. 383)

Yet, in this scenario, we can not be quite sure what to say. The anorexic does not want to die, and would deny that she is choosing to die; she would simply assert that she is choosing not to gain weight. She might even admit that her dying is foreseeable, although still not chosen.

In this kind of case, the anorexic's true desire is to not gain weight. She does not choose death nor has a true desire to die (and thus, perhaps, does not meet Fost's criteria for being left alone). The anorexic above does not desire to die but also does not desire to gain weight. What shall we say is the anorexic's *true* desire? Or (more appropriately), which true desire is the stronger desire? We simply do not know. The question is whether the anorexic desires not to gain weight more than she desires to continue living. Of course, one might simply ask the anorexic which is more important to her, but even that may not be helpful.

Suppose, for instance, that the anorexic says that she very much wants to live but she nonetheless continues to act in ways that endanger her life. Should we assume that her actions or her words better represent her desires? Before we immediately answer 'Her words', we must consider what our response would be were the conditions reversed; i.e. her actions were indicating that she wanted to continue living but her words were indicating that she wanted to die. As either the anorexic's actions or her words might truly represent her (stronger) desire, we cannot assume that we know which happens to represent her desire merely because one of them happens to be in accord with our own desires.

This analysis becomes even more complicated if the anorexic does not believe that her present habits will lead to her own death. We note that we do *not* establish that the anorexic is incompetent merely because she denies the physician's claim that her life is greatly endangered. First of all, it is much harder to know when a patient is in imminent danger than might first be believed (Dresser, 1984, p. 343). Secondly, if the physician is clearly quite willing to force-feed the patient and to manipulate or coerce the patient, it would be no suprise if the anorexic, fearing that the physician was trying to dupe her into eating, were unwilling to believe the physician's dire warnings.

The important question here involves how to determine when the anorexic is competent to make decisions about her own medical treatment. Dresser discusses five different possible criteria, as follows:

verbally or behaviourally. Most anorexics would meet this standard, although Dresser points out that 'its failure to require that [the anorexic] understand the proposed treatment means this test is likely to elicit uninformed consent from many anorexics who will then refuse to co-operate with treatment once they experience its demands' (Dresser, 1984, p. 349). Of course, we cannot assume that merely because anorexics would refuse to co-operate, this criterion must therefore be invalid. Nonetheless, insofar as we are not merely interested in competence (i.e. the *ability* to make a rational decision) but are also interested in the person's informed, autonomous decision, this standard does not seem to be appropriate.

A comparison The patient's decision is compared to the choice a reasonable person would make under similar circumstances. Dresser believes that this standard's 'focus on the reasonableness of the patient's choice allocates insufficient weight to individual freedom of choice' (p. 349). Yet, Dresser does not explain why that allocated weight is *insufficient.* After all, one might well claim that the anorexic's desires are weighed appropriately heavily on this account. When we examine what a reasonable person would say, we have to specify all of the relevant circumstances. In order to do this, we would have to understand something about the aetiology of anorexia. Were it, for instance, of biological origin, the 'relevant' circumstances (assuming that biological factors would not count as circumstances) would presumably not convince a reasonable person to act as the anorexic does. However, if anorexia is an adaptive behaviour necessitated by the circumstances that confront the anorexic, then a reasonable person might act that way. If we cannot specify the cause(s) of anorexia, then we can not specify how a reasonable person would react to the obtaining circumstances.

Reasons Another standard involves an examination of the reasons for the individual's decision to accept or refuse treatment. That is to say, if the reasons seem 'reasonable', then the person is deemed competent; if the reasons seem unreasonable, then the person is deemed incompetent. However, we must differentiate between the real and the stated reason. As Dresser points out, 'it is not possible to verify the basis for an anorexic's decision' (p. 351), in part (sometimes) because the anorexic may not trust her physician or therapist enough to disclose the reason (assuming, which may not be fair at all, that the anorexic knows the reason herself). Even if the anorexic does not know why she is doing what she is doing, however, her behaviour may still be quite adaptive. There is a further problem. As 'rationality is too vague and subjective a concept' (Dresser, p. 351), this standard does not seem appropriate. We note that we have some of the same problems as we do with the 'comparison' criteria.

Suppose, for instance, that the anorexic is unable to assert herself in her family context unless she resorts to this very extreme behaviour. Suppose further, that she has already tried all sorts of other (more moderate) ways to secure familial recognition of her as an independent being, but none have been successful. Is the anorexic's reason a good one? Perhaps so. If one is tempted to argue that no reason offered by the anorexic could be a good one, given the great extremes to which she goes, one seems to invalidate the worth of this criterion. Further, one would presumably thereby be committed to the necessary unreasonableness of the hunger striker's actions.

The fourth and fifth tests are based upon the individual's ability to understand the relevant information. However, Dresser points out that 'many anorexics exhibit an ability to understand the factual consequences of treatment and non-treatment' (p. 353). Indeed, often enough, the problem may not be cognitive, but affective; i.e. the anorexic may know the likely outcomes of different courses of action, but may value those outcomes in a much different way than many would claim is appropriate. Yet appropriate or proper affective orderings are notoriously difficult to establish.

If we use any of the possible criteria of competence offered above, we do not seem to have a non-question-begging way to establish that forced intervention is appropriate. Fost is correct to point out that unless we can find a clear way to distinguish between the competence of a hunger striker and the competence of an anorexic, then 'it is not clear why [the anorexic's] freedom should ever be curtailed' (p. 383). Fost suggests that paternalism would be justified if:

1. Imminent physical harm is likely.
2. Intrusion will probably protect the person from that harm.
3. The person is likely to say thank you at some later time.
4. The intrusion is generalisable, in the sense that those supporting it would wish the same for themselves. (pp. 383–4)

Yet we note that his comments are much less likely to yield the 'correct' result than he believes. As previously mentioned, Dresser points out the difficulty of predicting when imminent physical harm is likely. She also points out that professionals tend to overpredict the imminence of physical harm. When we couple these difficulties with the possibility that, although intrusion will probably protect that person from that harm presently, such an intrusion may *reduce* the likelihood of the patient's long-term recovery, we cannot be so certain about when intervention is the most appropriate course of treatment.

Fost's third condition is interesting precisely because we cannot all be sure what it would indicate. For, even if we knew (infallibly) that the anorexic would be thankful later, we would not know whether that gratitude would represent the anorexic's 'true' desires or her new desires. Presumably, one might be interested in whether or not the anorexic would be thankful in the future (e.g. for having been force fed against her will) for two reasons.

Firstly, insofar as one is thankful in the future, one is presumably as (if not more) pleased by the results of the procedure as one would have been, had the procedure not been performed. As it seems fair to assume that a patient would not be thankful if she thought that her present situation was worse than it would have been had nothing been done, the anorexic's being thankful (sometime in the future) would at least indicate that (for her own view) good had been done for her.

Secondly, insofar as the anorexic will be thankful, one might think that the procedure that the physician performs (even though presently against the anorexic's stated desires) is really in accord with the anorexic's 'true' desires (because after all she will be thankful in retrospect).

Fost's fourth condition is unhelpful for some of the reasons discussed earlier with respect to the 'reasonable person' standard. What treatment would we want were we in the anorexic's shoes? This question is much more difficult to answer than first appears. We need some way to specify the 'relevant' circumstances before we can make a sensible response to that question.

The account presented here is not intended to establish that no interferences with an anorexic's behaviour without her consent is morally permissible. Rather, this account is intended to suggest that: (a) such interferences should be performed as rarely as possible, and (b) such interferences cannot be justified by appealing to the 'true' desires of the anorexic (which are inaccessible to us, even if not inaccessible to the anorexic herself), or to how a reasonable person would want to be treated, etc.

Basically, we are without a helpful set of criteria by which to determine competence. Without such criteria, we cannot make appeals to autonomy considerations and must instead look to some other considerations for justifications. For instance, we might look at the treatment (or non-treatment) that looks like it will have the best long-term outcome for the anorexic herself. However, if we adopt this tack, we shall have to posit some 'objective' criteria by which to access the best outcome for the patient; for according to the patient's own values, gaining weight may not yield the best long-term outcome. Or, we might claim that more general good will be promoted if such interventions are permitted. However, such a policy could set a dangerous precedent, easily open to abuse, which would 'justify' many inappropriate practices.

CONCLUSIONS

This chapter does not involve an attempt to undermine the importance of patient autonomy. Much more research and discussion are needed to develop good, non-question-begging criteria for competence. Until they are found, however, we must be careful not to try to justify our actions by making specious claims either about what the patient 'really' wants or about what we would want, were we in a similar position. We hope that this chapter has been sufficiently logical and thought-provoking to the practical therapist such that their logical and provocative thoughts will spread to issues within eating disorders generally.

REFERENCES

Bruch, H. (1977) 'Atypical anorexia nervosa.' In R. Vigersky (ed), *Anorexia nervosa*, Raven Press, New York

—— (1978) *Eating disorders*. Routledge and Kegan Paul, London

Crisp, A.H. (1980) *Anorexia nervosa*. Academic Press, New York

Dresser, R. (1984) 'Feeding the hunger artists: legal issues in treating anorexia nervosa.' *Wisconsin Law Review*, *2*, 297–374

Fost, N. (1984) 'Food for thought: Dresser on anorexia.' *Wisconsin Law Review*, *2*, 375–84

Index